The Covenant and You

By the same author

Alaska Bahá'í Community: Its Growth and Development
Bahá'í Consultation Workbook
Bahá'í Teachings, Light for All Regions
Compassionate Woman: The Life and Legacy of Patricia Locke
Consultation
Developing Genius
Making the Invisible Visible: The Human Principles for Sustaining Innovation, (with Robert Rosenfeld)
Pondering the Fire Tablet: Reflections on Bahá'u'lláh's 'Fire Tablet'
Road Maps to the Future
Crazy Lovers of Bahá'u'lláh: Inspiring Stories of Little Giants

The Covenant and You

John Kolstoe

GEORGE RONALD
OXFORD

George Ronald Publisher Ltd
Oxford
www.grbooks.com

© John Kolstoe 2015
All Rights Reserved
Reprinted 2019

A catalogue record for this book is available from the British Library
ISBN 978-0-85398-594-5

Cover design: Steiner Graphics

Contents

Foreword by Dr William Roberts   vii
Preface   x
Acknowledgements   xii

Part I. Nature of the Covenant

   Introduction   3
1. The Eternal Covenant   5
2. The Greater Covenant   8
3. The Lesser Covenant   21
4. Behaviours   43

Part II. Reflections on Walking in the Light of the Covenant

   Introduction   59
5. Firmness in the Covenant   69
6. Oneness of Mankind   77
7. World Peace   94
8. Liberty, Submission and Guidance   106
9. Two Processes   121
10. Three Protagonists   137
11. Living the Life   153
12. Tests, Difficulties and a Radiant Life   191
13. Words and Deeds   230
14. Culture of Learning   239
15. Arts, Science, Work and Leisure   252
16. Socio-Economic Development: Bahá'í-inspired Projects   263
17. Crisis and Victory   279
18. Covenant-breaking   297
19. Teaching   305
20. The Pathway   322

Bibliography   349
References   355

Dedicated to those legions of deceased champions of Bahá'u'lláh whose sacrifice and love for the Covenant safely conveyed His Faith to those of us living today.
And to those champions, living and as yet unborn, whose love for the Covenant will ultimately bring to fruition the promise of the Báb

Foreword

'To be a Bahá'í simply means to love all the world;
to love humanity and try to serve it . . .'
'Abdu'l-Bahá[1]

References to the Covenant of Bahá'u'lláh have long been a mainstream element of the discourse in the Bahá'í community, but it appears that many do not have a clear understanding of what it is or how to apply it in daily life. It has been an elusive aspect among many, notwithstanding a general appreciation of its importance and presence.

A number of distinguished authors have written about this key and central aspect of the Faith and have offered uplifting elucidation of the principles and the history and import of the Covenant. Now, John Kolstoe has written inviting us into an understanding of its application and how it can be an active aspect of our lives.

Among the many statements by 'Abdu'l-Bahá concerning the Covenant are the following:

> The pivot of the oneness of mankind is nothing else but the power of the Covenant.[2]

And:

> The Covenant of God is like the sun – the brilliance and light of the Covenant radiates and shines forth from the faces of those who are firm in it.[3]

Where do we start? How can we operationalize this objective and how do we pursue this journey?

In my life, I have had the great privilege to be among those new believers in the midst of youth who were nurtured and encouraged in their emerging faith by devoted servants of the Cause who spent their lives striving to understand what it means to be a Baháʼí and to serve humanity as directed by the teachings of the Cause of God. The humble engagement by these venerable souls with wide-eyed youth has been a source of inspiration and a model of leadership marking a generation of believers, calling them to a firmness in the Covenant which could not have been otherwise anticipated.

Leading these extraordinary teachers were the Hands of the Cause of God and their auxiliaries, the Knights of Baháʼuʼlláh, itinerant teachers and accomplished administrators. How we loved them! This special collection of spiritual giants carried out among their many other responsibilities the mandate of promoting learning among the believers. They did this by making themselves accessible to the friends, often in informal surroundings at summer schools and conferences and even in local community meetings, pouring out their hearts, spending hours of time sharing their understanding of the Faith, and offering insights gleaned over time. In these close and intimate circles, segments of the Holy Text were studied, ideas were shared, questions were explored, and stories of service were told, all illuminating aspects of faith and devotion to its precepts and thereby establishing a close bond to the Covenant and its Centre.

This volume offers a similar opportunity to learn through the eyes of a believer who continues to strive to live a life of Baháʼí service. In the tradition of those unique teachers of yesteryear, John Kolstoe offers in this intimate space his observations and stories connecting our hearts with the Covenant. Here are real-life circumstances interwoven with spiritual intent that can lead to behaviour in line with the Covenant. He offers us descriptions of various themes of the Covenant and then in a pragmatic way invites us to a deeper appreciation through a series of experiences shared in story form. His capacity to create a space for reflection is magnetic. I suggest we will not come away from a reading of this book without feeling the love and wonderment of the Covenant. Joy of nearness to God can be realized through obedience and embracing His Law and Word!

In a talk delivered in New York at the Kinney home on 11 June 2012, 'Abdu'l-Bahá addressed those gathered:

> When you assemble. you must reflect the lights of the Heavenly Kingdom. Let your hearts be as mirrors in which the radiance of the Sun of Reality is visible. Each bosom must be a telegraph station – one terminus of the wire attached to the soul, the other fixed in the Supreme Concourse – so that inspiration may descend from the Kingdom of Abhá and questions of reality be discussed . . . The more perfect the love and agreement, the more the divine confirmations and assistance of the Blessed Perfection will descend.[4]

This statement made to the community in what was named the 'City of the Covenant' provides us with guidance about what is required to be a conduit of the light. To be firm in the Covenant is to be a conduit of that light.

True acts of kindness once completed are seldom mentioned again. But here I choose to make mention and celebrate acts of consequence made quietly over many years by John Kolstoe, which inform his capacity to invite us to draw nearer to the Covenant. Inspired by service, his view of the Covenant allows the topic to take flight from a mere recitation of ideals to a pattern leading to a life filled with joy and purpose. Kolstoe infuses into the language of this book the spirit of love, fidelity and longing held within his heart.

Join me in receiving this gift of a journey guided by Kolstoe along the path of learning about the *The Covenant and You*!

(Billy) Roberts

United States, June 2015

Preface

In the Bayán the Báb says that every religion of the past was fit to become universal. The only reason why they failed to attain that mark was the incompetence of their followers. He then proceeds to give a definite promise that this would not be the fate of the revelation of Him Whom God would make manifest, that it will become universal and include all the people of the world.
Shoghi Effendi[1]

How can that be? Is mankind finally able to overcome its incompetence and shortcomings that have so weighed it down in the past? Aren't we the same bunch of monkeys that have messed things up before? Or, is there something new to combat the viruses that have plagued the human race: anger, jealousy, greed, materialism, the love of leadership, and so on?

A strong antidote is at hand. It is the Covenant of Bahá'u'lláh. When people like you and me choose to walk in the light of the Covenant:

- A shift in human affairs is started.
- The shortcomings and foibles that have corrupted political systems and religions for eons gradually lose their power.
- The foundation is laid for peace and security on this war-torn planet.
- The world draws closer to fulfilling the Báb's promise.
- Mankind gets in harmony with the latest Word from God.

For over a century and a half the protective features of the Covenant have kept the Baháʼí Faith united and provided for its expansion to a global presence. At the same time, it has provided potential for unprecedented individual spiritual development and growth. That is because the Covenant calls ordinary believers like you and me to a new level of behaviour and a higher state of maturity.

How does the Covenant fulfil the Báb's prophecy? The answer lies in the dynamic relationship between the Covenant and you.

Acknowledgements

How can I sufficiently thank Chad Jones, whose search engines 'Ocean' and 'Sifter – Star of the West' were my tools of first resort in accessing the Sacred Writings? His creations are splendid examples of what can happen when talent is focused on serving the Covenant. Following a Protection Conference in Wilmette in 1975, I wrote a series of articles on the Covenant for the *Alaska Bahá'í News*. In the late 1980s I started expanding those articles for a book. When some other books on the Covenant came out, I set the work aside. A casual conversation with Billy Roberts in 2013 motivated me to look at it again. Billy and Tim Moore separately encouraged me to bring this work out of hibernation.

Illuminating and greatly appreciated comments on the manuscript were made by: Ray Hudson, David Hunt, and a few other people. Jack Finley provided some helpful illustrations. A big 'thank you' is due to each of them for their significant contributions.

It is a pleasure to again be working with the wonderful and most helpful staff at George Ronald, which is giving birth to this project after 40 years of intermittent gestation.

Finally, even through the fog of Alzheimer's, the radiance of my wife, Janet, was a constant support and source of inspiration until she was unshackled from that debilitating cage in May of 2014.

PART I

NATURE OF THE COVENANT

Introduction

O Son of Man! Veiled in My immemorial being and in the ancient eternity of My essence, I knew My love for thee; therefore I created thee, have engraved on thee Mine image and revealed to thee My beauty.
Bahá'u'lláh[1]

Even before humans appeared on Planet Earth, God's great love for mankind existed. In order for His *image* and *beauty* to become known to mankind and be engaged with the human experience, a vehicle was needed. That vehicle was and is the Covenant.

What is a covenant? It is a promise, or agreement, or contract. The Divine Covenant keeps people oriented to the teachings of the Founder. Simply put, a spiritual Covenant describes the essence of the religion and informs people what to do.

The various understandings of the Covenants of God are as different as the people who think seriously about them. Shoghi Effendi's secretary gave this explanation:

> As regards the meaning of the Bahá'í Covenant: The Guardian considers the existence of two forms of Covenant both of which are explicitly mentioned in the literature of the Cause. First is the covenant that every Prophet makes with humanity or, more definitely, with His people that they will accept and follow the coming Manifestation Who will be the reappearance of His reality. The second form of covenant is such as the one Bahá'u'lláh made with His people that they should accept the Master . . . [2]

THE COVENANT AND YOU

In December 1987, the Research Department of the Universal House of Justice prepared a compilation on the Covenant. The cover page says:

> A covenant in the religious sense is a binding agreement between God and man, whereby God requires of man certain behaviour in return for which He guarantees certain blessings, or whereby He gives man certain bounties in return for which He takes from those who accept them an undertaking to behave in a certain way. There is for example, the Greater Covenant which every Manifestation of God makes with His followers, promising that in the fullness of time a new Manifestation will be sent, and taking from them the undertaking to accept Him when this occurs. There is also the Lesser Covenant that a Manifestation of God makes with His followers that they will accept His appointed successor after Him. If they do so, the Faith can remain united and pure. If not, the Faith becomes divided and its force spent. It is a Covenant of this kind that Bahá'u'lláh made with His followers regarding 'Abdu'l-Bahá and that 'Abdu'l-Bahá perpetuated through the Administrative Order . . . [3]

Part I of this book is an overview of the three aspects mentioned above. The first short chapter, The Eternal Covenant, is followed by chapters on the Greater Covenant, the Lesser Covenant, and Behaviours.

While the Covenant for this age is the guide to help people stay in tune with the message of Bahá'u'lláh, it has extra features protecting people from their own incompetencies, weaknesses, and trouble-making. This makes it possible for the Bahá'í Faith to be a truly universal and uniting factor.

1

The Eternal Covenant

*O Son of Man! I loved thy creation, hence I created thee.
Wherefore, do thou love Me, that I may name thy name and
fill thy soul with the spirit of life.*
Bahá'u'lláh[1]

According to the traditions of Islam, there have been 124,000 Messengers from God, of whom 313 are regarded as Prophets receiving direct inspiration.[2] 'Abdu'l-Bahá explains that 'the Prophets are of two kinds. One are the independent Prophets Who are followed; the other kind are not independent and are themselves followers'.[3]

Traditions, myths and prophecies the world over suggest that every group of people in the world has received divine guidance. These traditions have so much in common that it is only natural to conclude that they come from a common source.[4]

An example of universality is the rainbow. People from diverse areas have similar metaphors of the rainbow. Finding a culture that does not give symbolic significance to the rainbow is a major challenge. Many people see the rainbow as a bridge to the next world.

Judeo–Christian–Islamic traditions see both a general and a specific symbolism. In general, it is a sign of God's ever-abiding love for mankind. Specifically, it symbolizes the promise of God not to destroy the world by flood again.

The visible rainbow is an arc – part of a circle. In potential it is a full circle. Twice, I have seen the full circle, both while flying, with the shadow of the plane on a cloud as the centre of the circle.

THE COVENANT AND YOU

Throughout the world a circle is considered a symbol of unity. It is continuous, with neither beginning nor end. Rainbows have the full spectrum of colours, just as is seen among the peoples of the world. Physically, it is potentially always there, but can only be seen when the conditions are right. Spiritual realities can only be seen when the soul is tuned in to them. To see the beauty of the rainbow, it is necessary to take time and gaze on it intently. Discovering spiritual realities also takes time and reflection.

Next time you see a rainbow you might pause for a moment to reflect on how it connects both all the people of the world and the wonders of the Covenant. When you see it, remember you are lucky – because, even though there in potential, it is not always obvious. The same is true of the Covenant.

'Abdu'l-Bahá wrote that 'all the forces of the universe, in the last analysis serve the Covenant'.[5] If all the forces are aligned with the Covenant, why isn't it obvious? Why doesn't everyone know of it? Visible or not, aware of it or not, the influence of the Covenant is there, like the sun.

No matter how dark and stormy the sky, the sun still shines. Without the sun's splendour, even when not visible, life on earth would cease. Dark, thick clouds often obscure the sun and diffuse its light. As clouds dissipate, the source of light is more easily located.

Present world conditions have been referred to as the 'dark and thorny stage' in human history. The Covenant is obscured by these dreary days. No matter how the storms rage in the dysfunctional world, the orb of the Covenant quietly shines on and the healing power works its miracle.

The lustre and intensity of both the physical sun and the Covenant are continuous. What changes is our capacity to see and acknowledge their impact. The clouds obscuring the Covenant decrease as we work to penetrate and dispel the number and density of intervening veils.

In the early dawn of an overcast day, people see dimly and

stumble around in the half-light. Even while the impact of the Covenant is not clear, some people see certain truths of this new Revelation: the oneness of mankind, the equality of men and women, the importance of universal peace, the harmony of science and religion and so on. These are understood by some keen-sighted and perceptive souls who see, albeit dimly, through the obscuring clouds of an unbelieving world. They intuitively grasp their truths without realizing that illumination comes from the Bahá'í Revelation. Gradually, the divine source will become more obvious to more people. In the meantime, those enlightened souls are advancing the Cause of God in their own way despite opposition in this 'dark and thorny stage' of human history.

2

The Greater Covenant

> *The Lord of the universe hath never raised up a prophet nor hath He sent down a Book unless He hath established His covenant with all men, calling for their acceptance of the next Revelation and of the next Book; inasmuch as the outpourings of His bounty are ceaseless and without limit.*
> The Báb[1]

This relationship was spelled out by Abdu'l-Bahá:

> His Holiness Abraham, on Him be peace, made a covenant concerning His Holiness Moses and gave the glad-tidings of His coming. His Holiness Moses made a covenant concerning the Promised One, i.e. His Holiness Christ, and announced the good news of His Manifestation to the world. His Holiness Christ made a covenant concerning the Paraclete (Muḥammad) and gave the tidings of His coming. His Holiness the Prophet Muḥammad made a covenant concerning His Holiness the Báb and the Báb was the One promised by Muḥammad, for Muḥammad gave the tidings of His coming. The Báb made a Covenant concerning the Blessed Beauty of Bahá'u'lláh and gave the glad-tidings of His coming for the Blessed Beauty was the One promised by His Holiness the Báb. Bahá'u'lláh made a covenant concerning a promised One who will become manifest after one thousand or thousands of years . . .[2]

Each Messenger (or Manifestation of God) brings the teachings necessary for the day in which He comes. They have much in common. Most prominent is that the new Teacher is different from what the religious leaders expect – They are opposed by the very authorities who were to prepare their followers for their advent.

Bahá'u'lláh fulfilled prophecies from all the Holy Books, yet this is rarely recognized. Different interpretations are placed on both the prophecies and fulfilling events. 'Evidence' that is obvious to one person is vigorously denied and disputed by someone else. Many people are so convinced of their own understanding that any other view is automatically dismissed. The more different from traditional thinking the interpretation is, the more vigorously it is protested.

Following are a few of the specific references in older religions to the coming of Bahá'u'lláh. They show continuity, even though they have convinced few followers of those Faiths.

Hinduism

According to Hindu scriptures, Krishna referred to the coming of an Avatar, which is a Divine Messenger. Special reference was made to the tenth Avatar, called 'Kalki', which implies the vanquisher of evil. In the Srimad Bhagavatam, part of the Hindu Scriptures, it says, 'Kalki will usher in the Golden age and a new race of good men.'[3]

Buddhism

Much of the wisdom of the Buddha has been collected in the Dhammapada, a collection of sayings in which there is a reference to a world Saviour called 'Maitreye, the Buddha of universal fellowship',[4] who would be, 'born into the world a fully Enlightened One, blessed and worthy, abounding in wisdom and goodness, unsurpassed as a guide to erring mortals.'[5]

Zoroastrianism

A Zoroastrian prophesy speaks of the Promised One, 'the World-Saviour S͟háh-Bahrám, Who would triumph over Ahriman [the spirit of evil] and usher in an era of blessedness and peace'.[6]

Judaism

The Hebrew Bible provides many prophecies about this age. One of these promises that 'nations shall not lift up sword against nation, neither shall they learn war any more'.[7] In contrast to that, Christ said, 'Think not that I am come to send peace on earth: I came not to send peace, but a sword.'[8] Christ seemed to deny that those prophecies referred to Him.

There are fascinating prophecies from Isaiah: 'and the government shall be upon his shoulder . . . and his name shall be called Wonderful, Counsellor, The mighty God, The everlasting Father, The Prince of Peace', and, 'Of the increase of His government and peace there shall be no end.'[9] Christ said, 'My kingdom is not of this world'[10] and 'Render therefore unto Caesar the things which be Caesar's, and unto God the things which be God's.'[11] The prophecy does not appear to fit the words of Christ.

The predictions of both Daniel and Isaiah find persuasive fulfilments in the coming of Bahá'u'lláh.

Christianity[12]

In the 24th chapter of Matthew, verses 15–24, Jesus said much about the 'latter days', including a warning of false prophets and how to tell the difference. In the book of John, He is recorded as saying, 'I have yet many things to say unto you but ye cannot bear them now. Howbeit when He the Spirit of Truth is come He will guide you unto all truth.'[13] The Bible has at least 17 references to the Glory of God, many of which clearly refer to Bahá'u'lláh. The most pointed is John's vision recorded in the book of Acts: 'But he (John), being full of the Holy Ghost, looked up steadfastly into heaven, and saw the glory of God, and Jesus standing on the right hand of God . . .'[14] That refers to two Persons. Since 'the Glory of God' is a title of Bahá'u'lláh, John's vision fits the appearance of Bahá'u'lláh and Christ standing together on the right hand of God.

Islam

The Prophet Muhammad made reference to the succession of Revelations under the Greater Covenant when He said, 'O, our Lord! For the day of whose coming there is not a doubt, thou wilt surely gather mankind together. Verily, God will not fail the promise.'[15] He also spoke of 'the day when the earth shall be changed into another earth'.[16]

Other

According to the Bahá'í Writings, the Founders of each of the above religions are Manifestations of God. Bahá'u'lláh further writes: 'Unto the cities of all nations He hath sent His Messengers, Whom He hath commissioned to announce unto men tidings of the Paradise of His good pleasure, and to draw them nigh unto the Haven of abiding security, the Seat of eternal holiness and transcendent glory.'[17]

The 124,000 Messengers from God mentioned in the Islamic traditions have appeared to people throughout the world.[18] Every group of people has had its Prophets and Holy Ones. Among the tribes of Africa, the Indians of the Americas, the islanders of the great oceans, there is evidence that each group had its own Messenger from God.

For instance, Patricia Locke together with two others researched American Indian oral history and discovered 23 individuals from different tribes who are considered by their tribes as Divine Messengers.[19] This is consistent both with Christ's statement in John 10:16 about other sheep, and the tradition in Islam mentioned above. The names and records of most of these Messengers have been lost. All that is left are stories, legends, traditions, prophecies, songs and visions that tell of a time when:

- there will be great trouble;
- people will forget their noble past;
- hope will be lost;
- a new Messenger from God will appear;
- He will unite all the people of world and bring about a time of peace and prosperity;
- hope, peace and happiness will come back to the people; and
- dignity and pride will be restored.

* * * * *

Despite the specific nature of prophecies, if their only purpose was to prepare mankind for the coming of the next Messenger from God, they have not seemed to work very well.

Why don't people rush to follow the new Messenger when He appears? True, a few perceptive souls immediately recognize the new Messenger based only on prophesy, but they are very few.

One thing all Manifestations have in common is that rather than being greeted with open arms, they are rejected. This rejection is most vigorous among the clergy who are the very ones who should be preparing their followers for the coming Voice of God. Moses had great difficulty convincing the Jews to follow Him. Christ was persecuted and crucified. Muhammad fled Mecca for Medina in the dark of night because of those ready to kill him. It was years before anyone would take Zoroaster seriously.

Even recognized fulfilments of the signs have failed to persuade many. For example, the Magi, three Zoroastrian priests, calculated the time and followed the star of Bethlehem to the birthplace of the Christchild. Where is the evidence that many Zoroastrians became Christians? According to the Gospels certain shepherds were given a special invitation to see that Holy Babe. How many shepherds became followers?

There are other lessons. The appearance of the Magi dramatically linked all religions together as having a common source, a point missed by many. Singling out the shepherds delivered several clear messages – which were generally ignored. The new Revelation was bypassing the established religious order. Christ would reach out to the humblest and lowliest members of the human family. The first to learn of a new Messenger are not necessarily the ones to promote the Cause and spread the teachings.

Despite the fact that Jesus spoke to at least 10,000 people, some New Testament scholars estimate that only about 40 could be called followers. No shepherds are mentioned. 'Abdu'l-Bahá commented, 'Consider the days of Christ . . . none but a small band followed Him.'[20] Even among the Apostles there were differences of opinion concerning His Station.[21]

One Christian scholar found 333 references in the Old Testament referring to the coming of Christ, but Jews don't see it that way. They even complain that Christians use their Holy Book (the Hebrew Bible, known to Christians as the Old Testament) against them. Muslims discern statements referring to Muhammad from Christian Scriptures, especially from the Book of Revelation, but that does not convince Christians.

A number of Christians accurately calculated the time for the coming of the Spirit of the New Day, such as Miller, Smith, Davis and Eddy in America, Wolff in Asia and Europe, Irving in England, Mason in Scotland, Kelber in Germany, among others.[22]

A colony was established on the slopes of Mount Carmel in Haifa – now called the German colony – anticipating the return of Christ. The mantel of one of the original dwellings reads, '*Der Herr ist nah*' (the Lord is near). Bahá'u'lláh pitched his tent next door to that very house shortly after it was built. Who from that house, or from the German colony itself, has, as yet, embraced the Cause?

They got the time right, but failed to find the object of their own calculations. Their own understandings became veils keeping them from recognizing Him when He did appear.

Prophecies do not have a good record of leading people to the next Messenger. Does that mean they are without purpose? Following are some questions to think about concerning prophecy in relationship to the Covenant for this age:

- Despite the fact that prophecies are both specific and allegorical, why haven't they been sufficient for people to recognize the next Messenger from God?
- Where is the evidence of fulfilment?
- What purpose, other than that of preparing people for the new Messenger, do prophecies serve?
- Why do symbolisms and veiled language often obscure rather than make fulfilment obvious?

Proof of interpretation

Many people claim to understand prophecy. However, only the divine Messengers have the keys to true understanding. This is explained by Bahá'u'lláh:

> . . . were the signs of the Manifestation of God in every age to appear in the visible realm in accordance with the text of established traditions, none could possibly deny or turn away, nor would the blessed be distinguished from the miserable, and the transgressor from the Godfearing.[23]

Only the Manifestation has full and complete understanding of the prophecies. His explanations are part of the proof of His sublime Station.

The New Testament records numerous instances in which Jesus interpreted prophecies of the Old Testament in ways that were not commonly understood. Ananias and Caiaphas, the leading clergymen of the day, saw Jesus's interpretations as blasphemy and gave counsel to Pilate that He be crucified.[24]

Bahá'u'lláh writes that 'Every hidden thing hath been brought to light . . .'[25] This completes the puzzle of Daniel, who prophesied that the meanings would be 'sealed till the time of the end'.[26] If Daniel did not understand his own vision, how should anyone else be expected to know the meaning? One of Bahá'u'lláh's earliest Writings, the *Kitáb-i-Íqán*, deals with understanding the prophecies and teachings of past Revelations – especially Judaism, Christianity and Islam. Accurate interpretation is part of the proof of the Manifestation.

A test

Sincerity, humility and detachment are all put to a formidable test when someone is asked to consider interpretations of prophecies that are different from his or her previous understanding.

Ironically, those who have studied prophecy the most are the ones who have the hardest time accepting other views. Their own understanding and interpretation become crystallized. Bahá'u'lláh used the term 'veils' for flawed human learning and understanding.[27]

Clergymen are the most vulnerable. Intellectual pride rears its ugly head. Some feel they 'know' the answer to prophetic mysteries. Many others become jaded to the mystery and leave it alone. Many focus on other issues and don't even want to discuss prophecy. Some see new and different interpretations as a threat to their authority and position. Prophecies, alone, have led few clergymen to the recognition of Bahá'u'lláh.

According to the Hopi of North America, mankind is facing the end of the fourth world and beginning of the fifth. There are many specific prophecies foretelling the greatness of this Day of God. They have ten specific prophecies, including the last that can be interpreted as predicting the destruction of the twin towers in New York City on 11 September 2001.[28] There is another one that seems to relate to the United Nations building in which people from all nations will gather to discuss international matters. Some Bahá'ís who are not Hopis have been led to the Faith through these prophecies. On the other hand, the Hopis who preserve and treasure the precious prophecies have not, as yet, perceived and embraced their fulfilment, although they did share these treasures with people who discovered Bahá'u'lláh aided by these prophecies.

Confirmation

Understanding that prophecy is fulfilled corroborates recognition. Interest in prophecy often develops AFTER someone has accepted Bahá'u'lláh.

Many people, with little or no interest in prophecy before becoming Bahá'ís, want to shout from the rooftops: 'Christ has returned.' They want everyone to know the good news that has just touched their hearts. They tend to forget that before they recognized Bahá'u'lláh, their own ears were deaf to such a pronouncement. One believer who had been married to a Bahá'í for ten years before accepting the Faith commented that his wife had been trying to tell him all that time that Christ had returned. It didn't penetrate until after he found his way to the Blessed Beauty through a very different route.

Continuity

Once there is an acceptance of the fulfilment of prophecy, the ability to see the pattern of progressive revelation is easy. It becomes a spiritual high ground from which to see the past, present and future as a continuous flow of the Eternal Covenant. The Covenant, then, provides an entirely new window through which to view and understand spiritual processes and unfolding world events.

Thrill of discovery

When an unknown becomes known, many other perplexing facts suddenly fall into place. Truth is assimilated in this manner: it is engraved on the soul and becomes YOURS. No one can take it from you. This thrill of discovery often has a major impact on new believers. When they first realize that prophecy has indeed been fulfilled, it is easier to embrace the totality of the Faith. It has the effect of opening a window to a whole new view of the world.

Symbolism

This becomes another issue. A symbol is anything that stands for or represents something else. The ability to use and manipulate symbols is a major distinction between human beings and other creatures. Symbols have the capacity to explain things on a deeper and more profound level than mere explanations. They connect what is known to what cannot be known.

As mentioned earlier, the rainbow is a good example. It is hard to find a culture that does not use the rainbow metaphorically – from a bridge to the next world or profound mysteries, to a pot of gold and/or mystical people.

Bahá'u'lláh gave an example of the value of symbols by quoting Sadiq: 'A true believer is likened unto the philosopher's stone,' going on to say, 'Reflect, how this symbolic language, more eloquent than any speech, however direct, testifieth to the non-existence of a true believer.'[29]

The concurrence of astronomical and spiritual signs is also interesting in this regard. In the intriguing year of 1844, near the time when the Báb revealed Himself, the Prussian astronomer and mathematician Friedrich Wilhelm Bessel became fascinated by the star Sirius. It was bright, yet irregular. He concluded that it must be not one, but two stars that were in line with each other. This was the first recorded note suggesting binary stars, sometimes called twin stars.[30] Nineteen years later, shortly before the events of the Riḍván garden, the telescope maker Alvan G. Clark actually saw and recorded the second star.[31]

The idea of twin luminaries first occurred to someone about the time that the Báb met with Mullá Ḥusayn. The visible evidence coincided with the Announcement of Bahá'u'lláh. It was as if the stars of heaven were announcing the Twin Manifestations of God for this Day. Despite the timing of this occurrence, it was noted by few and understood by none.

It is unlikely that either Bessel or Clark gave any thought to a metaphysical, let alone spiritual, significance to their discoveries. While these astronomical observances were an important factor for one physics professor to accept Bahá'u'lláh, they have not been persuasive for most people. Future generations may tie these events together and celebrate them, similar to the way that the star of Bethlehem was not given prominence in Christian traditions until long after the fact.

Like the symbolic interpretation of the rainbow as a bridge to the divine world, the symbols in myriad prophecies should have been, but were not always, a bridge to recognition of this New Day of God.

Identity and tradition

In the meantime, prophecies and traditional ceremonies are important. They form part of community identity and have served as an emotional protection. The stories are a belief held in common with other members of a religious community. That tie can become stronger than the prophetic or spiritual nature of the prophecy. For instance, in the Jewish community, in the celebration of the Seder the final intonation is often 'Next Year in Jerusalem'. This sustained and fortified the Jews for centuries during the Diaspora. A Bahá'í of Jewish background said that as a child she pleaded with her grandfather to let her go to the door during the ceremonial knock. She said, 'I knew, I just knew that one day I would open that door and there would be the Messiah.' After becoming a Bahá'í she realized that Bahá'u'lláh had fulfilled her expectation when she was a little girl.

This common unity and validating feature can take on a life of its own, introducing the danger that prophecies become more important than their fulfilment, making it more difficult, rather than easier, for people to accept the completion.

Some Bahá'ís try to blend the old and the new. The 'Last Wednesday' celebration is still celebrated by some Persian Bahá'ís. Held on the last Wednesday before Naw-Rúz, it probably dates back to Zoroastrian days of these Bahá'ís' forebears. Part of it involves jumping over open fires, in the idea that inappropriate thoughts and habits are dropped in and consumed by the fire. Many Bahá'ís of Christian background continue to celebrate Christmas with their families. A Bahá'í of Jewish background was married to an Eskimo, giving their daughter a dual heritage. Living in Alaska at the time, the child learned quite a bit of her Eskimo background, but nothing of her Jewish heritage. They lived in a small town without a synagogue, a rabbi or an active Jewish community. One day this Bahá'í rounded up all the Jews in town and hosted a Seder so that her daughter could experience something of her Jewish heritage. A pattern was started. The Jews in town continued getting together for traditional Holy Days even after the Bahá'í moved away.

These are examples of how religious rituals can become traditions that extend beyond their religious roots.

The problem is that, while traditions contribute toward a sense of stability and security, they also make it more difficult to accept the true meaning and significance of the tradition.

* * * * *

Many religious communities claim finality for their Revelation. Bahá'u'lláh gave a different perspective. Rather than claiming finality, He made specific statements concerning the next Messenger from God. The most graphic is: 'Whoso layeth claim to a Revelation direct from God, ere the expiration of a full thousand years, such a man is assuredly a lying impostor.'[32]

This statement clearly states the coming of another Manifestation of God, but specifies a period of time during which there will be NO direct Revelation, nipping in the bud any such pretensions, while affirming there WILL be others.

But, what about the most recent stage in this long process? That is, the Lesser Covenant for this age?

3

The Lesser Covenant

Nowhere in the sacred scriptures of any of the world's religious systems . . . do we find any provisions establishing a covenant or providing for an administrative order that can compare in scope and authority with those that lie at the very basis of the Bahá'í Dispensation.
Shoghi Effendi[1]

Each Manifestation appears when there are two human conditions: one is that people have lost the fire of faith and are at a low point spiritually; the other is that they have reached the point in their evolution at which they have the capacity to move to the next stage of development.

Among the many challenges for each new Messenger is to find capable souls who can be the instruments to recreate and educate the human spirit. This search is carried out among a population that is not only resistant to change, but violently hostile to those Divine Manifestations Who come for human revival.

The first step is to enkindle souls that are receptive to the Voice of the Lord of the Age. This is a selection process. It is not always the most capable people, but those most likely to be attuned to the Word of God. As Jesus put it: 'for many be called, but few chosen'.[2]

Bahá'ís are that thin sliver of humankind that has been selected in this age as participants in the matrix for the building the World Order. They come from all strata of society, a true cross-section of mankind, geographically and in other ways. Far-flung, this universal sample encompasses every ethnic and cultural background, with varying intellectual capacities, the gifted and the ordinary, the energetic and the casual, the mystic and the rational, the wealthy and those in poverty, the spiritually perceptive and sensitive and those with more practical inclination, scholars and illiterates, those with penetrating wisdom and keen insight and those of modest endowments. This miniscule community of the Greatest Name was selected to be a safe haven for the development of the institutions mankind so sorely needs.

Their love for Bahá'u'lláh is what unites them. It is the power of the Covenant that keeps the community from being fragmented by secondary issues that so often divide humanity. These are features that enable the world-wide Bahá'í community to be entrusted with the awesome privilege and responsibility for the development of this Administrative Order for all mankind.

The basics

How is this done? A rough comparison can be made to a school. In many schools, when a teacher has to leave the room, chaos enters. If a good teacher has to be gone for any length of time, two things are done: one is leaving a detailed lesson plan; the other is having a qualified substitute.

Through the *Kitáb-i-Aqdas* and the *Kitáb-i-'Ahd*, specific instructions – or lesson plans – were provided. With the appointment of 'Abdu'l-Bahá, a qualified leader was found to supervise the instructions for an unruly, undisciplined, immature and severely fragmented humanity.

Upon the passing of 'Abdu'l-Bahá, mankind was still not capable of sustaining the guidance for the new day without assistance. So, as the Centre of the Covenant, He continued the process with his own Will and Testament and the appointment of Shoghi Effendi as the Guardian. Although Shoghi Effendi was only six years old when the appointment was written, 'Abdu'l-Bahá saw in the child the qualities needed for the Guardianship. The document was kept hidden and secret until the passing of 'Abdu'l-Bahá.

Among Shoghi Effendi's signal achievements was the launching of the Ten Year Spiritual Crusade. He passed away at the mid-point of that divinely revealed plan, leaving the world with five more years to complete it.

The Hands of the Cause,[3] as custodians and 'Chief Stewards'[4] of the Faith, had the responsibility of completing the Guardian's plan. They realized that, according to the *Kitáb-i-Aqdas*, only the Universal House of Justice could be the channel for infallibility. Therefore, at the critical juncture of the conclusion of the World Crusade, the second of the twin institutions of the Administrative Order, the Universal House of Justice, was elected.[5] This provided the continuation of infallible guidance under the Covenant.

Continuity

Any organization is vulnerable during a time of transfer of authority. Historically, that is when governments topple and dynasties end. The strength of the Covenant of Bahá'u'lláh is demonstrated by the fact that the Faith has been able to remain united for more than a century and a half despite numerous attempts at division.

There have been five major transfers of authority within the Bahá'í community during its formative years. Through all of these, the Covenant has protected the Faith, leaving it united, intact and unscathed.

Before the Declaration of the Báb there was a transfer that followed the normal pattern. Students of Siyyid Káẓim were just that, students. Shortly before his death, Siyyid Káẓim said the Promised One was on earth and his followers should search for Him. Mullá Ḥusayn was the first to begin his search. After fasting for 40 days, he, together with his brother and nephew, set out on their quest. He became the first to believe.

While some of the followers of Siyyid Káẓim embraced the Faith of the Báb, the majority did not. Several claimed the mantle of leadership for themselves and splinter groups were formed. That was business as usual. This was before the Báb promised that this Cause would never be divided. That promise changed forever the problems that have historically arisen during the vulnerable time when the mantle of authority changes.

The first threat to cohesion came to light with Bahá'u'lláh's Declaration in the Riḍván Garden, in 1863, when He announced that He was 'Him Whom God Will Make Manifest'. The jealousy of Mirzá Yaḥyá, Bahá'u'lláh's younger half-brother, knew no bounds. He continued to cause grave difficulties. Except as a bad example, Mirzá Yaḥyá left no lasting impact. His attempt to seize power faded into oblivion after his death. Most of the Bábís embraced the Cause of Bahá'u'lláh and became Bahá'ís.

The second transfer of authority and challenge was with the passing of Bahá'u'lláh. Even though He had clearly appointed 'Abdu'l-Bahá as the Centre of His Covenant, it did not take long before the Master's half-brother, Muḥammad-'Alí, fired by jealousy and a love of leadership, together with a few others, tried to undermine the authority of 'Abdu'l-Bahá. The efforts of those few detractors also came to naught, leaving no permanent breach.

The third threat to the integrity of the Cause came when 'Abdu'l-Bahá appointed Shoghi Effendi as Guardian of the Cause of God. Again, there were those who sought leadership and other dissidents who tried to undermine his authority, especially his jealous great-uncle Muḥammad-'Alí and other members of both his immediate and extended family, as well as Ahmad Sohrab – who had served as 'Abdu'l-Bahá's secretary. The efforts of those who tried to cause division came to naught. The integrity of the Faith was maintained.

The fourth period of vulnerability was with the passing of the Guardian. Prior to his passing in 1957, he had appointed certain prominent Bahá'ís as Hands of the Cause and, as just mentioned, referred to them as 'Chief Stewards' of the Faith. This gave them the legal authority under the laws of Israel to continue to function as the head of the Faith from the World Centre. They became responsible for completion of the Guardian's Ten Year Spiritual Crusade.

After his funeral, 27 of the Hands met and reached several conclusions. One of the first was that it had not been possible, under the Covenant, for the Guardian to appoint a successor. That led to the realization that when the Ten Year Crusade was concluded, without a Guardian the world would be deprived of infallible guidance. Only the formation of the Universal House of Justice would give mankind the benefit of such guidance.

There has not been a lot of speculation as to why there was no second Guardian. Most Bahá'ís accept it as part of the mysterious plan of God. It really doesn't matter. We still have the Guardianship with the copious interpretations of the Guardian, and the Universal House of Justice functions well in its own sphere. The Cause of God moved forward at this fragile juncture because of the selfless action of the Hands of the Cause. They were a group of highly talented, successful and strong-willed individuals. History is filled with fights for leadership among the most prominent of any group when the leader dies. What the Hands had in common, in addition to being firm in the Covenant, was their utter devotion to the Guardian and lack of personal ambition for leadership in the Faith.

From among this group there was one, and only one, Mason Remey, who aspired to personal leadership. He announced that he should be the second Guardian. He got no support from the other Hands. He did have a small following among some disenchanted and/or self-seeking believers. His leadership did not last long.

There have been a few times in history when one, two or three great people have put aside perceived personal benefit for the common good; but, nearly 30? Never before!

The Hands of the Cause:

- ❖ maintained the integrity of the Faith;
- ❖ oversaw the successful completion of the Ten Year Spiritual Crusade;
- ❖ called for an election of the International Bahá'í Council[6] which the beloved Guardian said would 'effloresce' into the Universal House of Justice; and finally,
- ❖ called for the first election of the Universal House of Justice.

This fifth and final transfer of authority, the election of the Universal House of Justice, took place during Riḍván of 1963. The Hands of the Cause specifically asked that they *not* be elected. They stated that each one wished to resume the specific instructions given them by the Guardian that would not be possible if elected to the Universal House of Justice.

Members of 56 National Spiritual Assemblies gathered in Haifa, Israel at Riḍván 1963 for that election. With no campaigning, without nominations, with no prior platforms, people from different parts of the world, few of whom knew one another, prayerfully gathered for this election.

The clear choice for the nine who were elected was completed with the very first balloting.

The cheers and tears of joy at the announcement of the nine members elected to the Universal House of Justice were overwhelming. The only sombre people present were those who had just been elected. They stood, stunned, heads bowed, contemplating the weight that had been thrust upon them. Their acclamation by those who were present was nothing less than a celebration of the victory of this incomparable Covenant of God, which had protected the infant Cause of God through extremely troubled waters.

Prayers for the House of Justice should be an important part of every believer's daily routine. Such prayers do two things.

While one person's petition to God to help the House may have little impact, thousands, nay millions, do. Secondly, those prayers more strongly connect the individual with the spirit and objectives of the House, facilitating the execution of its plans.

Having successfully survived those five times of vulnerable transition shows the strength of the Covenant. In the more than a century since the martyrdom of the Báb, that Covenant has kept the Faith united and provided for its expansion to a global presence, with adherents from every ethnic, religious and cultural background. This achievement has no parallel in all of recorded history. It is part and parcel of the fulfilment of the Báb's promise.

Since then, a few misguided and self-serving souls have tried to cause trouble, but none have succeeded at penetrating the protective shield of the Covenant. From the time of the Báb's promise that this Cause would not be divided, all attempts to divide the Faith have been short-lived or failed almost immediately.

In a world based on power relationships, one successful transfer of power of such magnitude would be miraculous. But, five times!

I was an enrolled Bahá'í during the last two transfers. What stood out is the universal support each time. Even though I lived in a culture that dotes on conspiracy theories, I never heard one dismissive word of dissent or suspicion of manipulation or that something was being withheld. Only the protection of the Covenant could achieve this.

Five documents specifically spell out the features of the Covenant through which the promise of the Báb is being realized.

The Kitáb-i-Aqdas

Described by the beloved Guardian as the 'Most Holy Book', the 'Mother Book' and the 'charter of the future world civilization' and of the World Order of Bahá'u'lláh, this book covers every aspect of being a Bahá'í. In regard to the Lesser Covenant, it spells out successorship, defines infallibility and interpretation, inaugurates the Universal House of Justice, gives the terms of authority and provides for its continuity.[7]

The Kitáb-i-'Ahd

This Will and Testament of Bahá'u'lláh clearly appointed 'Abdu'l-Bahá as Centre of His Covenant, and deliberately subordinated Muḥammad-'Alí to 'Abdu'l-Bahá. This seemingly simple step nipped in the bud any potential schism. It conferred infallibility of interpretation exclusively on 'Abdu'l-Bahá. This eliminated any pretensions Muḥammad-'Alí might have had to insubordination.

The Will and Testament of 'Abdu'l-Bahá

Along with the *Kitáb-i-Aqdas*, the Guardian has called this a charter of the future world civilization and of the World Order of Bahá'u'lláh.[8] Among the many topics covered, it spells out the general framework for the Administrative Order; formally establishes the Guardianship; defines the relationship between the Guardian and the Universal House of Justice; calls for the formation of secondary houses of justice; and specifies the functions of related institutions, including the Hands of the Cause.

'The Dispensation of Bahá'u'lláh'

A long letter written by Shoghi Effendi in 1934 has been titled 'The Dispensation of Bahá'u'lláh'. It is the sixth letter found in *The World Order of Bahá'u'lláh*. Amatu'l-Bahá Rúḥíyyih Khánum, the widow of Shoghi Effendi, writes that in it he 'considered he had said all he had to say'.[9] It is an elucidation of the Stations of Bahá'u'lláh, the Báb, 'Abdu'l-Bahá and the Administrative Order.

The 'Dispensation' describes the functioning of the Administrative Order and delineates the relationships among its component parts. It shows that authority in the Faith passed from Bahá'u'lláh to 'Abdu'l-Bahá as the Centre of the Covenant and from there to the Administrative Order, of which the Guardianship and the Universal House of Justice are its twin institutions.

The Constitution of the Universal House of Justice

This document, drafted by the Universal House of Justice shortly after its formation, spells out the legal authority and functions of the House by itemizing five specific duties:

1. Preserve the Sacred Texts
2. Advance the interests of the Cause
3. Enact laws and ordinances
4. Promulgate and apply laws and principles, and
5. Adjudicate disputes.

The best overview of the system was provided by the Guardian when he wrote:

> To direct and canalize these forces let loose by this Heaven-sent process, and to insure their harmonious and continuous operation after His ascension, an instrument divinely ordained, invested with indisputable authority, organically linked with the Author of the Revelation Himself, was clearly indispensable. That instrument Bahá'u'lláh had expressly provided through the institution of the Covenant, an institution which He had firmly established prior to His ascension.[10]

And:

The Covenant which, despite the determined assaults launched against it, succeeded, unlike all previous Dispensations, in preserving the integrity of the Faith of its Author, and in paving the way for the advent of the One Who was to be its Center and Object, had been firmly and irrevocably established.¹¹

Infallibility

The range of infallibility is outlined in the Will and Testament of 'Abdu'l-Bahá and clarified by the interpretation of the Guardian. 'Indisputable authority' is the pinnacle of power and authority. This constitutes a primary element of the Lesser Covenant. No human institution can claim anything like it. It is a restrictive gift from God.

Part of its great beauty and virtue is its finality. In the secular world, when a leader or institution makes a decision it sometimes settles disputes, but often does not. At times, that decision sets off endless wrangling and division that sometimes end in bloodshed and war. With divine infallibility, the matter is settled. There is no basis for further dispute.

Many times Bahá'ís have disagreed with one another on various issues. Rather than arguing, they have turned to authoritative sources, and issues were settled. This benefit is a bounty of the Covenant.

God provided this Revelation with two forms of infallibility: innate and conferred. That which is innate exists by its very nature, such as water being wet. That which is conferred is limited to specific matters.

Only Universal Manifestations have innate infallibility. This has also been called 'the Most Great Infallibility [which] is confined to the One Whose station is immeasurably exalted beyond ordinances or prohibitions and is sanctified from errors and omissions'.¹²

Conferred infallibility is bestowed by the Manifestation of

THE LESSER COVENANT

God. In this Dispensation, for the first time, humanity has the exact Words of the Messenger Himself, in writing, concerning His successor and the infallibility that was conferred. The Blessed Beauty, Bahá'u'lláh, appointed 'Abdu'l-Bahá as the Centre of His Covenant and confirmed upon Him infallible interpretation of His Word. Anything 'Abdu'l-Bahá said was as if Bahá'u'lláh Himself had said it. This was implied in the *Kitáb-i-Aqdas* and confirmed in the *Kitáb-i-'Ahd*.

In His *Will and Testament*, the Centre of the Covenant appointed Shoghi Effendi as the Guardian and infallibility for interpretation and protection was conferred upon him:

> Shoghi Effendi was asked several times during his ministry to define the sphere of his operation and his infallibility. The replies he gave and which were written on his behalf are most illuminating. He explains that he is not an infallible authority on subjects such as economics and science, nor does he go into technical matters since his infallibility is confined to 'matters which are related strictly to the Cause'. He further points out that 'he is not, like the Prophet, omniscient at will', that his 'infallibility covers interpretation of the Revealed Word and its application', and that he is also 'infallible in the protection of the Faith'. Furthermore, in one of the letters, the following guideline is set forth:
>
>> '. . . It is not for individual believers to limit the sphere of the Guardian's authority, or to judge when they have to obey the Guardian and when they are free to reject his judgment. Such an attitude would evidently lead to confusion and to schism. The Guardian being the appointed interpreter of the Teachings, it is his responsibility to state what matters which, affecting the interests of the Faith, demand on the part of the believers, complete and unqualified obedience to his instructions.'[13]

The Universal House is the unique institution 'which God hath ordained as the source of all good and freed from all error...'[14] It will provide mankind with infallible guidance throughout this Dispensation. It was also given the specific 'power to enact laws that are not expressly recorded in the Book and ... also it hath power to repeal the same.'[15]

On the matter of its own infallibility, the Universal House of Justice has written:

> The Universal House of Justice shares with the Guardian the responsibility for the application of the Revealed Word, the protection of the Faith, as well as the duty 'to insure the continuity of that divinely appointed authority which flows from the Source of our Faith, to safeguard the unity of its followers, and to maintain the integrity and flexibility of its Teachings'. However, the Universal House of Justice is not omniscient...[16]

Historically, in both religious and secular systems, people who had absolute authority often abused it. Within the framework of their societies, their authority was similar to infallibility: not because it was free of error, but because it was final. Now, the important feature of final authority has been removed from leaders who can be corrupted and abuse it. This essential element is under the protection of the Covenant. Still, opposition is an everpresent danger.

Continuity of spiritual guidance was described by the Guardian when He wrote:

> The Covenant of Bahá'u'lláh had been instituted solely through the direct operation of His Will and purpose. The Will and Testament of 'Abdu'l-Bahá, on the other hand, may be regarded as the offspring resulting from that mystic intercourse between Him Who had generated the forces of a God-given Faith and the One Who had been made its sole

Interpreter and was recognized as its perfect Exemplar.[17]

An example of that divine relationship was illustrated by an incident told by Hand of the Cause Ugo Giachery. He said he was in the Master's house and overheard a conversation when a Persian family arrived. They presented the Guardian with a copy of the *Kitáb-i-Íqán* in the handwriting of 'Abdu'l-Bahá which had been sent to one of their ancestors.[18] The Guardian accepted it graciously and all went their several directions.

A short time later Shoghi Effendi came running down the stairs shouting, 'Ugo, Ugo, look at this.' The copy had a margin note in Bahá'u'lláh's handwriting. It was something the Guardian had never seen before. However, he had used the same wording in the Introduction to *The Dawn-Breakers*. It was as if he had translated something from Bahá'u'lláh that he had never seen! To me, this shows the divine, mystical connection running through the Lesser Covenant.

Administration

The Guardian explained the administration of the Cause as an integral part of the Faith and the perfect instrument for carrying forth the provisions of the Covenant when he wrote:

> It should be remembered by every follower of the Cause that the system of Bahá'í administration is not an innovation imposed arbitrarily upon the Bahá'ís of the world since the Master's passing, but derives its authority from the Will and Testament of 'Abdu'l-Bahá, is specifically prescribed in unnumbered Tablets, and rests in some of its essential features upon the explicit provisions of the Kitáb-i-Aqdas. It thus unifies and correlates the principles separately laid down by Bahá'u'lláh and 'Abdu'l-Bahá, and is indissolubly bound with the essential verities of the Faith. To dissociate the administrative principles of the Cause from the purely

spiritual and humanitarian teachings would be tantamount to a mutilation of the body of the Cause, a separation that can only result in the disintegration of its component parts, and the extinction of the Faith itself.[19]

Just a few months after receiving the staggering news that he was appointed Guardian of the Faith, Shoghi Effendi wrote a long letter dated 5 March 1922 to the believers of the West.[20] That letter not only stated the bases of the organization of the Faith, it also made clear that the administration is embryonic and evolving. During his lifetime, Shoghi Effendi made many adjustments in the system and the Universal House of Justice continues to make necessary changes according to time and circumstances.

An illustration of the far-reaching changes that continue to take place is the establishment of what are now called local Spiritual Assemblies. One day they will become local Houses of Justice with vastly expanded duties. Changes are necessarily gradual and only the Universal House of Justice can say when the time is right.

Leadership

Leadership in the secular world has historically been both a great blessing and an enormous curse. It has vast capacity for both good and evil. While people of good will can and do use authority wisely and to the best interests of all concerned, self-serving people have all too often heaped great evil on those whom they were to serve.

There are several problems with the contemporary models of leadership. Many well-intentioned people have entered a position of authority with altruistic motives. Sometimes, but not always, these are changed for the worse. But the temptation is always there.

It has been said that power corrupts, but this is only partly true. The real problem is that power can create an aura of invincibility. That is what makes people vulnerable to corruption. People in positions of authority can come to believe that the law does not apply to them. Sometimes it is sinister, but often not; rather, it is a slow erosion of standards.

Albert Speer, in his book *Inside the Third Reich*, detailed the slow erosion of his moral standards by association with Hitler's hierarchy. Speer was an architect. From the start, his interest and focus was in the design and construction of government buildings, not political matters. He paid scant attention to Hitler's aims. It wasn't until after the downfall of the Third Reich, while Speer was in prison, that he realized that over the course of months he came to endorse views that had been repugnant to him earlier. In retrospect, he was stunned by the complete shift in his notions of right and wrong. But it had been so gradual that he did not notice the change as it was happening. That has happened to countless others in various human situations.

Corruption can start by cutting corners as a means to achieve lofty objectives. It is particularly dangerous when authority figures control those who are to enforce the rules. Sometimes people overlook and accept the wrongdoings of those in authority because of misplaced feelings of admiration, intimidation or fear of reprisal. The result is that the one in authority does not receive the same level of scrutiny as others do. There may be bitter criticism by avowed opponents, but those words are taken less seriously because their motives are suspect.

Another problem is distance from the generality of mankind. Leaders can enter an almost cocoon-like experience. It is easy to get out of touch with what is going on, and not even be aware of the growing gap.

There is another, more subtle, problem, sometimes referred to as 'group think'. That is when close advisers have a reluctance to disagree with the authority figure. There is a tendency to find information and say things to support the leader's point of view. Those close to the one in authority may develop a common mind-set that supports the authority figure. The rise of Nazism, the bombing of Pearl Harbor, the Bay of Pigs fiasco and the disaster in Syria have all suffered from 'group think'. The leaders all had top-level advisers who failed to sufficiently warn against potential disastrous results. This is not necessarily from ulterior motives; often it is only a misguided display of loyalty. But it can create a treacherous curtain of deference around authority figures that easily invites a distortion of reality and leads to corruption.

In order to resolve this problem, Bahá'u'lláh declared: 'From two ranks amongst men power hath been seized: kings and ecclesiastics.'[21]

Despite His privileged family connections, Bahá'u'lláh spurned offers of worldly leadership and clearly showed His attitude when He wrote:

> By the righteousness of God, my Well-Beloved! I have never aspired after worldly leadership. My sole purpose hath been to hand down unto men that which I was bidden to deliver by God, the Gracious, the Incomparable, that it may detach them from all that pertaineth to this world, and cause them to attain such heights as neither the ungodly can conceive, nor the froward imagine.[22]

This shows a clear sense of mission. However, it was not to be achieved through personal leadership – not even strong, charismatic leadership, even though that quality was part of His natural endowment.

A lofty goal without strong, individual leadership creates a dilemma: leaderless societies do not thrive. Anarchy leads to chaos and wanton destruction. Both secular and spiritual authority is needed. How can that be achieved without personal leadership?

In order to provide the blessings of enlightened leadership without the negative elements that have accompanied personal leadership, Bahá'u'lláh created two new channels, the rulers and the learned: 'It is incumbent upon everyone to aid those daysprings of authority and sources of command who are adorned with the ornament of equity and justice. Blessed are the rulers and the learned among the people of Bahá.'[23]

Leadership can be formal or informal. In a formal sense, there are institutions and individuals that have specific, legal authority. There is also informal leadership, similar to what is seen among all animals. Whenever two or more creatures are involved in some activity – from playing to hunting to social activities – there are clear leadership roles. Every wolf pack has an alpha female leader; every herd of wild horses likewise has a leader. Even in a litter of newborn pups, one usually stands out as the leader. Among chickens, the pecking order changes when a new chicken is added.

Humans display similar patterns. From children at play to family dynamics to any other group, leaders emerge. Sometimes leadership changes within a single group, depending on the specific activity. Informal leadership among Bahá'ís will be discussed in Part II.

The new roles established by Bahá'u'lláh are explained by Shoghi Effendi as follows:

> In this holy cycle the 'learned' are, on the one hand, the Hands of the Cause of God, and, on the other, the teachers and diffusers of His Teachings who do not rank as Hands, but who have attained an eminent position in the teaching work. As to the 'rulers' they refer to the members of the Local, National and International Houses of Justice.[24]

This is more than a minor adjustment. It is the total realignment of both the selection and the operation of leadership. One astounding change is that no one can seek or aspire to any position among either the rulers or the learned. There is no place for those who harbour a personal desire for leadership. In the secular world, people become rulers through several means. Some are rulers by birthright – such as kings; some come to power through struggle – such as wars, coups or insurrections; others attain power through political processes, including contentious elections based on power relationships.

Bahá'u'lláh extolled the importance of the two new institutions when he wrote, 'Please God, the peoples of the world may be led, as the result of the high endeavours exerted by their rulers and the wise and learned amongst men, to recognize their best interests.'[25]

Rulers

For the institution of the rulers, Bahá'u'lláh created major shifts in the way leaders function. One was replacing confrontational modes of negotiations and decision-making with a consultative model. Another was basing deliberations on mutual respect rather than power relationships.

Another potent feature is that within the Universal House of Justice there is an ultimate authority. The fractious bickering, contentions and armed conflicts of today continue because there is no agreed-upon final authority to settle disputes. There are attempts within the secular world to provide stability through institutions such as the United Nations, the International Court of Justice (World Court) and a wide variety of agencies to combat world hunger and other maladies. While they are making some progress and providing experience in global living, they do not have the allegiance and respect necessary for their moral authority to be binding.

Only with unswerving loyalty and commitment to the agreed-upon final authority can the bloody wrangling that currently plagues mankind reach an end. Bahá'u'lláh provided the Universal House of Justice as the capstone for world peace and stability.

Bahá'u'lláh retained the concept of free and democratic elections but removed the negative elements that too often accompany the process. Specifically, He removed the features of partisanship, parties, nominations, campaigns and electioneering. This denies positions of leadership to those with personal ambitions. As a result, no individual can seek an office. The office seeks the individual.

In my experience, those elected to Spiritual Assemblies fall into one of three broad categories. First of all, there are those who love the work and thrive on it. They wholeheartedly put their best efforts into the matters at hand, relishing the task.

Secondly, there are those who are indifferent to it personally, but take on their elected responsibilities as a matter of duty. They work diligently and tirelessly at their tasks, but their satisfaction is in knowing they are serving Bahá'u'lláh, not in the nature of what they are doing or a sense of personal achievement.

The third group consists of those who would rather do anything EXCEPT serve in this capacity. Some of these people don't bother to show up for meetings. There are others who serve in spite of their preference not to, because of love for Bahá'u'lláh. It takes a great deal of personal strength for people who would rather be elsewhere to overcome their personal reticence.

One highly competent individual who was a member of a National Spiritual Assembly for many years would deliberately miss national Conventions in the hope he would not be re-elected. But, when re-elected against his personal desire, he would serve, and he served well. I even heard a member of the Universal House of Justice mutter tearfully, just after his first election, 'This is not the way I can best serve.' But he did, and for many years! Another member of the House of Justice jokingly said, 'Those who think they would like to serve on the Universal House of Justice should try it for a while.'

How can you corrupt people who would rather not be there in the first place?

Only the rulers, as a group, can make binding decisions, and that can only be done when the body is in a duly called session.

Learned

Members of the institution of the learned act in harmony with the rulers, but have different functions. The learned are selected, usually for very specific qualities needed for the Bahá'í community at a particular time and place.

Despite the implication of their title, the learned are not necessarily the most knowledgeable people. The specific characteristic is suggested in the quotation above on page 37. That is, they are *learned among the people of Bahá*. One way to look at it is that they have within themselves a measure of the essence of being a Bahá'í. They may or may not be a storehouse of vast knowledge, either for matters relating to the Faith or other subjects. That is beside the point. This point was made by Bahá'u'lláh in a prayer for the Hands: 'They utter not a word on any subject ere Thou hast spoken, for their ears are attuned to hear Thy command . . .'[26]

A protection, both for them and for others, lies in the fact that they cannot tell people what to do. They can advise, suggest, inspire and give guidance, but only the rulers, as an institution, not as individuals, can make authoritative decisions.

Hands of the Cause were first and foremost among the learned. After the passing of Shoghi Effendi and the election of the Universal House of Justice, the House soon realized two things. One was that the function of the Hands was vital and the second was the House of Justice had no authority under the Covenant to appoint future Hands. This led to the institution of the Counsellors. They serve for specific time periods with defined duties and, unlike the Hands, theirs is a function, not a station. That is, the Hands had a unique spiritual station without end. The Counsellors have specific duties to perform for a limited period of time. Counsellors, in turn, appoint Auxiliary Board members to assist them in their work. Board members can appoint assistants. While both the institution of the rulers and individual believers should listen respectfully to what the learned have to say, there is no obligation to follow that advice.

The importance of the institutions of the rulers and the learned is stated by Bahá'u'lláh as follows:

> They are My trustees among My servants and the manifestations of My commandments amidst My people. Upon them rest My glory, My blessings and My grace which have pervaded the world of being. In this connection the utterances revealed in the *Kitáb-i-Aqdas* are such that from the horizon of their words the light of divine grace shineth luminous and resplendent.[27]

Finally, there is this summary by the Guardian:

> Let no one, while this System is still in its infancy, misconceive its character, belittle its significance or misrepresent its purpose. The bedrock on which this Administrative Order is founded is God's immutable Purpose for mankind in this day. The Source from which it derives its inspiration is no one less than Bahá'u'lláh Himself. Its shield and defender are the embattled hosts of the Abhá Kingdom. Its seed is the blood of no less than twenty thousand martyrs who have offered up their lives that it may be born and flourish. The axis round which its institutions revolve are the authentic provisions of the Will and Testament of 'Abdu'l-Bahá. Its guiding principles are the truths which He Who is the unerring Interpreter of the teachings of our Faith has so clearly enunciated in His public addresses throughout the West. The laws that govern its operation and limit its functions are those which have been expressly ordained in

the Kitáb-i-Aqdas. The seat round which its spiritual, its humanitarian and administrative activities will cluster are the Mashriqu'l-Adhkár and its Dependencies. The pillars that sustain its authority and buttress its structure are the twin institutions of the Guardianship and of the Universal House of Justice. The central, the underlying aim which animates it is the establishment of the New World Order as adumbrated by Bahá'u'lláh. The methods it employs, the standard it inculcates, incline it to neither East nor West, neither Jew nor Gentile, neither rich nor poor, neither white nor colored. Its watchword is the unification of the human race; its standard the 'Most Great Peace'; its consummation the advent of that golden millennium – the Day when the kingdoms of this world shall have become the Kingdom of God Himself, the Kingdom of Bahá'u'lláh.[28]

This is a brief summary of the administrative scheme. But, what are ordinary Bahá'ís to do?

4

Behaviours

O Son of Dust! Verily I say unto thee: Of all men the most negligent is he that disputeth idly and seeketh to advance himself over his brother. Say, O brethren! Let deeds, not words, be your adorning.
Bahá'u'lláh[1]

The Greater Covenant is the relationship among the revealed religions. The Lesser Covenant relates to this Dispensation and gives a shift of focus both to everyday life and the immediate workings of the plan of God. It provides both an entirely different way to view the world and a blueprint for behaviour. But, what are individual believers to do about it?

Natural and spiritual pathways

'Abdu'l-Bahá said:

> From the time of the creation of Adam to this day there have been two pathways in the world of humanity; one the natural or materialistic, the other the religious or spiritual. The pathway of nature is the pathway of the animal realm. The animal acts in accordance with the requirements of nature, follows its own instincts and desires. Whatever its impulses and proclivities may be it has the liberty to gratify them; yet it is a captive of nature. It cannot deviate in the least degree from the road nature has established. It is utterly lacking spiritual susceptibilities, ignorant of divine religion and without knowledge of the Kingdom of God. The animal possesses no power of ideation or conscious

intelligence; it is a captive of the senses and deprived of that which lies beyond them. It is subject to what the eye sees, the ear hears, the nostrils sense, the taste detects and touch reveals. These sensations are acceptable and sufficient for the animal. But that which is beyond the range of the senses, that realm of phenomena through which the conscious pathway to the Kingdom of God leads, the world of spiritual susceptibilities and divine religion – of these the animal is completely unaware, for in its highest station it is a captive of nature.[2]

That is not to say that animals do not have intelligence and emotions, or are not sensitive to a wide range of relationships. Animals can and do learn many things. Even though certain animals are far superior to man in specific traits – such as physical strength or eyesight – none are known to be superior to man in the aggregate or in ideational matters. Their capabilities are minimal compared to humans, who have options to move beyond the natural limits of other creatures. The Covenant facilitates the process.

'Abdu'l-Bahá elaborated on this theme when He said:

The imperfect members of society, the weak souls in humanity, follow their natural trend. Their lives and actions are in accord with their natural propensities; they are captives of physical susceptibilities; they are not in touch or in tune with the spiritual bounties. Man has two aspects: the physical, which is subject to nature, and the merciful or divine, which is connected with God. If the physical or natural disposition in him should overcome the heavenly and merciful, he is, then, the most degraded of animal beings; and if the divine and spiritual should triumph over the human and natural, he is, verily, an angel. The Prophets come into the world to guide and educate humanity so that the animal nature of man may disappear and the divinity of his powers become awakened. The divine aspect or spiritual nature consists of the breaths of the Holy Spirit. The second birth of which Jesus has spoken refers to the appearance of this heavenly nature in man. It is expressed in the baptism of the Holy Spirit, and he who is baptized by the Holy Spirit is a veritable manifestation of divine mercy to mankind. Then he becomes just and kind to all humanity; he entertains prejudice and ill will toward none; he shuns no nation or people.[3]

All the peoples of the earth have been the beneficiaries of guidance from on high. Bahá'u'lláh wrote:

> He hath called into being His creatures, that they may know Him, Who is the Compassionate, the All-Merciful. Unto the cities of all nations He hath sent His Messengers, Whom He hath commissioned to announce unto men tidings of the Paradise of His good pleasure, and to draw them nigh unto the Haven of abiding security, the Seat of eternal holiness and transcendent glory.[4]

This guidance has been given in many forms. Basically it is the battle each human being has within himself between good and evil inclinations. 'Abdu'l-Bahá explained it this way:

> Man has the power both to do good and to do evil; if his power for good predominates and his inclinations to do wrong are conquered, then man in truth may be called a saint. But if, on the contrary, he rejects the things of God and allows his evil passions to conquer him, then he is no better than a mere animal.[5]

There is an American Indian story of the grandfather who explained to his young grandson that everyone had within himself a good dog and a bad dog, fighting each other for control. The grandson asked which one wins. The grandfather wisely answered, 'Whichever one you feed.'

The Covenant is food for the 'good dog'.

Laws and principles

When I was studying the Faith, but before enrolling, I gambled for small stakes and was moderately successful. One day I was playing a card game for money and was not doing well. While losing, the thought struck me that this might not be right according to Bahá'í teachings. I had recently purchased a copy of *God Passes By* but had not read it. It occurred to me there might be something in there about gambling. So, I looked it up and discovered that there is a law of Bahá'u'lláh interdicting gambling. After looking up the word 'interdict', I found that my hunch was right. That was the last $3.00 I contributed to gambling.*

Neither good judgement nor discipline led me to give up the folly of gambling; not even losing. It was because I was trying to become a Bahá'í, was no longer ignorant of the law, and chose to follow it. Later I realized that following the law was an early step in forming a relationship with the Covenant. I had heard the word, but that was about all. Still later it occurred to me that by following that simple law, a baby step had been taken toward something great in my spiritual development. It was quite a bit later that the enormity of the implications struck me. Even though I knew little of the Covenant and had no real appreciation of its colossal implications, simply by choosing to follow Bahá'í law and no longer gamble, I was doing my part toward building the Christ-promised Kingdom of God on earth – the World Order of Bahá'u'lláh.

---

*   Anyone who wants a well-rounded education and to expand his or her vocabulary should read the writings of Shoghi Effendi. Creative writing teachers who are not Bahá'ís have recommended *God Passes By* as a model of superlative English.

A law is a command or rule that must be followed. A principle is a standard or belief that is a guide for action. Laws indicate specific behaviours – such as the obligatory prayers. Principles are more abstract and influence choices or options – such as the equality of men and women.

The Guardian called the interaction of laws and principles 'the warp and woof of the fabric of its future World Order . . .'[6]

A loom is used for weaving – usually, the warp strands are fixed to the loom vertically, and held taut. The woof strands are usually woven horizontally, in and out of the warp strands. It takes them both, tightly interwoven, to produce the strong and enduring fabric. Laws and principles are the fabric of life for the individual and of the World Order itself.

Laws

In the secular world, most laws set the limits of what a person is allowed to do. They are like fences or the white lines on the edge of roads showing that it is illegal or dangerous to cross them.

Divine laws are different. They generally define the paths to follow safely to a desired destination, or like the white line down the middle of an airport runway, guiding the pilot for the safest landing.

A power and miracle of the Covenant is that it transforms the appreciation of laws. In the secular world, laws are often thought of as onerous duties you are obliged to follow. Divine laws are guidance you want to follow both because of love for Bahá'u'lláh and recognition that following them is the best means to attain enduring happiness, both for the individual and society.

Divine law, as a pillar of the Covenant, was mentioned in the opening of Baha'u'lláh's Most Holy Book:

> The first duty prescribed by God for His servants is the recognition of Him Who is the Dayspring of His Revelation

and the Fountain of His laws ... It behoveth every one who reacheth this most sublime station, this summit of transcendent glory, to observe every ordinance of Him Who is the Desire of the world. These twin duties are inseparable. Neither is acceptable without the other.[7]

Ignoring His laws suggests that the Station of Bahá'u'lláh is either not understood or not accepted. Passive belief is insufficient. Hand of the Cause Horace Holley referred to passive belief as a form of denial. Bahá'u'lláh writes:

> Know verily that the essence of justice and the source thereof are both embodied in the ordinances prescribed by Him Who is the Manifestation of the Self of God amongst men ... Were His law to be such as to strike terror into the hearts of all that are in heaven and on earth, that law is naught but manifest justice. The fears and agitation which the revelation of this law provokes in men's hearts should indeed be likened to the cries of the suckling babe weaned from his mother's milk ... [8]

Divine laws are not for God's benefit. Obedience does nothing for Him. He is a loving God and desires nothing but the best for His creatures. Even when laws seem unduly harsh and the purpose is not understood, they are not punitive. God is not being mean or cruel. 'Abdu'l-Bahá said: 'The world of humanity may be likened to the individual man himself; it has its illness and ailments. A patient must be diagnosed by a skilful physician. The Prophets of God are the real Physicians. In whatever age or time They appear They prescribe for human conditions.'[9] Not all prescriptions are easy or pleasant to take. Some pills are bitter medicine.

If the laws were easy to follow, where would the challenge be? Where would be the opportunity for spiritual growth? How could the sincere be distinguished from the nominal or passive believer?

BEHAVIOURS

It is clear that doing bad things to ourselves does not bring joy to Bahá'u'lláh. However, the only harm is what the person does to himself. Bahá'u'lláh's sorrow is like a parent who grieves when a child makes a foolish mistake. Nothing we do, or do not do, harms Him.

The most complete list of Bahá'í laws is found in *A Synopsis and Codification the Laws and Ordinances of the Kitáb-i-Aqdas* This work was started by the Guardian and completed under the direction of the Universal House of Justice. It was published as a single volume in 1973 and is included as a separate section of the English edition of the *Kitáb-i-Aqdas*. The *Codification* lists laws, ordinances and exhortations into four categories:

   A. Prayer;
   B. Fasting;
   C. Laws of Personal Status; and
   D. Miscellaneous Laws, Ordinances, and Exhortations.

No one is expected to know all the laws upon accepting Bahá'u'lláh. They are learned over time as one deepens in the Faith. The more a person learns, the greater becomes the desire both to learn more and to comply more completely. Both the responsibility and the desire to act accordingly increase gradually. The law of marriage is a good example. If a new Bahá'í gets married without following the marriage law because he or she is not aware of it, it is quite different from a deepened Bahá'í doing the same thing.

Other than the Guardian's grouping, Bahá'í laws can be divided into five general categories:

1. Those you must do, such as the obligatory prayers.
2. Those that are encouraged but not required, such as getting married.
3. Matters that are neither encouraged nor discouraged, such as eating meat.

4. Those that are discouraged but not prohibited, such as smoking.
5. Those that are forbidden, such as murder, gossip and backbiting.

Obeying Bahá'í laws is not a simple dichotomy between right and wrong, good and bad. That simplistic division masks the nature of spiritual growth. There are levels of obedience from doing the minimum to doing more. For instance, the law concerning the marriage dowry states a minimum to be paid as well as a maximum. There is a different range for rural and city dwellers. Whatever is done is acceptable.[10]

The main issue is purpose or motivation:

- At one level, someone will do something or not do it for fear of punishment. How many blistering sermons have spouted hell-fire and damnation in an effort to scare people into righteousness?
- Related to that is the fear of getting caught and facing the embarrassment of being found out.
- Hope for some kind of reward is also a powerful motivator. Bahá'u'lláh called reward and punishment the 'two pillars' of justice.[11]
- Concern over one's reputation keeps many people doing what is right. This includes the desire to win the good favour of God.
- There is also obedience from a sense of duty. That is, doing the right thing or not doing a wrong thing with neither the fear of punishment nor hope for reward; nor concern over praise or blame. Doing the right thing is done for no reason other than it is the right thing to do.
- It is a real achievement when doing the right thing is automatic. That is, when doing anything other than the right thing is not even considered.
- Near the top of the list in terms of motivation is when

the mere thought of disobedience is repugnant and/or sickening.
- ➢ The purest reason is the desire to bring pleasure to God. This should not be an attempt to make God pleased with you. It is doing something that would bring pleasure to Him. Toward the end of the 'Fire Tablet' Bahá'u'lláh writes: 'He [referring to Himself] hath risen up in faithfulness at the place of sacrifice, looking toward Thy pleasure, O Ordainer of the worlds.'

Enforcement

In most societies, law enforcement comes from external pressures. This includes such items as the police force, the court system, fines, jail sentences and (in some countries) executions. Some religious communities use disfellowship, restriction from certain sacraments, or fear of eternal punishment. 'Abdu'l-Bahá explained:

> . . . there are two safeguards that protect man from wrongdoing. One is the law which punishes the criminal; but the law prevents only the manifest crime and not the concealed sin; whereas the ideal safeguard, namely, the religion of God, prevents both the manifest and the concealed crime, trains man, educates morals, compels the adoption of virtues and is the all-inclusive power which guarantees the felicity of the world of mankind.[12]

Under the Covenant people are called to a higher level of maturity than ever before. It is self-monitoring, with limited outside pressure. People are expected to obey the laws even when no one is watching and there is no possibility of getting caught. As one Bahá'í likes to say: 'There is no coach; there is no referee; there is no policeman.' The best enforcement of any law is the desire to follow it.

At the same time, it is nobody else's business whether or not I say the obligatory prayers. However, when there is a problem that is harmful to the community or other human beings, external censure is needed. In extreme cases sanctions can be imposed such as removal of administrative rights. Strange as it seems in today's materialistic culture, one of the punishments is that the individual can no longer contribute money to Bahá'í funds.

That is not to say there is no punishment for doing wrong. As one Bahá'í writer stated it: 'God does not enter in, to judge and punish. We judge and sentence ourselves, and administer the punishment! We cannot escape the consequences of our actions! In this respect the Universe is sternly automatic.'[13]

A person's spiritual development is the flawless recorder of her or his priorities, behaviour and motivation. That, too, can be tricky. While striving to be spiritual is laudable, it can also be limiting. Obeying laws for the love of God, not for perceived personal benefit – no matter how laudable – is what produces the greatest and most beneficial spiritual growth.

The Báb made this clear in one of His prayers: '. . . shouldst Thou ordain evil for a servant by reason of that which his hands have unjustly wrought before Thy face, Thou wouldst test him with the benefits of this world and of the next that he might become preoccupied therewith and forget Thy remembrance.'[14] Can desire for a better life in the next world be a test? That is certainly a novel idea.

Even being obedient can have its pitfalls. 'Abdu'l-Bahá is reported to have said, 'Holding to the letter of the law is many times an indication of a desire for leadership. One who assumes to be the enforcer of the law shows an intellectual understanding of the Cause, but that spiritual guidance in them is not yet established.'[15]

The spirit of the law is more important than the letter. Bahá'u'lláh writes: 'Walk in My statutes for love of Me and deny thyself that which thou desirest if thou seekest My pleasure.'[16]

And further, Bahá'u'lláh revealed a prayer that says, 'Assist them, by Thy grace, to love Thee and to conform unto that which shall please Thee.'[17] However, that, too, can be taken to extremes. For instance, Sufi mystics and certain charismatic Christians hold that their spiritual station, not the law, leads them in the right way. That has produced many problems.

In today's world it is commonplace to try to defeat the spirit or purpose of a law without violating the letter. This is often seen in political or business transactions.

The ideal way of adhering to the spirit is illustrated in the law of Ḥuqúqu'lláh that every believer is to pay. Adib Taherzadeh explained: 'Bahá'u'lláh always insisted that no one should be solicited to pay the Ḥuqúqu'lláh, and even that payment should not be accepted unless the individual was willing to observe the Ḥuqúq with the utmost joy.'[18] Isn't that interesting? No one is to pay Ḥuqúqu'lláh unless the payment brings him joy!

Principles

Principles are guides for behaviours and choices rather than specific actions. For instance, elimination of prejudice is an important Bahá'í principle. But, how is that applied?

If in a group of people someone makes a racial slur, there are several ways to deal with it. No matter how inappropriate and reprehensible the remark is, an appropriate response depends on the circumstances and the relationship with others who are present. At times it is best to confront it directly. At other times, it is best to ignore the comment. You may choose to have nothing more to do with a group that condones such talk. There are other options such as changing the subject, saying something to soften tension, making an observation that counters the comment without being confrontational and so on.

The need is to build bridges to people. It is possible that the

Grand Dragon of the Ku Klux Klan can find the Faith, but reacting to stupid things he says about race will not touch his heart. It is true that a direct rebuttal may be appropriate and prove beneficial for others who are present. The trick is finding the best way to apply the principle in any given situation.

Principles such as the oneness of mankind, the equality of men and women and the oneness of religion are lenses through which Bahá'ís see the world. They give insights and attitudes toward life that should distinguish Bahá'ís from others. Often a believer will be praised for her or his view on something when in reality the individual is simply reflecting Bahá'í principles. 'Abdu'l-Bahá wrote:

> Should any one of you enter a city, he should become a centre of attraction by reason of his sincerity, his faithfulness and love, his honesty and fidelity, his truthfulness and loving-kindness towards all the peoples of the world, so that the people of that city may cry out and say: 'This man is unquestionably a Bahá'í, for his manners, his behaviour, his conduct, his morals, his nature, and disposition reflect the attributes of the Bahá'ís.' Not until ye attain this station can ye be said to have been faithful to the Covenant and Testament of God. For He hath, through irrefutable Texts, entered into a binding Covenant with us all, requiring us to act in accordance with His sacred instructions and counsels.[19]

I am not aware of any complete list of Bahá'í principles. There was a talk recorded in *The Promulgation of Universal Peace* in which 'Abdu'l-Bahá mentioned twelve items which, for many years, became known as the twelve principles of the Faith, but it is far from a complete list.

In parsing the section of *The World Order of Bahá'u'lláh* headed, 'World Unity the Goal', starting on page 202, I counted 95 items that could be considered principles of the Faith.

Compliance

Show me someone who has followed all the teachings 100%! Perfection belongs to the central figures of the Faith. The rest of us, no matter how sincere, nor how hard we try, fall short. Describing gradualism, Bahá'u'lláh writes:

> Know of a certainty that in every Dispensation the light of Divine Revelation hath been vouchsafed unto men in direct proportion to their spiritual capacity. Consider the sun. How feeble its rays the moment it appeareth above the horizon. How gradually its warmth and potency increase as it approacheth its zenith, enabling meanwhile all created things to adapt themselves to the growing intensity of its light. How steadily it declineth until it reacheth its setting point. Were it, all of a sudden, to manifest the energies latent within it, it would, no doubt, cause injury to all created things . . . In like manner, if the Sun of Truth were suddenly to reveal, at the earliest stages of its manifestation, the full measure of the potencies which the providence of the Almighty hath bestowed upon it, the earth of human understanding would waste away and be consumed; for men's hearts would neither sustain the intensity of its revelation, nor be able to mirror forth the radiance of its light. Dismayed and overpowered, they would cease to exist.[20]

In a letter to a believer, 'Abdu'l-Bahá stated the process:

> Verily, I beseech the Lord of Hosts to increase thy faith each day over that of the previous day, to confirm thee through His Holy Spirit, to give thee capacity to partake of the lights of knowledge and wisdom, to make thee a herald of the Covenant in those regions, and to instruct thee in that which thou knowest not . . .[21]

This process implies there will be mistakes. Why else would there be so many prayers for forgiveness? The more we learn and progress spiritually, the higher the standard we should try to live up to. Just as a little child is not expected to know and abide by all the rules of social life, so anyone enrolling in the Faith starts on a learning curve in the process of becoming a Bahá'í. Becoming a Bahá'í has been compared to attending a university from which one never graduates.

The fulfilment of the Báb's prophecy continues, albeit unevenly, despite problems along the way. As long as individuals, institutions and the communities remain strong and firm in the Covenant, humanity will enjoy the protection and benefits of this great plan of God. How long it takes depends on the degree to which ordinary Bahá'ís, like you and me, do our part.

What should you and I do about it? Part II, 'Walking in the Light of the Covenant', explores that question.

PART II

REFLECTIONS ON WALKING IN THE LIGHT OF THE COVENANT

Introduction

> *Having created the world and all that liveth and moveth therein, He, through the direct operation of His unconstrained and sovereign Will, chose to confer upon man the unique distinction and capacity to know Him and to love Him – a capacity that must needs be regarded as the generating impulse and the primary purpose underlying the whole of creation . . .*
> Bahá'u'lláh[1]

A professor of theology at a Christian seminary once remarked, 'Religion is the most ingenious device thought of by man to exclude God from his life.' He went on to explain, 'It is if man says, "Look here, God, we will worship you once a week, but stay out of my life the rest of the week."' It has been more than 60 years since I heard him say that. Over those years even worship once a week has diminished.

The Revelation of Bahá'u'lláh allows no room for separating religion from daily life. Whether or not people are aware of it, to know and worship God are the most important challenges for every human being every day. These two purposes are so important that daily reminders are embedded in the daily obligatory prayers.

All the precious gifts of the world in which we live – natural or manmade – can be used either to serve the divine purpose or as powerful temptations and lures for endless distractions and misdirection.

Bahá'ís are fortunate. They have the Covenant that gives the clearest possible guidance to lead people in the proper direction while protecting against ever-present and appealing distractions. At the same time, a 'seeing eye' enables perceptive souls to understand how all the forces of the universe can serve that divine purpose.

Part I of this book summarized the core of the Covenant. An apple has a core, but it also has the tasty flesh dependent on the core. In the same way, the core of the Covenant not only keeps the Faith strong and united, it nourishes human behaviour and clarifies how each of the treasures and challenges of life on earth can aid in knowing and worshipping God and protect against the dangers leading away and distracting from that spiritual journey. At the same time, making efforts to fulfil these twin mandates develops the qualities and attributes needed for the next world. This is just one of the ways in which everything serves the Covenant.

The questions remain: how does anyone know and worship God? How can anyone know the Unknowable Essence? What does it mean to worship? In what ways does anyone worship? How are these part of daily life? These puzzles are so profound that they are easily ignored, but they have been in the shadow of life throughout history.

To know God

In the opening paragraph of the *Kitáb-i-Aqdas*, Bahá'u'lláh wrote with clarity and strength: 'The first duty prescribed by God for His servants is the recognition of Him Who is the Dayspring of His Revelation and the Fountain of His laws . . .'[2] And in another place: 'If it be your wish, O people, to know God and to discover the greatness of His might, look, then, upon Me with Mine own eyes, and not with the eyes of any one besides Me.'[3]

The same theme was stated by Jesus when He said 'no man cometh unto the Father, but by me'.[4] All revealed religions place knowing God as the highest priority, but one that can only be found through the Manifestation.

Full recognition is rare. There is a Tablet in the handwriting of Bahá'u'lláh that indicated that Aḥmad, for whom the famous Tablet is named, was one of only a few people to get a glimpse of Bahá'u'lláh's inner reality.[5]

In 'Abdu'l-Bahá's talk reported in *The Promulgation of Universal Peace*, starting on page 422, several pages are devoted to an elaboration on what it means to know God. There is no simple answer and it is a life-long pursuit.

To worship God

The first paragraph of the *Kitáb-i-Aqdas* goes on to say that when someone recognizes the Voice of God for this age, there is an obligation: 'to observe every ordinance of Him Who is the Desire of the world. These twin duties are inseparable. Neither is acceptable without the other.'

Daily behaviour is the measure of obedience. Worship involves more than pious meditation. The monastic life is no longer acceptable; Bahá'u'lláh wrote: 'O concourse of monks! Seclude not yourselves in your churches and cloisters. Come ye out of them by My leave, and busy, then, yourselves with what will profit you and others.'[6] Worship includes the limitless possibilities of service.

A person's religion is not so much what may be claimed as a belief, but how life is lived. Where someone invests time, money and energy describes that person's beliefs.

In the Western world, self-serving materialism has become the dominant religion. The major branches are acquiring things, entertainment, sports, and the cult of the individual. These have an impact on all we see and do. Self-absorption and self-gratification are the offspring of materialism, appealing to man's baser instincts. Materialism makes people feel entitled to luxuries and to expect them. Governments are overthrown and riots occur when material resources do not reach expectations. Every day is so filled with the noise, activity and gadgets of materialism that it is difficult to find the time and space for quiet reflection to think seriously about more important matters.

Even religious observances, rather than providing guidance for doing God's Will, understanding the purpose of life and constructive living, are often reduced to social activities, traditions, superstitions, habits, convictions born of imagination, demagoguery and/or warped ideology. Bahá'u'lláh described the difference between the apparent and the ideal when He wrote:

> Follow not, therefore, your earthly desires, and violate not the Covenant of God, nor break your pledge to Him. With firm determination, with the whole affection of your heart, and with the full force of your words, turn ye unto Him, and walk not in the ways of the foolish. The world is but a show, vain and empty, a mere nothing, bearing the semblance of reality. Set not your affections upon it. Break not the bond that uniteth you with your Creator, and be not of those that have erred and strayed from His ways. Verily I say, the world is like the vapour in a desert, which the thirsty dreameth to be water and striveth after it with all his might, until when he cometh unto it, he findeth it to be mere illusion. It may, moreover, be likened unto the lifeless image of the beloved whom the lover hath sought and found, in the end, after long search and to his utmost regret, to be such as cannot 'fatten nor appease his hunger'.[7]

All religions have had the dynamism and teachings of their Founders. Believers were expected to apply those teachings in their lives, and the faith and sincerity with which they have done this have enriched them throughout history. There has also been a wide range of understandings and misunderstandings that has led to lack of clarity, divisions and disputes.

The Covenant takes us a step further. The definition given by the Universal House of Justice includes the phrase 'whereby God requires of man certain behaviour(s) . . .'[8] The core of the

Covenant furnishes spiritual nourishment and guidance for those behaviours.

All behaviours are based on current circumstances and past experiences. The paradox is that it these are not the reality of either the past or the present, but the perception of them. That perception can be based on either fact or illusion or, more often, a combination.

Are there two or three prongs?

Optical illusions demonstrate how easy it is to see even simple items in different ways. This being true of visual things, how much more is it true of complex matters of the physical world, of the heart or the soul?

There is a truism that we see things, not as they are, but as we are. How something is understood is shaped by culture, traditions, biases, habits, world-views and a host of other things. The result may be far from objective reality.

The Covenant provides a clear standard by which even the ordinary events of life can be properly understood and viewed. With the appointment of 'Abdu'l-Bahá as the Centre of the Covenant, the Exemplar of the Bahá'í life and the sole Interpreter of the teachings, there is clear and indisputable authority. With the subsequent appointment of Shoghi Effendi as the only authorized interpreter, protection and guidance under the Covenant were affirmed and continued.

Now, with the leadership of the Universal House of Justice, believers continue to have clear and immediate divine guidance. This extensive umbrella of protection is available to mankind for the first time.

Stated another way, 'Abdu'l-Bahá and the Guardian have infallible interpretation on every matter because of, and only because of, the Covenant. That not only covers the administrative structure of the Faith and understanding the Sacred Writings, it goes much further. It also means that whatever they interpret, from ways to worship to diet to leisure time activities, are words from God. For example, the Centre of the Covenant spoke of the medicinal value of food; he permitted eating meat but said that in the future people would be vegetarians. He gave a warning about leisure activity: there is a danger that pastime may degenerate into waste of time.[9]

In addition to laws and rules, there are principles individuals are to apply according to their circumstances. These features are the greatest possible assistance anyone can have for living according to the primary purpose of life. The Universal House of Justice, while it cannot interpret, gives divine guidance on those things not explicitly mentioned in the Texts. (It is appropriate here to restate the vital, distinctive and complementary functions of these twin institutions. The Guardian interpreted, but could not legislate. The Universal House of Justice legislates, but cannot interpret.) By analogy, these institutions are lamps and the Covenant shines through them providing illumination, not just for Bahá'ís, but for the entire world.

It is hard to walk in the light of the Covenant while living in cultures so out of tune with the Will of God. The process of walking in the light is so private and personal, that in the unsurpassed teaching Tablet known as the Tablet of Aḥmad, Bahá'u'lláh advised Aḥmad concerning a new believer, 'let him choose the path to his Lord'.

There are powerful, immediate obstacles in following the Covenant. Overcoming these problems starts with accepting the preeminent place of the Covenant in the scheme of life, paying proper attention to available guidance, thinking about the advice, and taking it seriously.

Then, there is the fact that even clear directions are not

always easy to follow because the culture screams the opposite. For instance, the cause of peace – from peace of mind to international accord – is one of the two overarching standards of this day. Yet the Western world delivers a daily barrage of contrary messages, polluting the mental and emotional environment. Even seemingly innocent items are laden with a glorification of discord and violence: sports, entertainment, computer games, confrontational politics, arts, put-down humour, music and literature. The daily news dwells on wars, personal and public confrontations and disasters. The problem is compounded by the fact that this pollution is not only thrust upon people: it is what people demand. Any news media must report a full array of violence, controversy, conflict and mayhem in order to stay in business.

Changing from a contentious culture applauding violence to one honouring peace is hard, gradual, unpopular, and filled with spurts forward and slips backward. A letter written on behalf of the Guardian stated, 'When a person becomes a Bahá'í, he gives up the past only in the sense that he is a part of this new and living Faith of God, and must seek to pattern himself, in act and thought, along the lines laid down by Bahá'u'lláh.'[10] It is hard for people to overcome their environment. People are like fish living in polluted water. Fish raised in polluted water have difficulty surviving when transferred into clear, wholesome and nutritious water. A gradual transition is needed.

Before I enrolled as a Bahá'í, some of my opinions on social, personal and moral issues were consistent with Bahá'í teachings. Some were not. The Faith provided illumination that settled a host of issues, enabling me to live more easily both in the world about me as it is, while trying to remain in harmony with the Covenant.

The greatest benefit was in helping me see the clear distinction between civil, secular or conventional standards, and Bahá'í values. There is an enormous relief and liberation from the endless disputes and wrangling over such divisive issues as human rights, partisan politics, abortion, use of alcohol or mind-altering substances, capital punishment, sexual licence and/or orientation and a host of other matters that are divisive and waste a great deal of time and energy. Vast amounts of ill-will, hardship and destruction are created from idle disputes that are high on emotion and short on facts.

Attempting to walk in the light of the insights provided by the Covenant contributes to being constructively at peace and living alongside the differing opinions and behaviours of Western civilization, knowing that a better world, while still in an embryonic form, is alive and well – just waiting to be born. This provides the strength and vision to see beyond the immediate conditions.

Without the light of the Covenant, people become slaves to their animal appetites. Bahá'u'lláh writes that behaving like beasts of the field is unworthy of man.[11] The degree to which anyone rises above the animal level is a tribute to the impact of the spiritual aspects of life and connection to the Covenant, whether or not the individual is even aware of that relationship.

On my first pilgrimage, Hand of the Cause John Ferraby casually remarked that there are good and bad people in every religion. He added, 'The hope is that the average will improve with each succeeding Dispensation.'

Then comes practical application, or doing something about it. 'Abdu'l-Bahá described three elements necessary to accomplish anything: knowledge, volition and action. He said:

> Unless these three conditions are forthcoming, there is no execution or accomplishment. In the erection of a house it is first necessary to know the ground, and design the house suitable for it; second, to obtain the means or funds necessary for the construction; third, actually to build it.[12]

Acknowledging the Covenant is the first step towards re-creating the individual life and building the New World Order. The will and desire of individuals to move out of their respective comfort zones to apply the teachings of the Faith is the second step. Actually, taking small baby steps in righting a disoriented world is the ultimate third and final step, in which everyone is called upon to find something that can further the Cause and better the world, without waiting for someone to tell them what to do. In the aggregate, these baby steps create the New World Order.

During the interregnum between the passing of the Guardian and the election of the Universal House of Justice, the Hands of the Cause in the Holy Land wrote:

> The work of Bahá'u'lláh lies before us to be completed. No one generation will do this; a thousand years at least are required to carry out and mature the specific provisions of His Dispensation. But to each man his opportunity, to each generation its tasks . . . Great moments in history require great deeds; great men are not necessarily those best qualified to be great, but rather those who see their chance and seize it, with love and courage, when it offers itself. The records of our Faith show that its heroes and heroines, its saints and martyrs, sprang mostly from the rank and file, but what they possessed, which raised them to the summits of fame and glory, were vision and faith.[13]

In a prayer, Bahá'u'lláh asked that we be given strength to do the right thing and emphasizes the importance of this, both for the individual and all of mankind. He asked God 'to aid Thy servants to observe what Thou hast commanded them in Thy days – commandments through which the sacredness of Thy Cause will be demonstrated unto Thy servants and the affairs of Thy creatures and of Thy realm will be set aright.'[14]

The Covenant – the tangible expression of that sacredness

– exerts a powerful influence on our daily lives to the extent that we let it. It can help clear away the clutter, vapour and illusions of materialism as a new model of life develops. Understanding how the Covenant influences behaviour in the everyday world is the subject of Part II.

The behaviours required are not easy. If they were easy, where would the challenge be? Where would the growth be? The Covenant is the roadmap for a two-fold path: one for the individual's spiritual destiny to know and worship God; the other bringing humanity ever closer to the glorious future promised by the Báb.

The following chapters attempt to penetrate some of the veils obscuring this brilliant illumination, making it both more attractive and easier to walk in the light of the Covenant.

5
Firmness in the Covenant

Today the most important principle of faith is firmness in the Covenant, because firmness in the Covenant wards off differences. Therefore, you must be firm as mountains.
'Abdu'l-Bahá[1]

The word 'cord' is used frequently in the Bahá'í Writings to illustrate that strong bond needed to endure whatever trials may come. *Clinging to Thy cord, the cord of Thy glory,* and *the golden cord* are some examples. Bahá'u'lláh writes in the *Kitáb-i-Aqdas*:

> Cling, O ye people of Bahá, to the cord of servitude unto God, the True One, for thereby your stations shall be made manifest, your names written and preserved, your ranks raised and your memory exalted in the Preserved Tablet.[2]

The metaphor is based on the hazardous travel of nomadic times. If someone was being chased by people who would do him harm, and he came upon a shaykh's camp, he could grab and hold a cord or rope supporting the tent. That created two conditions: First of all, the one 'clinging to the cord' was pledging his loyalty and submission to the owner of the tent. Secondly, it was expected that the shaykh would extend his protection to the one clinging to the cord.

Clinging to the cord of the Covenant is pledging support and allegiance to its conditions and thereby becoming a beneficiary of its provisions.

Firmness in the Covenant covers a vast range of issues. In the *Tablets of the Divine Plan*, 'Abdu'l-Bahá addresses the 'armies of God' and says much about them:

To attain to this supreme station is, however, dependent on the realization of certain conditions:

The first condition is firmness in the Covenant of God. For the power of the Covenant will protect the Cause of Bahá'u'lláh from the doubts of the people of error . . .

The second condition: Fellowship and love amongst the believers . . . O ye friends! Fellowship, fellowship! Love, love! Unity, unity!³

The degree to which fellowship, love, and unity reflect the true relationship among Bahá'ís is the degree to which Bahá'ís are realistically firm in the Covenant and working toward peace and security both in their individual lives and in the world.

Just as exercise is needed to keep the physical body in shape, there are spiritual exercises to keep the relationships with the Covenant strong. For many Bahá'ís, the most vital practices are: obligatory prayer and fasting, saying the Greatest Name 95 times every day, reciting the verses of God morning and evening and bringing oneself to account each day.

In some ways it is like an art, skill or profession. Capacity

FIRMNESS IN THE COVENANT

and passion grow over time and are dependent on practice. One musician said if he missed a day of practice, he could tell the difference. If he missed two days, the critics could tell. If he missed three days, his fans could all tell the difference. How much more is this true of prayer!

Today's confrontational world is filled with limited unities, be they business, political, religious, associations or others. 'Abdu'l-Bahá said, 'From these limited unities . . . only limited outcomes proceed . . .'[4] They often cannot survive the many pressures that arise and tend to divide people. A company may endure, but individuals come and go. Personality disputes are often the basis of disruptive problems. They sometimes disintegrate to the point of destroying organizations from the inside. It is the strong, enduring attachment to the Covenant that gives Bahá'ís the strength needed to look beyond the enormous internal and external strains that afflict all people.

How does this work? Bahá'ís are no different from anyone else when it comes to having differences of opinion.

While listening to a recorded talk by a well-known, knowledgeable Bahá'í, I felt that the speaker said some things that were different from my understanding. These were the kinds of differences that caused serious divisions, sects and even bloodshed in the past. Instead of antagonism, because of the Covenant, I could concentrate on the different ideas and insights the speaker provided. While giving serious consideration to the different opinions, an opportunity was provided to bask in the luxury of thinking deeply about this different perspective, mindful that it was not a matter of one being right and the other wrong, but of understandings. If it needed to be resolved, divine institutions would settle the matter without confrontation or contention.

Before my book *Consultation* was published, I had written a series of articles on the subject for the *Alaska Bahá'í News*. These were distributed throughout the Bahá'í world. In one local Spiritual Assembly in a different country, the secretary used them for deepening before their meetings.* One member of the Spiritual Assembly, whom I knew well and who was a highly regarded international figure, said at one point, 'Boy, do I disagree with John on this.' He went on about how wrong I was. The secretary glanced at the article and interrupted by saying, 'But, he's quoting 'Abdu'l-Bahá here.'

Immediately, this devoted believer changed his tune and embraced the idea. That is the power of the Covenant and a tribute to his obedience to the Covenant. Otherwise, the issue could have led to significant estrangement.

The Writings contain a long list of specific behaviours for believers to follow. Here are more than a dozen items listed by 'Abdu'l-Bahá that can be related to being firm in the Covenant. These focus on relationships with other people.

> Be thou severed from this world, and reborn through the sweet scents of holiness that blow from the realm of the All-Highest. Be thou a summoner to love, and be thou kind to all the human race. Love thou the children of men and share in their sorrows. Be thou of those who foster peace. Offer thy friendship, be worthy of trust. Be thou a balm to every sore, be thou a medicine for every ill. Bind thou the souls together. Recite thou the verses of guidance. Be engaged in the worship of thy Lord, and rise up to lead the people aright. Loose thy tongue and teach, and let thy face be bright with the fire of God's love. Rest thou not for a moment, seek thou to draw no easeful breath. Thus mayest thou become a sign and symbol of God's love, and a banner of His grace.[5]

There are specific instructions for mothers:

> . . . suckle your children from their infancy with the milk

---

* I do not recommend that. In my estimation, only the Sacred Writings should be used for deepening material before a meeting of this sort.

of a universal education, and rear them so that from their earliest days, within their inmost heart, their very nature, a way of life will be firmly established that will conform to the divine Teachings in all things.

For mothers are the first educators, the first mentors; and truly it is the mothers who determine the happiness, the future greatness, the courteous ways and learning and judgment, the understanding and the faith of their little ones.[6]

A well-known Tablet of Bahá'u'lláh starts, 'Be generous in prosperity, and thankful in adversity . . .'[7] It lists nearly 40 specific items. The very number of items can be overwhelming, easily set aside and/or ignored, creating an apparent paradox. Trying to do everything can be daunting. How can anyone remember everything, let alone apply them? It would be like trying to lift and move a whole pile of rocks in one trip. It cannot be done. Only by moving one rock at a time can the pile can be moved.

The following steps offer some ideas:

1. Think and pray seriously about one selected item to understand what it means in practical terms.
2. Discuss the idea with others. Not only does this enrich your views and understandings; the act of discussing embeds and strengthens determination. At the same time it generates ideas about how to apply it.
3. Find some specific activity that is a normal part of your life to which that item can be applied.
4. Do it.
5. When you feel the time is right, concentrate on one other specific item.

One instruction in the *Kitáb-i-Aqdas* is: *to engage in some occupation.* On one level that is as simple as having a job. An extra bounty is that Bahá'u'lláh likened that activity to a form of worship, when done in the spirit of service.

Arthur came from a wealthy family and had no particular aim in life when he discovered the Faith. Upon learning of the requirement to engage in an occupation, he interpreted this as meaning he should find a profession. So, he went on to college, although he had been inclined to lead a life of leisure. He continued to find many creative ways to serve the Faith. Not only did his strength increase, this spilled over to other areas as he applied great vigour to a long list of activities. Decades later he had led a fulfilling life of devoted and tireless service. It all started from a desire to fulfil one part of being firm in the Covenant. Select one item at a time, as Arthur did.

Throughout the world today there are enormous problems that result from unemployment. In the words of Bahá'u'lláh: 'when occupied with work one is less likely to dwell on the unpleasant aspects of life'.[8] Newspaper headlines scream out the reality of that statement every day. Work is needed, not just for material reasons but for spiritual ones as well. If no jobs are available the challenge is finding constructive and worthwhile alternatives. There is no room for anyone to sit idly by. As Bahá'u'lláh writes: 'The basest of men are they that yield no fruit on earth.'[9] Doing something constructive is part of being firm in the Covenant, whether or not the 'occupation' is a paying job. For example, stay-at-home mothers have an arduous occupation, but the material benefits are non-existent.

'Occupation' can also refer to activities that are not related to employment. To be engaged in an occupation in that sense implies being aware of the physical, material and emotional needs of those around you. But that is not enough. The next step is doing what is reasonable and appropriate to make life better for those who share, or occupy, space with you. That can be as simple as making people glad you are there. When done in the spirit of service the relationship with the Covenant is strengthened.

But there is more to it than doing something. To be 'engaged' takes it out of a passive role into commitment and passion. For instance, being a teacher is more than being in the teaching profession. It is when the passion of teaching is in the teacher. This means the teacher doing her or his best and finding ways to improve both the activity and the relationships with others in the course of the 'occupation'.

Conscientiously working on just one element of the Faith helps progress in the other aspects as well. You will discover a host of applications that are purposeful, and ultimately of service to mankind. Finding worthwhile things to do becomes an automatic response when the focus is on the Covenant. This also helps you, and those around you, maintain balance as human beings.

Being firm in the Covenant is not something to be accomplished, like building a box and then being done with it. It is a journey, not a destination; a life-long, constant and wonderful process. The following Hidden Word implies a journey:

O Son of Being! Walk in My statutes for love of Me and deny thyself that which thou desirest if thou seekest My pleasure.[10]

Life has provided me with many incredible experiences, simply because, as a Bahá'í, I chose to pursue whatever challenges were set before the believers. My non-Bahá'í friends stand in awe of what I have seen and done. Among my greatest regrets is that I cannot adequately convey to them that these wonders are available to anyone who chooses to cling to the cord of the Covenant!

Furthermore, by clinging to that cord, both understanding and wonder expand toward the ideal of: 'O Lord, increase my astonishment at Thee!'[11]

Being firm in the Covenant is a starting point. But, how are priorities set? What are the chief and distinguishing characteristics of the Bahá'í Faith?

6

Oneness of Mankind

> *In every Dispensation the light of Divine Guidance has been focused upon one central theme . . . In this wondrous Revelation, this glorious century, the foundation of the Faith of God, and the distinguishing feature of His Law, is the consciousness of the oneness of mankind.*
> 'Abdu'l-Bahá[1]

This may be the most far-reaching and dramatic change brought with the Bahá'í Revelation. There is a difference between oneness and unity. Even though people sometimes use the terms interchangeably, there is a profound yet subtle distinction.

Oneness is indivisible while unity is made up of component parts. Oneness can exist in the abstract, unity cannot: it needs a focus, or object. It is like the difference between a chemical compound or alloy and a mixture. If you mix salt and pepper together, the grains can be separated and each grain retains its inherent property. When they are put together there is unity in diversity.

A compound is different. Combining two parts of hydrogen with one part of oxygen produces water, a substance different from either of its component parts. Copper and tin, two soft metals, can be melted and combined to make an alloy, bronze – much stronger than either component.[*]

The Guardian indicated the broad sweep of this feature:

> Let there be no mistake. The principle of the Oneness of Mankind – the pivot round which all the teachings of Bahá'u'lláh

---

[*] Its discovery, about 6,500 years ago, was a major tool in the development of civilization.

revolve – is no mere outburst of ignorant emotionalism or an expression of vague and pious hope. Its appeal is not to be merely identified with a reawakening of the spirit of brotherhood and good-will among men, nor does it aim solely at the fostering of harmonious cooperation among individual peoples and nations. Its implications are deeper, its claims greater than any which the Prophets of old were allowed to advance. Its message is applicable not only to the individual, but concerns itself primarily with the nature of those essential relationships that must bind all the states and nations as members of one human family. It does not constitute merely the enunciation of an ideal, but stands inseparably associated with an institution adequate to embody its truth, demonstrate its validity, and perpetuate its influence. It implies an organic change in the structure of present-day society, a change such as the world has not yet experienced. It constitutes a challenge, at once bold and universal, to outworn shibboleths of national creeds – creeds that have had their day and which must, in the ordinary course of events as shaped and controlled by Providence, give way to a new gospel, fundamentally different from, and infinitely superior to, what the world has already conceived. It calls for no less than the reconstruction and the demilitarization of the whole civilized world – a world organically unified in all the essential aspects of its life, its political machinery, its spiritual aspiration, its trade and finance, its script and language, and yet infinite in the diversity of the national characteristics of its federated units.

It represents the consummation of human evolution – an evolution that has had its earliest beginnings in the birth of family life, its subsequent development in the achievement of tribal solidarity, leading in turn to the constitution of the city-state, and expanding later into the institution of independent and sovereign nations.

The principle of the Oneness of Mankind, as proclaimed

by Bahá'u'lláh, carries with it no more and no less than a solemn assertion that attainment to this final stage in this stupendous evolution is not only necessary but inevitable, that its realization is fast approaching, and that nothing short of a power that is born of God can succeed in establishing it.[2]

In relationship to mankind, our oneness is our common spiritual essence and heritage as children of the one God. No individual can be separated from that spiritual reality.

Unity refers to the coming together of people based on a desire to accomplish a specific mission. The members of a soccer team are united on two levels. One is to score points. The other is to keep the opponents from scoring. Whether or not they like the same kind of music or food is irrelevant. That which defines them as soccer players is the ability to work with the other team members to score and defend. Musicians in an orchestra have unity in diversity when they make good music. Beyond that, anything they have in common is incidental.

Without a foundation of the oneness of mankind, it is difficult to see how any unity could be anything but limited. Unity is dependent on an object. There may or may not be carryover to other areas of concern. Without a commitment to oneness, personality, priority changes or other differences pose a real danger of undermining the unity. Diversity then becomes a problem and not a benefit. Many worthwhile groups have had their unity shattered by internal friction when there is no underlying commitment to the oneness of mankind. Based on oneness, unity survives inevitable challenges.

In a public talk, 'Abdu'l-Bahá explained: 'When we observe the human world, we find various collective expressions of unity therein.' He goes on to mention a number unities that focus on specific things, saying, 'All these unities are imaginary and without real foundation, for no real result proceeds from them.' He called them 'limited unities' with 'limited outcomes'.[3]

There was a small town with a dedicated, active Bahá'í community. During mass teaching days, a team came into town with aggressive street teaching techniques. This was in stark contrast to the deliberate, methodical methods the resident Bahá'ís had been practising with success. There was open anger that the teaching team was destroying the image the Bahá'ís had carefully created. Any other group would have been destroyed by this profound difference. It was an enormous tribute to their strength in the Covenant and the underpinning and acceptance of the oneness of mankind that the community survived what some had thought of as a vulgar and undignified onslaught. They not only survived, ultimately they were better off because of the experience.

In another community, there was a strong difference of opinion concerning direct street teaching in contrast to indirect teaching, including 'living the life'. The Spiritual Assembly decided they needed to go on a retreat to hash out the issue. The members first thought of going to Green Acre in Maine, but decided the problem was bigger than that. So, they considered a retreat at the Temple in Wilmette. They finally decided that the entire Spiritual Assembly should request a three-day visit to Haifa. While there, they met at the far edge of the garden in front of the Shrine of the Báb, each one vigorously and loudly proclaiming his point of view. This was before the building of the Seat of the Universal House of Justice, when groups were small. During a break at the Eastern Pilgrim House, members of the House of Justice appeared and visited with the pilgrims. One member of the House put his arm around the Bahá'í who was most vociferous about direct teaching and said, 'The important thing is that the dignity of the Faith be upheld.' Another member, who happened to be with the most conservative voice, said it was important that everyone hear of the coming of Bahá'u'lláh. Those comments shattered the contention among the members. Because of its commitment to oneness the Spiritual Assembly was able to

ONENESS OF MANKIND

consider the issue rationally and devise reasonable plans of action. Ten years later, when I moved into the community, that experience remained a highlight. Only the love of Bahá'u'lláh, firmness in the Covenant and the underlying appreciation of the oneness of mankind had been able to keep their unity from being shattered.

To the uninformed, unity is something that is nice, when other problems have been solved. That thinking sees unity as frosting on the cake – nice, but not essential. From the Bahá'í perspective, unity, based on oneness, comes first. There is no issue that cannot be resolved if there is unity with that firm foundation. On the other hand, no lasting resolution is possible for any major issue if unity is limited.

The Guardian explained, 'For the bedrock of the Bahá'í administrative order is the principle of unity in diversity, which has been so strongly and so repeatedly emphasized in the writings of the Cause.'[4] He used the administrative order as the focus for unity, to be applied by people who were fully committed to the oneness of mankind.

In a prayer for Spiritual Assemblies 'Abdu'l-Bahá writes, 'We have gathered in this spiritual assembly, united in our views and thoughts, with our purposes harmonized to exalt Thy Word amidst mankind.'[5] Note that the unity and harmony are focused on a single purpose: *to exalt Thy Word amidst mankind.* It does not matter if everyone has different tastes in music or food, or anything else. Unity is applied when working together, with our diversities, to promote the administrative order in advancing the Word of God for the whole world. Outside the council chamber, let each one enjoy her or his individuality.

Recognizing the oneness of mankind is not natural. If it were, it would not be necessary for the Manifestation of God to call it to our attention. Breathing is natural, so Bahá'u'lláh

---

* This was the first translation that Shoghi Effendi included in his long letter of 5 March 1922, his first letter outlining the scope of the administrative order.

did not have to tell us to breathe. A challenge for Bahá'ís is to make the oneness of mankind natural and commonly accepted.

Man's physical evolution seems fairly well complete. Social evolution remains a work in progress. As Shoghi Effendi implied in the quotation mentioned earlier, the principle of the oneness of mankind is like a capstone signaling the culmination of human evolution.

This dynamic process can be seen from the perspective of the Tower of Babel. Bahá'u'lláh confirmed that event when He wrote,

> The divers and widely-known languages now spoken by the peoples of the earth were originally unknown, as were the varied rules and customs now prevailing amongst them. The people of those times spoke a language different from those now known. Diversities of language arose in a later age, in a land known as Babel. It was given the name Babel, because the term signifieth 'the place where the confusion of tongues arose'.[6]

The story of Babel is covered in nine short verses of the 11th chapter of the Book of Genesis. Whether literally true, a compression of historical facts or a metaphor, there are many lessons. With few details, it describes what must have been a highly advanced material civilization. Also, there must have been a social order with a high level of unity. Both of these would be necessary to even consider, let alone undertake, the colossal project of building a tower high enough to reach heaven. There is no indication of slave labour or the kind of heavy equipment so essential for today's massive projects. The logistics stagger the imagination.

According to Genesis, when God saw what was happening He didn't like it, so He confounded the people by taking away the most important tool needed for the project: the ability to communicate. At least a few people must have been able speak each of the languages visited upon the people. Apparently each language group went off by itself to the several parts of the world.

Thousands of years after this massive division and dispersal, Bahá'u'lláh was sent to mankind commanding people to come together, to unite and speak a common language. Isn't that what they did before? What is going on here? Can't God make up His mind? It appears as if humanity is being taken full cycle. Or is there some other explanation for this strange turn of events?

The following is nothing more than my speculation, and not verifiable. It may well be over-simplified, incomplete and flawed, yet it seems consistent with events, and I find it a useful model with which to think about the oneness of mankind. This is especially helpful in view of the huge quantity of superficial evidence that refutes the idea that we are all basically the same.

Is it possible that God saw that mankind had developed as much as it could homogeneously, and ambitions had taken a materialistic direction? The Tower of Babel is often seen as a metaphor for human arrogance, 'joining partners with God', seeing themselves as equal with God. Also, perhaps God wanted variety, rather than uniformity. Perhaps He wanted people to pay attention to spiritual matters rather than concentrate on the material. Is it possible that mankind had to be divided into separated groups in order for distinctive capabilities and cultural norms to develop in furtherance of social evolution? Is it further possible that after sufficient time, enough differences had evolved and matured that the family of man could be called back together to share what each had gained over eons of separation? Just think of the wide variety of world-views. Each culture has its own traditions, myths and mores. Together they can give great insight into ultimate realities.

While it is true that much of what has been learned by each group over the centuries has been drowned out by the noise and weight of Western civilization, there is much that lives on and can be of benefit as a new world is being built. This is especially true of the many perspectives, cultural priorities and world-views that are needed to grapple with global issues.

How did all the cultural differences of attitude, traditions, outlook and priorities develop, and how does that relate to both the oneness of mankind and unity in diversity?

The oneness of mankind implies that mankind is spiritually indivisible at its core. Our spiritual reality is present from the moment of conception. Water can take on different properties of odour, colour and taste. Yet, it remains water. So, too, people take on different characteristics, yet remain spiritual beings.

There is an analogy from nature. Over the plains of central western Amazonia, in Brazil, a rain cloud deposits its load. Two drops, let's call them Rachel and Tim, from the same cloud – which is the source of their essential oneness – fall to earth, side by side. They land atop a low rising hill. Rachel, a millimeter to the south, flows down the hill into a small stream that feeds the Japurá River. Rachel is then swept away into the raging, churning, creamy waters of the Solimões River. Tim falls slightly to the north and finds his way down the hill into the black waters of the Negro River.

The two drops meet again just beyond Manaus in Central Brazil, only Rachel and Tim could not possibly recognize each other. Both have taken on the characteristics of the environment through which they've passed. Tim, from the Negro river of the north, is now dark. Rachel, from the water of the Solimões, has become creamy brown, almost white. Even after the two rivers meet, and run side by side for nearly four miles, they mix only at their fringes.

Just as with humans, the colour distinction is the most obvious but not the most important difference. The greater problem is their distinctive cultures. The two rivers have different temperatures, acidity and current speeds. All they seem to have in common is being wet. It will be nearly 100 miles before Rachel and Tim become indistinguishable as two drops of the Amazon.

ONENESS OF MANKIND

So it is with mankind. The oneness of mankind is like the essential wetness of both Rachel and Tim. Their diversity has resulted from the traits picked up on their separate cultural journeys. The unity of their diversity is illustrated by their coming together to form the Amazon River.

Humanity is now at the confluence of the many streams of life. We have been brought together – though not yet united – from varied ancestral experiences. It is no wonder that our differences are easily seen, since our ancestors coursed through such diverse channels of human history. At this stage of mankind's reunion, the common humanity is easily missed.

Whatever the divine purpose, getting people back together seems more difficult than separating them in the first place. Over the centuries each group has developed deep-seated suspicions and prejudices against those who are different.

This could well be a survival trait. History is filled with stories of trusting people who encountered hostile neighbours. Invariably, the hostile ones won the day. The castles in Europe, with their moats and parapets with watch-towers, arrow-slits and gaps from which boiling oil or rocks could be hurled at would-be intruders, were not built as 21st-century tourist attractions. They were built because there was reason not to trust those who might come to visit.

My forebears, the Vikings, travelled in order to 'vik' – that is, to rape, pillage and plunder. They were not welcome guests. Those being visited, who survived, were rightfully wary and suspicious. They wisely did what they could to protect themselves from the hordes that would do them harm, including building fortresses and being suspicious of strangers.

Bahá'ís of today are faced with the incredible challenge of uniting the scattered family of man, even though not all members of that family agree that getting together with historical enemies is a good idea. The dilemma is explained by Bahá'u'lláh:

The Book of God is wide open, and His Word is summoning mankind unto Him. No more than a mere handful, however, hath been found willing to cleave to His Cause, or to become the instruments for its promotion. These few have been endued with the Divine Elixir that can, alone, transmute into purest gold the dross of the world, and have been empowered to administer the infallible remedy for all the ills that afflict the children of men.[7]

The imagery of changing base metal into gold is mind-boggling. If those elements had nervous systems and voices, you can imagine the immense pain, anguish and crying there would be. Excruciating grief and wailing would accompany each atom going through that transformation. Yet, mankind must endure that painful process to establish the reality of the oneness of humanity. Mankind has a voice and, throughout the world, is crying out and acting out in hostile ways in protest over the painful changes taking place.

The transformation would not be possible except for the power of the Covenant. As 'Abdu'l-Bahá said: 'It is indubitably clear that the pivot of the oneness of mankind is nothing else but the power of the Covenant.'[8]

Part of the challenge is helping people who see only the differences among people and are blind to essential unity. For them, the differences are obvious. Mention commonality to a bigot and you are apt to get a long and detailed list showing the contrary. Characteristics and incidents are used to 'prove' not only differences, but how those who are different are inferior and less worthy. They may even argue that people who have different values, see the world differently, or react in unfamiliar and even disgusting ways, are terribly flawed. Severe bigots even wonder if anyone outside their group can really be considered fully human. Neither ironclad reason nor DNA evidence can penetrate the armour of a racist's ignorance. Only Bahá'u'lláh and the Divine Elixir of the Covenant can transmute those base perceptions into golden thoughts.

Following are a few examples of the Divine Elixir at work.

Michael, a white man, was born and raised in the southern United States in the 1930s, when Jim Crow laws were in full force, the Ku Klux Klan was at its peak and black people were still being lynched. He had the full slate of prejudice and antagonism that was part of the culture in which he was raised.

One day he had to take a bus and the only seat available was next to a black person. He refused to sit next to such a person. The driver told him everyone had to be seated before he could start the bus. So, Michael sat on the edge of his seat as far away from the black person as possible. When the bus started he stood up and remained standing until a seat became vacant in the white section. Not long after he learned of Bahá'u'lláh and became a believer. A few years later I was sitting with him in the kitchen of the house he was renting in North Carolina. He was considering whether he should buy a house or build one. He was certain he was going to be evicted from where he was living. It was a vigorously segregated community. The night before a black couple had spent the night in his house. That would be sufficient cause for eviction. Many years later he had two grown daughters and was delighted when he got a black son-in-law and he thoroughly loves his black grandchildren. Only the Divine Elixir of the Covenant could change his base perceptions into golden ones.

Elmer was born and raised in the hills of Kentucky. He told me that as a youth he had accepted as a fact that blacks had horns and tails. He said he was told, and believed, that was why they wore hats and long trousers. It was during the Second World War that he and his wife embraced the Faith. With the launching of the Ten Year Crusade in 1953 they pioneered to Fairbanks, Alaska, and Elmer with his Kentucky accent set out to teach the Faith mainly among the black population he found there. As he explained to me, 'I had so much hate in my heart that I just had to do something about it.'

Jim had been an ordained preacher in a black Baptist church in Texas, before coming to Alaska. Elmer was assigned to a room at a construction site that he was to share with Jim. Jim was wary of this southern white man when Elmer first entered the room, it didn't take long before they became trusted friends and Elmer introduced Jim to the Faith. Jim became an energetic Bahá'í. He once told me, 'I didn't know white men could be Christians until I met the Bahá'ís.' When Elmer left Fairbanks there was a by-election for the Spiritual Assembly. The result was eight blacks and one white – a grand tribute to Elmer's tireless efforts and his legacy.

Elmer, this white man from Kentucky, had become a staunch member of the National Association for the Advancement of Colored People. Upon his tragic death in an industrial accident, his funeral was adorned with the largest floral wreath I had ever seen, given by the NAACP of Fairbanks; this, for the white man from Kentucky whose heart, once full of hate, was transmuted into pure gold by Bahá'u'lláh's Elixir.

Jeffrey had a well-earned reputation for being hard to get along with. His stepson had married an Eskimo woman and he would not allow her in his house when he was home. It was all right for her to visit her mother-in-law when he wasn't there, but she was not to be in the house when he got home.

Under a strange set of circumstances he ended up attending a Bahá'í conference to which he had NOT been invited. His heart was touched by what he experienced and he soon enrolled in the Faith. During a fireside a short time later he not only attended, but had provided transportation for his stepson and his wife and two other Eskimo women. I was talking about the power of God to change hearts. With beautiful irony, he pulled his curved, meerschaum pipe from between his teeth and said with a customary scowl, 'But, John, you can't change people.' It was silent for a time as he looked around the room at the people of different races sitting there because of him. His face lightened as he looked around the room and added, 'Or, maybe you can.'

More base metal was transmuted!

The Bahá'í World Congress held in New York in 1992 took place during the height of the war in Bosnia, pitting three ethnic groups against each other in bitter conflict: Serbians, Croatians and Montenegrins. New York reporters were covering the Bahá'í Congress and one interviewed a Serbian Bahá'í and a Croatian Bahá'í at the same time. He thought it was incredible that during this time of intense turmoil there could be these two individuals who could embrace each other as brothers. They were living in extremely hostile and antagonistic environments. Their people were torturing and killing each other. It did not seem possible to the reporter that people from such contentious cultures could embrace each other with obvious amity, simply because they were Bahá'ís. That is the wonder of base metals turning to gold.

There are countless other cases where the Elixir has worked its magic in the lives of individuals. The next grand breakthrough will be when that healing balm is applied to large numbers of humanity. That would be like the two rivers that meet at Manaus going downstream and gradually blending as they form the Amazon. When the time is ripe, and only God can determine that, the often-promised and eagerly anticipated entry by troops will take place. That will be the wholesale application of the Divine Elixir.

The efforts of the Bahá'ís to bring the Faith to the masses of humanity in the 1960s and 1970s demonstrated several things. First of all, it showed that people were ready for the Message of Bahá'u'lláh. At the same time it showed that the Bahá'í community was not ready to absorb them. People accepting Bahá'u'lláh did not automatically embrace His teachings. Thank God the Universal House of Justice established the Institute process to build the capacity to educate large numbers of people when they enter the Cause. In my judgement, the masses will not enter the Faith until the Bahá'ís are able to accommodate them.

Since this is an age of such mass confusion, specific steps must be taken to promote the oneness of mankind. One is to study and think deeply about this most significant feature. Another is to talk about it. The most important part is reflecting it in our lives. 'Abdu'l-Bahá writes:

> When delivering the glad tidings, speak out and say: the Promised One of all the world's peoples hath now been made manifest. For each and every people, and every religion, await a Promised One, and Bahá'u'lláh is that One Who is awaited by all; and therefore the Cause of Bahá'u'lláh will bring about the oneness of mankind, and the tabernacle of unity will be upraised on the heights of the world, and the banners of the universality of all humankind will be unfurled on the peaks of the earth. When thou dost loose thy tongue to deliver this great good news, this will become the means of teaching the people.[9]

A pernicious part of the problem today is that many people think of themselves as free from prejudice. Their cultural bias produces a mindset that makes them blind to the prejudices they unconsciously harbour. Many people think the way they view the world is the way the world is. Furthermore, they think that anyone who sees things differently is wrong to varying degrees. They do not consider that to be a prejudice. That is just the way they think things are.

After a high school shooting, a sociology teacher gave her students an assignment to observe and make notes in the lunchroom, focusing on who was sitting with whom. They discovered that the students tended to sit with people who were like themselves, according to race, interests or social standing. The class then discussed what impact this might have on social attitudes. Their conclusion was that lunchroom seating contributed to a mentality and attitude of divisiveness: a we–they mentality. The teacher next had her students sit with groups that were different from themselves. At first this was awkward and the students reported feeling uncomfortable. They continued. Ultimately, the students began to like the idea of interacting with people who were different and even noted that students who were not part of the class were showing a greater acceptance of students who were different.

Bahá'ís can fall into the same trap of clinging together rather than reaching out. One time there was an Intercalary Day party in a small country where people had gathered from various areas. There were many active youth who were having a grand time in the open air downstairs. A few people had gathered upstairs where refreshments were being prepared. When I arrived upstairs, there was a local girl who was not a Bahá'í sitting by herself. Her husband was downstairs with the others. She was obviously bored, paging through some magazines. At the same time there was a group of pioneers from different parts of the country, who had not seen each other for a long time and were clustered together having a fine conversation. In their understandable excitement at being together, they completely ignored the local girl sitting by herself. As far as I know, she never became attracted to the Faith.

One way to demonstrate the oneness of mankind is, like Elmer, to reach out to people who are different, not in spite of their differences but because of them. Deliberate attempts can be made to do business with people from different cultures.

While it is important to find people who are competent to perform certain tasks, when that is determined, it is a great step toward diversity to gravitate toward professionals who are minorities or women. This offers encouragement in an age when racial and gender inequality still rages. Blending the need for competence and the value of a minority view, the Guardian wrote:

> So great and vital is this principle that in such circumstances, as when an equal number of ballots have been cast

in an election, or where the qualifications for any office are balanced as between the various races, faiths or nationalities within the community, priority should unhesitatingly be accorded the party representing the minority, and this for no other reason except to stimulate and encourage it, and afford it an opportunity to further the interests of the community.[10]

Competence, important as it is, is only part of the need. A good photographer uses bright lights. Lights of less intensity are also used strategically to cut shadows and soften glows. The same thing is true in human affairs. While penetrating insight is prized, a different perspective, even if less intense, may well be what is needed to get the most appropriate view of a given situation.

In the final analysis, it is up to the Bahá'ís to be the channel for the Divine Elixir to enter the body of mankind. Deliberately mingling socially with people who are different is not natural. However, in order for the Elixir to be applied, Bahá'ís need to seek out people who are different. This is the colossal transformation bringing mankind into the Golden Age of the World Order of Bahá'u'lláh.

In writing about the oneness of mankind, Shoghi Effendi emphasizes:

> One word more in conclusion. The proclamation of the Oneness of Mankind – the head corner-stone of Bahá'u'lláh's all-embracing dominion – can under no circumstances be compared with such expressions of pious hope as have been uttered in the past. His is not merely a call which He raised, alone and unaided, in the face of the relentless and combined opposition of two of the most powerful Oriental potentates of His day – while Himself an exile and prisoner in their hands. It implies at once a warning and a promise – a warning that in it lies the sole means for the salvation of

ONENESS OF MANKIND

a greatly suffering world, a promise that its realization is at hand.[11]

While the oneness of mankind is the chief and distinguishing feature of the Faith, 'Abdu'l-Bahá said that working toward world peace is also a top priority. These are two essential and primary ingredients for facilitating the monumental changes mankind must go through before it can deal with the problems of this age on a meaningful level.

7

World Peace

That all nations should become one in faith and all men as brothers; that the bonds of affection and unity between the sons of men should be strengthened; that diversity of religion should cease, and differences of race be annulled – what harm is there in this?. . . Yet so it shall be; these fruitless strifes, these ruinous wars shall pass away, and the 'Most Great Peace' shall come.
Bahá'u'lláh[1]

These words, uttered to the Cambridge University orientalist Edward Granville Browne during his interview with Bahá'u'lláh in April 1890, were both a prophecy and a statement of a pre-eminent focus for Bahá'ís.

The Universal House of Justice outlined the application of that thought in its 1985 publication *The Promise of World Peace*. Deep-rooted problems were noted that defy political solutions – which it described as a chimera. It wrote:

> World order can be founded only on an unshakeable consciousness of the oneness of mankind, a spiritual truth which all the human sciences confirm. Anthropology, physiology, psychology, recognize only one human species, albeit infinitely varied in the secondary aspects of life. Recognition of this truth requires abandonment of prejudice – prejudice of every kind – race, class, colour, creed, nation, sex, degree of material civilization, everything which enables people to consider themselves superior to others.[2]

It went on to point out major barriers: doubts, misconceptions, prejudices, suspicions and narrow self-interests.

The primary question raised was how the present world with its entrenched pattern of conflict can change to a world in which harmony and cooperation will prevail.

The major stumbling blocks pointed out in that document are:

- racism;
- disparity between rich and poor;
- unbridled nationalism;
- religious strife;
- women's lack of emancipation;
- lack of universal education; and
- communications problems – the need for an auxiliary, universal language.

So much of the world's attention focuses on negative elements. News organizations thrive by dwelling on the negative. A reporting truism is: 'Bleeds, leads'. In one survey, 9 out of 10 opening stories for local television news programmes were disasters: earthquakes, fires, wars, corruption, murders, accidents and so on. A plane crash killing scores of people makes the news. Never is there a report of the thousands of planes that have landed safely on that same day. Public opinion polls are increasingly popular and they tend to focus on what divides people rather than what unites.

The reality is that in the wake of natural disasters, human compassion and helpfulness come out of hiding. Strangers rush to the aid of those afflicted by a flood or earthquake. Those emergencies tend to bring out both the best and the worst in people, and generally the good far outweighs the bad. There is a greater amount of good in the world than there is evil. Otherwise, tragedies would never make the news – they make the news because they are the exception rather than the rule. Dark forces are noisy and obvious. The good are often hidden and quiet.

Bahá'ís have even more reason to have a positive and optimistic view of the world in matters both large and small. They have the assurance of a better world that is slowly being built. Seeing with the vision of Bahá'u'lláh, positive signs are clear and this builds confidence. When Bahá'ís deliberately look for the best, they are sharing a brighter view of life and doing more than they realize to promote world peace.

In her inaugural address as Research Professor of the Bahá'í Chair for World Peace at the University of Maryland, Hoda Mahmoudi quoted the American historian Howard Zinn as saying:

> There is a history of wars and a history of kindness. But it's like the newspapers and the historians. They dwell on wars and cruelty and the bestial things that people do to one another and they don't dwell a lot on the magnificent things that people do for one another in everyday life again and again. It seems to me it only takes a little bit of thought to realize that if wars came out of human nature, out of some spontaneous urge to kill, then why is it governments have to go to such tremendous lengths to mobilize populations to go to war.

The most important thing any Bahá'í can do is support whatever projects are given by the Universal House of Justice. The stronger the relationship to the Covenant, the more resilient believers become in confronting the challenges that people face. In families, schools, workplaces, communities, among peers and social settings, there is something simple and practical that can make a big difference. That is radiating the joy of knowing Bahá'u'lláh. This has a far more profound effect than may be realized. Bringing joy and happiness into the lives of others makes each one an agent of change for the better.

It is worth repeating a statement from 'Abdu'l-Bahá in which He was speaking specifically about peace:

Be thou of those who foster peace. Offer thy friendship, be worthy of trust. Be thou a balm to every sore, be thou a medicine for every ill. Bind thou the souls together. Recite thou the verses of guidance. Be engaged in the worship of thy Lord, and rise up to lead the people aright. Loose thy tongue and teach, and let thy face be bright with the fire of God's love.[3]

Bahá'u'lláh as well as 'Abdu'l-Bahá provided the model for doing small but significant things about global issues. Not that any of us can, or should try, to replicate what they did, but we can learn from them.

In His letters to the kings and rulers* of the world, Bahá'u'lláh clearly announced who He was. For us, when talking with other people about the problems of the world, it is helpful to clearly state the source of our views, and as appropriate, let people know the source and that it is not just our personal opinion. Quoting His Words is best.

He spelled out the specific problems that each of the rulers were confronting and gave advice about how to deal with them. He then predicted what would happen if they did not do as He suggested. While you and I don't have omniscience, we can learn from this example. Comments on events of the day should be based on facts, not far-flung and hypothetical speculation. Stating the right for each country to protect itself is consistent with what Bahá'u'lláh said, as is the need for an international police force. Going much beyond that can lead to unintended quagmire. Bahá'u'lláh wrote:

> The Great Being, wishing to reveal the prerequisites of the peace and tranquillity of the world and the advancement of its peoples, hath written: The time must come when

---

* These are collected in *The Proclamation of Bahá'u'lláh* published by the Universal House of Justice in 1967, as well as in *The Summons of the Lord of Hosts*, published in 2002.

the imperative necessity for the holding of a vast, an all-embracing assemblage of men will be universally realized. The rulers and kings of the earth must needs attend it, and, participating in its deliberations, must consider such ways and means as will lay the foundations of the world's Great Peace amongst men. Such a peace demandeth that the Great Powers should resolve, for the sake of the tranquillity of the peoples of the earth, to be fully reconciled among themselves. Should any king take up arms against another, all should unitedly arise and prevent him. If this be done, the nations of the world will no longer require any armaments, except for the purpose of preserving the security of their realms and of maintaining internal order within their territories. This will ensure the peace and composure of every people, government and nation. We fain would hope that the kings and rulers of the earth, the mirrors of the gracious and almighty name of God, may attain unto this station, and shield mankind from the onslaught of tyranny . . . The day is approaching when all the peoples of the world will have adopted one universal language and one common script. When this is achieved, to whatsoever city a man may journey, it shall be as if he were entering his own home. These things are obligatory and absolutely essential. It is incumbent upon every man of insight and understanding to strive to translate that which hath been written into reality and action . . . That one indeed is a man who, today, dedicateth himself to the service of the entire human race. The Great Being saith: Blessed and happy is he that ariseth to promote the best interests of the peoples and kindreds of the earth. In another passage He hath proclaimed: It is not for him to pride himself who loveth his own country, but rather for him who loveth the whole world. The earth is but one country, and mankind its citizens.[4]

There is much in this statement that individuals can apply

in daily life. Sharing those thoughts with other people helps create a climate of hope and expectation. At the same time they silence many of the negative views of hopelessness that are so prevalent in today's society.

Bahá'u'lláh told the rulers of the world to compose their differences. Individuals can apply that advice to help people as much as is reasonably possible, to settle disputes as amicably as possible. By making local and domestic situations more peaceful, an important step is made for peace in the world.

Plentiful and obvious as problems are, a step forward can be taken by quoting from the Peace Message:

> The Great Peace towards which people of good will throughout the centuries have inclined their hearts . . . is now at long last within the reach of the nations . . . World peace is not only possible but inevitable. It is the next stage in the evolution of this planet – in the words of one great thinker, 'the planetization of mankind'.[5]

Perhaps one the greatest lessons is that while there is no evidence that the kings and rulers changed their behaviour as a result of Bahá'u'lláh's letters, His Words set in motion a continuing process. Look at the positive steps, despite the disastrous world wars of the past century. True, are also many and inevitable setbacks.

- ➤ Rivalries have shifted. Armed hostilities are increasingly with dissident terrorists and organized crime and less with conflicting nations. Shooting differences among nations have changed to less bloody economic competition.
- ➤ World travel has become more accepted, frequent, simpler and safer.
- ➤ Devastating events, such as earthquakes and floods, draw immediate and compassionate international response.

> Cultures (including foods) from all parts of the world are becoming familiar in most major and many smaller cities as populations become more diverse in individual countries.
> Never before have there been so many meetings of representatives of various nations to discuss global problems through the sponsorship of the United Nations and its agencies. While many of these meetings have produced meagre results, or agreements that are ignored, these first, faulty steps are crucial.

The above are early fulfilments of some of the advice Bahá'u'lláh gave to kings and rulers who did not heed His Words. The ideas lived on and are developing in the world despite initial neglect.

So, too, for us as individuals, when we promote the ideas of peace, it is unrealistic to expect immediate agreement. That is not important. It is part of the ongoing process and the world is slowly catching up. Sharing Bahá'u'lláh's teaching on peace introduces a note of optimism at a time when the world's negatives reign. Another important step is preparing those with whom we come in contact to look for and accept as signs of hope the elements of progress that gradually unfold before our eyes.

One day I was talking with a banker friend of mine about the need for a universal currency. He vigorously protested how unrealistic and impractical it was. A few weeks later I overheard him talking to someone else. He was speaking about the need for a universal system of currency, almost as if it were his idea. What Bahá'u'lláh told the rulers did not take place right away. When His ideas are shared, they probably will not sink in immediately either, but their truth will live on.

Turning to the example of 'Abdu'l-Bahá, we can learn both from what He said and what He did. When 'Abdu'l-Bahá was released from imprisonment, believers all over the world asked Him to visit their countries. There was no way He could visit them all. In a letter He wrote to the Bahá'ís of Bombay, India in response to one of their invitations, He said that if He did go to India, it would not be during monsoon season. Anyone who has been in India during monsoons can appreciate His practicality! He never went.

He agreed to travel to the West. Three of the most outstanding reasons were for 1) advancing awareness of the Covenant; 2) promoting the oneness of mankind; and 3) warnings of the war, looming on the horizon. His recorded comments from the West – published in English in *Paris Talks*, *'Abdu'l-Bahá in London*, *The Promulgation of Universal Peace* and *'Abdu'l-Bahá in Canada*, as well in *Star of the West* magazine including talks in Germany and Hungary – are filled with warnings on the danger of the probable war and the importance of world peace.

Here is just one example of the strong language He used:

> Today there is no greater glory for man than that of service in the cause of the Most Great Peace. Peace is light, whereas war is darkness. Peace is life; war is death. Peace is guidance; war is error. Peace is the foundation of God; war is a satanic institution. Peace is the illumination of the world of humanity; war is the destroyer of human foundations. When we consider outcomes in the world of existence, we find that peace and fellowship are factors of upbuilding and betterment, whereas war and strife are the causes of destruction and disintegration . . . Consider the restlessness and agitation of the human world today because of war. Peace is health and construction; war is disease and dissolution . . . If two nations were at war in olden times, ten or twenty thousand would be sacrificed, but in this century the destruction of one hundred thousand lives in a day is quite possible. So perfected has the science of killing become and so efficient the means and instruments of its accomplishment that a whole nation can be obliterated in a short time. Therefore, comparison with the methods and results of ancient warfare is out of the question.[6]

He emphasized the importance of thoughts when He said:

> I charge you all that each one of you concentrate all the thoughts of your heart on love and unity. When a thought of war comes, oppose it by a stronger thought of peace. A thought of hatred must be destroyed by a more powerful thought of love. Thoughts of war bring destruction to all harmony, well-being, restfulness and content.[7]

'Abdu'l-Bahá did more than talk about peace. He took four specific actions: warnings, preparations, prayer and designing a preventative programme.

Warnings: His public talks during His trip to the West were filled with warnings about the coming war (World War I). He clearly outlined the steps being taken by various governments and business interests that would inevitably lead to war. The number of talks on the subject indicates how strongly He felt about the subject.

Preparations: He instructed Bahá'ís in Palestine to build granaries and stockpile grain against the future food shortage that would be caused by the impending war. This was a major reason cited by King George V of England to confer a knighthood upon Him.

Prayer: For 'Abdu'l-Bahá, prayer was far more than a noble venture and pious activity. It is reported that one night, before a potentially bloody encounter, He stayed up all night pacing back and forth and praying.* He revealed many prayers oppos-

---

* There were at least two other recorded times when 'Abdu'l-Bahá stayed up all night praying, with dramatic results. The first was when he was 12 or 13 years old, praying for the return of His Father. The very next day information was received that started the process leading to

ing war. Most notable was the long prayer from the general *Tablets of the Divine Plan*. This prayer was revealed at Bahjí in April 1916, starting with: 'O God, my God! Thou seest how black darkness is enshrouding all regions . . .'

Prevention: He is reported to have wept when He read the Treaty of Versailles, the peace treaty between Germany and the Allied nations ending World War I, signed in the Palace of Versailles on 28 June 1918. He warned of worse conflicts yet to come because of the onerous conditions of the treaty. A few world leaders shared 'Abdu'l-Bahá's scepticism about the ultimate outcome of the retributions demanded in the treaty. However, most important and far-reaching was the fact that during the height of the war, in 1916 and 1917, 'Abdu'l-Bahá penned His monumental *Tablets of the Divine Plan* – the guide to building a world in which war is no longer an option.

Following are some lessons that can be gleaned from 'Abdu'l-Bahá's method:

1. Look ahead to see what problems need urgent attention.
2. Warn appropriate people about impending problems.
3. Use prayer intensively.
4. Take practical steps to avert or minimize the impact of a potential problem.
5. Take appropriate action to prevent future problems.

The *Tablets of the Divine Plan* continue to give guidance on at least two levels. One is the basis for all teaching plans, starting with the first Seven Year Plan which began in 1937. Toward the end of one teaching plan, a member of the Universal House of

---

Bahá'u'lláh's return. The other time was over the difficulty of obtaining land for the Shrine of the Báb. 'Abdu'l-Bahá stayed up all night in prayer. The next day the reluctant owner rushed to 'Abdu'l-Bahá, begging Him to buy the land.

Justice was asked what was going to be next. His answer was to read the *Tablets of the Divine Plan*. Anything not yet accomplished would be part of the next plan.

In addition to the global scope, those letters are filled with items that anyone can take as a personal goal. This is especially true of the four general letters. Bahá'ís living in areas with specific letters are able to find a host of ideas that are yet to be completed.

The rulers of the world devote an enormous amount of conscientious effort, energy and thought to finding material solutions for world peace. Their efforts are not working. 'Abdu'l-Bahá explained why:

> Today the world of humanity is in need of international unity and conciliation. To establish these great fundamental principles a propelling power is needed. It is self-evident that the unity of the human world and the Most Great Peace cannot be accomplished through material means. They cannot be established through political power, for the political interests of nations are various and the policies of peoples are divergent and conflicting. They cannot be founded through racial or patriotic power, for these are human powers, selfish and weak. The very nature of racial differences and patriotic prejudices prevents the realization of this unity and agreement. Therefore, it is evidenced that the promotion of the oneness of the kingdom of humanity, which is the essence of the teachings of all the Manifestations of God, is impossible except through the divine power and breaths of the Holy Spirit. Other powers are too weak and are incapable of accomplishing this.[8]

He also identified the alternative to what world leaders are powerless to accomplish: 'Blessed are the nameless and traceless poor, for they are the leaders of mankind.'[9] That is nowhere more true than on the issue of world peace.

WORLD PEACE

When Manúchir Khán told the Báb that he was going to bring the Message of this New Day to the Shah, the Báb replied,

> Not by the means which you fondly imagine [through the power of the Shah] will an almighty Providence accomplish the triumph of His Faith. Through the poor and lowly of this land, by the blood which these shall have shed in His path, will the omnipotent Sovereign ensure the preservation and consolidate the foundation of His Cause.[10]

This was an affirmation of Christ's prediction that 'the meek shall inherit the earth'.[11]

World peace will not, it cannot, come from the top down. It is the ordinary people of the world, like you and me, not the secular leaders, who spread the teaching of Bahá'u'lláh. That is the spiritual foundation for the inevitable world peace.

World peace and the oneness of mankind are the two essential features needed to create the climate in which the world's endless problems can be properly and meaningfully addressed. Problems, whether from nature or human enterprise, or an interaction of the two, demand the best thinking and commitment that humankind can produce.

In order to find practical ways to apply remedies to personal and global problems as the features of the oneness of mankind and world peace gain acceptance, it is important to look at the differences among liberty, submission and guidance. The next chapter explores these.

8

Liberty, Submission and Guidance

Liberty must, in the end, lead to sedition,
whose flames none can quench.
Bahá'u'lláh[1]

Liberty

In the Western world, terms like freedom and liberty have become sacred. However, hidden in the shadows are severe though little appreciated limitations. Bahá'u'lláh brought them into full light in the *Kitáb-i-Aqdas*:

> Consider the pettiness of men's minds. They ask for that which injureth them, and cast away the thing that profiteth them. They are, indeed, of those that are far astray. We find some men desiring liberty, and priding themselves therein. Such men are in the depths of ignorance.[2]

The emerging philosophies of the Age of Reason (also called the Age of Enlightenment) of the 17th and 18th centuries unleashed a thirst for both the scientific method and for liberty. An immediate result was found in the American Declaration of Independence (1776). Liberty, without being defined, is listed as a basic human right, second only to life itself. Shortly thereafter, the loud battle cry of the French Revolution (1789-99) was 'liberty, equality and fraternity'. Liberty has been regarded as the foundation not only of the Western idea of democracy, but of every appealing aspect of Western civilization.

LIBERTY, SUBMISSION AND GUIDANCE

For many people the mere suggestion of restrictions or regulations sets off intense emotional responses, in spite of the fact that today's headlines are filled with stories of people who have run amok in the name of personal freedom and liberty. Bahá'u'lláh predicted the kinds of problems that come from lack of understanding when He said that men seeking liberty are in the 'depths of ignorance'. Few people, even among the most enlightened Western thinkers, comprehend this truth.

Bahá'u'lláh categorically asserts the need to limit freedom. It is matter of balance. He goes on to say:

> Know ye that the embodiment of liberty and its symbol is the animal. That which beseemeth man is submission unto such restraints as will protect him from his own ignorance, and guard him against the harm of the mischief-maker. Liberty causeth man to overstep the bounds of propriety, and to infringe on the dignity of his station. It debaseth him to the level of extreme depravity and wickedness.[3]

There are bloody encounters throughout the world where people are sacrificing their lives for liberty. What people really want are security, stability, status and freedom from oppressive tyranny. They are under the delusion that liberty will get it for them. Western media and leaders feed that notion. They credit liberty with far more virtue than it deserves. As a result, lives are sacrificed in the quest for liberty, based on the hope of gaining something it cannot deliver.

Revolutions and uprisings in the Balkans, Africa and the Middle East have all too often led to chaos and other problems that are as bad or worse than the oppressions from which people wanted freedom. They are fighting to get what they think the West has, without a history or the understanding that it is essential to harness liberty. Their quest for freedom and liberty fulfils Bahá'u'lláh's assertion that 'liberty must, in the end, lead to sedition, whose flames none can quench'.

The rule of law is so taken for granted by most Westerners that its significance is often overlooked. At the same time, Westerners seem to assume that everyone has that same foundation. Unbridled liberty creates and feeds problems instead of solving them. Attempts to impose Western democracy on people of different cultures have repeatedly failed.

If liberty cannot protect people from the above dangers, what protection is there? Bahá'u'lláh answered that question in the *Kitáb-i-Aqdas*:

> Regard men as a flock of sheep that need a shepherd for their protection. This, verily, is the truth, the certain truth. We approve of liberty in certain circumstances, and refuse to sanction it in others. We, verily, are the All-Knowing.[4]

Submission

Rather than dismissing liberty, Bahá'u'lláh redefined it:

> Say: True liberty consisteth in man's submission unto My commandments, little as ye know it. Were men to observe that which We have sent down unto them from the Heaven of Revelation, they would, of a certainty, attain unto perfect liberty. Happy is the man that hath apprehended the Purpose of God in whatever He hath revealed from the Heaven of His Will that pervadeth all created things. Say: The liberty that profiteth you is to be found nowhere except in complete servitude unto God, the Eternal Truth. Whoso hath tasted of its sweetness will refuse to barter it for all the dominion of earth and heaven.[5]

It seems counterintuitive that submission is the key to true liberty. In reality, the only freedom anyone has is the freedom to choose that to which to be subservient and to devote her or his life. There is a certain irony in the fact that freedom of choice

LIBERTY, SUBMISSION AND GUIDANCE

determines that to which we become enslaved. Following are some of the potential masters that can become addictive, without the person even being aware of it. Whether any specific item is good or bad is beside the point. Some of them are even essential. Problems arise when anything assumes importance beyond moderation. Then, each one of the following has the potential to take command, become unduly important and unconsciously take over life and be the individual's master. In effect, they become a religion.

- **Creature needs:** food, shelter, clothing, transportation, rest, physical activity, sex drive.
- **Emotions:** love, hate, envy, pride, joy, jealousy, etc.
- **Quests:** striving for success, hopes and dreams, careers, better health, the need to win, wealth accumulation, desire for leadership, acquisitiveness, social standing, greed, seeking peace and tranquillity.
- **Ideologies:** racism, self-centredness, nationalism, political or religious doctrines and idealism, love of anything but service to God.
- **Substances:** drugs, alcohol, food fetishes, tobacco.
- **Interests:** sports, entertainment, travel, metaphysics, fishing, group affiliations, hunting, hobbies, the paranormal, education, the arts, science, etc.

We usually have no idea how much these things take over life. But they do. It is an extremely subtle enslavement. Lives increasingly revolve around these items.

Some things, such as drugs and alcohol, are obvious. Other things, such as food and shelter, are generally subtle. While there are legitimate health reasons why people can avoid certain foods, being a gourmand can become a fetish and take over sensible choices. Some people will devote their lives to getting the right kind of house in the right neighbourhood. In these cases, food and shelter have become the masters, taking over the persons' life. This misdirected attention was described by 'Abdu'l-Bahá as follows:

> Man is submerged in the affairs of this world . . . Desire and passion, like two unmanageable horses, have wrested the reins of control from him and are galloping madly in the wilderness. This is the cause of the degradation of the world of humanity. This is the cause of its retrogression into the appetites and passions of the animal kingdom. Instead of divine advancement we find sensual captivity and debasement of heavenly virtues of the soul. By devotion to the carnal, mortal world human susceptibilities sink to the level of animalism.[6]

Anything in which a person invests time, money and energy is the real driving force of that person's life, defining real priorities. These may be very different from what that person claims to believe. Those actions become those *unmanageable horses* 'Abdu'l-Bahá was talking about that take anyone on wild journeys into whatever wilderness their appetites seek. Without recognizing it, people become slaves to their own priorities, diverting attention from the real purpose for existence and denying true liberty.

When I pioneered to a place lagging behind in civilized development and, therefore, where cars were out of place, I was surprised to feel a sense of liberation by not having a car. While I had not realized it, rather than my owning a car, it owned me. There was daily dependence on it. Mechanical breakdowns could not be tolerated. The village had not, at that time, overstepped the bounds of moderation and I remember saying how wonderful it was not to be 'owned by an automobile'.

At another pioneering post that also lacked many of the amenities of civilization, I was liberated from telephones, radios and TV. It was a year before we got a telephone. When we got one, we actually lost some freedom. Dependence on the social necessities of civilization is an unwitting, but real, loss of personal liberty and freedom. Today, hand-held electronic gadgets can be useful items, or gods that enslave a lot of people.

How many writers and artists escape the demands of civilization to 'get away from it all' in order to unleash creativity? Away from the so-called benefits of civilization, they can call upon their inner creative energy and bask in the freedom it provides, away from the cacophony and distractions of the modern world. Thoreau had Walden and Sibelius his cabin in the woods. Those are just two examples of the enormous liberty gained from solitude. Even in writing this, on several occasions I camped out where there were no telephones, television or internet connections in order to better concentrate. It was wonderful!

Guidance

Personal guidance comes from upbringing, peer and social pressures, learning from experience, or trying to follow some external standard. The greatest external standard comes from religious scriptures. They all give guidance, including some form of the 'Golden Rule'. Bahá'u'lláh, wrote:

> The Prophets and Messengers of God have been sent down for the sole purpose of guiding mankind to the straight Path of Truth. The purpose underlying their revelation hath been to educate all men, that they may, at the hour of death, ascend, in the utmost purity and sanctity and with absolute detachment, to the throne of the Most High.[7]

A major question is: what guidance does the Bahá'í Faith offer that is different? The Writings provide three specific avenues. While these were given particularly to the Bahá'ís, anyone can take advantage of them.

First and foremost is the rich depository of the fully authentic Word of God, aimed specifically for this time in history. This includes the infallible interpretations of 'Abdu'l-Bahá and the Guardian. People who are not Bahá'ís might regard these nuggets as sources of profound wisdom, and they are right. For Bahá'ís they are more. They are flawless guidance from God, to be respected and followed as such.

A second source is the guidance of the Universal House of Justice. Everything the House says is a marching order from God. Anyone can seek advice from the House, but whoever asks for such advice should be prepared to follow it. If you are not willing to do whatever it says, it is better not to ask. A member of the House of Justice mentioned that even House members are reluctant to ask advice of the House unless they are absolutely certain they are prepared to follow whatever advice is forthcoming.

Still a third means of finding guidance is consultation.[8] Bahá'u'lláh wrote that

> consultation is acceptable in the presence of the Almighty, and hath been enjoined upon the believers, so that they may confer upon ordinary and personal matters, as well as on affairs which are general in nature and universal.
>
> For instance, when a man hath a project to accomplish, should he consult with some of his brethren, that which is agreeable will of course be investigated and unveiled to his eyes, and the truth will be disclosed. Likewise on a higher level, should the people of a village consult one another about their affairs, the right solution will certainly be revealed. In like manner, the members of each profession, such as in industry, should consult, and those in commerce should similarly consult on business affairs. In short, consultation is desirable and acceptable in all things and on all issues.[9]

LIBERTY, SUBMISSION AND GUIDANCE

Consultation, while it is a 'lamp of guidance', does not provide infallible answers. Bahá'u'lláh acknowledged that reality when He described the action to be taken when consultation is inconclusive:

> If consultation among the first group of people assembled endeth in disagreement, new people should be added . . . Whereupon the consultation shall be renewed, and the outcome, whatever it is, shall be obeyed. If, however, there is still disagreement, the same procedure should be repeated once more, and the decision of the majority shall prevail. He, verily, guideth whomsoever He pleaseth to the right way.[10]

With the clear sense of direction that is available, the issue remains: how to take advantage of it? There are enormous barriers in trying to follow the available guidance. Overcoming the barrage of cultural factors that compete with following the true path is a huge personal challenge. Bahá'u'lláh warned:

> The civilization, so often vaunted by the learned exponents of arts and sciences, will, if allowed to overleap the bounds of moderation, bring great evil upon men. Thus warneth you He Who is the All-Knowing. If carried to excess, civilization will prove as prolific a source of evil as it had been of goodness when kept within the restraints of moderation.[11]

Just as a child needs a certain amount of freedom to develop its potential while learning to accept necessary limits, so too, with all of us the freedom to develop our spiritual potential is dependent on the extent to which we become servants of God. Left to our own devices, the secular idea of liberty will deprive us of our greatest freedom. The Hindu mystic Rabindranath Thakur (Tagore), captured the idea in his plea: 'Free me from my own free will.' Bahá'u'lláh neatly summarized that idea in a prayer:

Ordain Thou for me, O my God, the good of this world and the world to come, and grant me what will profit me in every world of Thy worlds, for I know not what will help or harm me.[12]

Since I do not know what will help or harm me, the wisest course of action is to voluntarily put myself in the hand of the One Who does. Bahá'u'lláh gave wonderful details of what that means with five simple but all-inclusive standards: trustworthiness, fidelity, fear of God, truthfulness, and courtesy. In His elegant words:

> Adorn your heads with the garlands of trustworthiness and fidelity, your hearts with the attire of the fear of God, your tongues with absolute truthfulness, your bodies with the vesture of courtesy.[13]

Trustworthiness

Bahá'u'lláh gave an eloquent description of this first standard:

> We will now mention unto thee Trustworthiness and the station thereof... We gazed on one of the Beauties of the Most Sublime Paradise, standing on a pillar of light, and calling aloud saying: 'O inmates of earth and heaven! Behold ye My beauty, and My radiance, and My revelation, and My effulgence. By God, the True One! I am Trustworthiness and the revelation thereof, and the beauty thereof. I will recompense whosoever will cleave unto Me, and recognize My rank and station, and hold fast unto My hem. I am the most great ornament of the people of Bahá, and the vesture of glory unto all who are in the kingdom of creation. I am the supreme instrument for the prosperity of the world, and the horizon of assurance unto all beings.' Thus have We sent down for thee that which will draw men nigh unto the Lord of creation.[14]

As a result of this teaching, when the Bahá'ís of Persia started businesses, they became renowned for their trustworthiness. Their businesses flourished in a culture where cheating was normal. The trustworthiness of these believers was an early evidence that the 'prosperity of the world' will result from this virtue.

Fidelity

In a Tablet to one whom Bahá'u'lláh had named 'Vafa' – which means Fidelity – He wrote the following:

> It behoveth thee, however, to exert thine utmost to attain the very essence of fidelity. This implieth to be well assured in thy heart and to testify with thy tongue to that whereunto God hath testified for His Own exalted Self, proclaiming: 'Verily, self-subsisting am I within the Realm of Glory.' Whoso is enabled in these days to solemnly affirm this truth, hath attained unto all good, and the heavenly Spirit shall descend upon him in the daytime and in the night season, shall graciously assist him to glorify the Name of his Lord and suffer him to unloose his tongue and uphold with his words the Cause of his Lord, the Merciful, the Compassionate. And none can ever achieve this except he who hath purged his heart from whatsoever is created between heaven and earth, and hath entirely detached himself from all but God, the sovereign Lord, the Almighty, the Gracious.[15]

Fear of God

This phrase, common to practically all religions, has perplexed their followers for ages. For many people it has the punitive connotation of damnation and the hell fire of a mean and angry god. When Bahá'u'lláh writes, 'Bring thyself to account ere thou art summoned to a reckoning, on the Day when no man shall have strength to stand for fear of God, the Day when the hearts of the heedless ones shall be made to tremble',[16] a new understanding of the phrase comes into focus.

While punitive fear – which is so common in hell-fire and brimstone sermons – may help some people live better lives, it is limited. The heedless may encounter severe punishment, but what about the faithful, obedient and sincere and their fear of God?

One of the definitions of fear given in Webster's unabridged dictionary is: 'reverential awe'. That definition applies to the following injunction by Bahá'u'lláh:

> We have admonished Our loved ones to fear God, a fear which is the fountain-head of all goodly deeds and virtues. It is the commander of the hosts of justice in the city of Bahá. Happy the man that hath entered the shadow of its luminous standard, and laid fast hold thereon. He, verily, is of the Companions of the Crimson Ark, which hath been mentioned in the Qayyúm-i-Asmá.[17]

Related to that is also the fear of not wanting to disappoint a loved one. One teenage girl in Iran was put in jail for the crime of teaching children's classes. She later told me that she was convinced she was going to be killed. The officials told her that if she recanted her faith, they would let her go free. She believed that whether or not she recanted, they would kill her. Then she thought, after she was dead, she would come face to face with Bahá'u'lláh. If she recanted, her first task would be to explain why she had renounced Him. The fear of that encounter so strengthened her that every future threat served only to embolden her. The fear was not so much of what might happen to her, but of disappointing Bahá'u'lláh.

Truthfulness

Trustworthiness and fidelity are 'garlands' for the head, which can be thought of as attitudes. The fear of God is related to the heart, or emotions. All these are basically internal. Bahá'u'lláh linked truthfulness to the tongue, and courtesy to vesture. These are external – outward appearance and behaviour, relating to other people.

Important as it is, truthfulness is often in short supply. It is commonplace for people to hedge a little on the truth with 'little white lies'. Even being late for a meeting will motivate many people to invent a plausible excuse instead of being honest and open about it. The story of the Greek philosopher Diogenes of Sinope, carrying a lamp looking for an honest man, illustrates how long-standing and common it is to be deceitful and how uncommon it is to be entirely truthful.

Very often, the ruse lies in what is not said as much as a downright lie. Partial truths are sometimes the most misleading. Scam artists, politicians and advertisers are adept at this type of deception.

Yet, this virtue is so important that Bahá'u'lláh said that falsehoods facilitate corruption and injustice while leading to wars. He said the tranquillity of nations was based on honesty:

> In these days truthfulness and sincerity are sorely afflicted in the clutches of falsehood, and justice is tormented by the scourge of injustice. The smoke of corruption hath enveloped the whole world in such wise that naught can be seen in any direction save regiments of soldiers and nothing is heard from any land but the clashing of swords. We beseech God, the True One, to strengthen the wielders of His power in that which will rehabilitate the world and bring tranquillity to the nations.[18]

Rehabilitate the world and bring tranquillity to the nations? That is a big order. How can truthfulness do that?

When you think about it, a high percentage of laws are written and public energy invested to combat the lack of truthfulness. If truthfulness were the basis of human behaviour, it would not be necessary for people to swear in a court of law that they were telling the truth; a person's word would be an oath; commercial, legal and social relationships would be revolutionized; the many laws and much energy that go into countering deception could focus on the *rehabilitation* and the *tranquillity* of humankind.

But there is more. He also states that seeking truth is the means of dispelling ignorance:

> We ask thee to reflect upon that which hath been revealed, and to be fair and just in thy speech, that perchance the splendours of the day-star of truthfulness and sincerity may shine forth, and may deliver thee from the darkness of ignorance, and illumine the world with the light of knowledge.[19]

It is an enormous challenge to be completely truthful at all times and under all circumstances. Yet, this is expected of Bahá'ís. This is another area in which believers are to take the lead in correcting a major problem in society that, as a whole, underrates, trivializes or ignores truthfulness as the normal and accepted standard of behaviour.

Courtesy

Bahá'u'lláh writes:

> I admonish you to observe courtesy, for above all else it is the prince of virtues. Well is it with him who is illumined with the light of courtesy and is attired with the vesture of uprightness.[20]

LIBERTY, SUBMISSION AND GUIDANCE

I was once asked if a certain person was a Bahá'í. He was so courteous that my friend thought he must be a Bahá'í. It so happened that he was not, but I have never been more pleased with a false accusation – that someone would assume a person was a Bahá'í because the courtesy he displayed was associated with being a Bahá'í.

* * * * *

These five standards: trustworthiness, fidelity, fear of God, truthfulness and courtesy are essential tools for building the New World Order. Through submission to the above counsels it is possible to take advantage of the abundant guidance for living. With those counsels as a perspective, it is possible to be comfortable with many of the pursuits mentioned earlier – such as food and shelter, sports and entertainment – that could otherwise enslave. Furthermore, these virtues confer the freedom to use all things, including modern conveniences, in the path of service.

Today's materialistic world is dependent upon less worthy standards. The world is so mired in materialism that any hint of economic slowdown produces worldwide fear and leads to panic. Conventional wisdom holds that NOTHING should interfere with economic growth. A defence of slavery in the 19th century was that it was essential to the economy. It is a classic irony that the unbridled pursuit of economic growth and development is a major cause for civilization to 'overleap the bounds of moderation'.

Progress in food production, communications and electronics are increasingly dependent upon substances that have proven to be harmful when misused or taken in large quantities. Garbage dumps are filled with materials that are known to be carcinogens or lethal and are leaching into water and food supplies.

Science has identified many of the unintended consequences of development. Meaningful action on many issues is ignored, considered not worth worrying about or seen as a threat to the economy. Financial and political leaders take the lead in masking and/or trivializing dangers, even when there is clear evidence of a problem and the means for immediate corrective action are available.

Man's contribution to global warming is both real and hotly debated. The alarming increase in respiratory and neurological problems as well as the increasing variety of mental illness are all parts of the 'evil' Bahá'u'lláh warned of from lack of moderation. Garbage accumulation in the world's oceans is a major global problem that is understood by only a handful of people and ignored by most, including government leaders.

Not everyone's immune system can cope with the onslaught of physical, spiritual and cultural pollutants invading the environment. The two unmanageable horses of passion and desire 'Abdu'l-Bahá spoke of keep dragging mankind into the wilderness of unintended consequences as they gallop out of control. That wild ride is not over.

Any disruption of material progress is shunned and there is massive resistance to corrective measures, especially when they will lead to an immediate financial loss. People want the convenience and luxury of the latest technical developments and have little interest in finding out, let alone paying to prevent, problems that might develop later. The thirst for more of the perceived advantages of materialism camouflages its dangers. Our dysfunctional civilization is but an early sign of Bahá'u'lláh's warning that 'civilization . . . if allowed to overleap the bounds of moderation, [will] bring great evil upon men'.[21]

However, two processes are going on simultaneously and they are the dynamics of human progress, as the next chapter will show.

9

Two Processes

*Soon will the present-day order be rolled up,
and a new one spread out in its stead.*
Bahá'u'lláh[1]

Great things come in twos. There are the Twin Manifestations for this age; there is the dual nature of the Manifestations: not only are they divine, but human, with much greater sensitivity than the rest of us; there is also the junction of two epic cycles: the closing of the Prophetic Cycle after thousands of years, and the opening of the 500,000-year Bahá'í Cycle; the exclusive right of interpretation was given to two – 'Abdu'l-Bahá and the Guardian; the Guardian said of 'Abdu'l-Bahá that in Him 'the incompatible characteristics of a human nature and superhuman knowledge and perfection have been blended and are completely harmonized';[2] there are two branches or arms of the Administrative Order – the Guardianship and the Universal House of Justice.

The Revelation for this age comes with two modes of redemption, one for the individual and the other collective. Bahá'u'lláh writes:

> The first is to liberate the children of men from the darkness of ignorance, and guide them to the light of true understanding. The second is to ensure the peace and tranquillity of mankind, and provide all the means by which they can be established.[3]

Added to this is the dual purpose of man – to know and worship God.

The world is going through convulsions today such as it has never seen before. As Bahá'u'lláh stated in the *Kitáb-i-Aqdas*:

> The world's equilibrium hath been upset through the vibrating influence of this most great, this new World Order. Mankind's ordered life hath been revolutionized through the agency of this unique, this wondrous System – the like of which mortal eyes have never witnessed.[4]

The Lord's Prayer states a common objective for Christians and Bahá'ís: *Thy kingdom come, Thy will be done in earth, as it is in heaven.*[5] A major distinction is that while the Christians ardently pray for it, the Bahá'ís not only pray for it, but are building its foundation. It is still in its embryonic state, and not all Bahá'ís are fully conscious of the importance of what they are doing.

So the parade of twos continues as the old decays and the new emerges!

The vehicle for both life and growth is challenge and response. We have little control over the challenges we face, but we have some control over responses. We humans are called upon to carry on two functions. One is building the Kingdom of God on earth. The second is developing individual spiritual capacity. Working for the first produces the second.

The Kingdom of God will be established, no matter how many or few individuals live up to their individual spiritual potential. Mason Remey's life illustrates this point. When he became a Covenant-breaker, he forfeited his spiritual destiny. However, while he was a faithful Bahá'í, he used his architectural skills to design three temples – for Africa, Australia, and Haifa. The good he did continues to contribute to building the Kingdom of God on earth, despite his defection. This illustrates how the Faith progresses, even when individuals take themselves out from under the protection of the Covenant.

Duality is either two things working against each other or

two things working in tandem. Both are found within the Bahá'í world. For things working against each other, the recurring cycles of crises and victories is a reflection of the basic physical principle that for every action there is an equal and opposite reaction.

On a personal level there is the ongoing challenge of changing from an old, basically material being into a new, spiritually oriented creature. Within Bahá'í communities there is the difficult contrast of putting aside the cultural and traditional ways of doing things and adopting the Bahá'í model; and the challenge of dealing with varied personalities. Some people are easy to get along with and some are not. Learning how to function based on a Bahá'í perspective with people with whom we disagree or have little in common, other than the love of Bahá'u'lláh, is a major challenge. This is a continuous stumbling block, filled with both successes and failures.

There was a little poem that Rúḥíyyih Khánum liked to recite:

There is so much good in the worst of us,
And, so much bad in the best of us,
That ill becomes any of us,
To say anything about the rest of us.

Within the world about us there is the duality of, on the one hand, the dying of hopelessly dysfunctional civilizations, while at the same time there is an incredible flourishing of the ideas enunciated by Bahá'u'lláh, such as the elimination of prejudice, equality of men and women and the harmony of science and religion. There is the stunning decay and destruction of the old world order and the simultaneous, though gradual and uneven, emergence of the new. This provides much material for both hope and despair.

The Guardian commented about this confusing period in history:

> What we witness at the present time . . . is the adolescent stage in the slow and painful evolution of humanity, preparatory to the attainment of the stage of manhood, the stage of maturity, the promise of which is embedded in the teachings, and enshrined in the prophecies, of Bahá'u'lláh. The tumult of this age of transition is characteristic of the impetuosity and irrational instincts of youth, its follies, its prodigality, its pride, its self-assurance, its rebelliousness, and contempt of discipline.[6]

In addition to the tumult of negative impulses he mentioned, adolescence is also a time when altruism and idealism emerge. Ask a group of youth what they want to do with their lives and a surprising number will express lofty sentiments: helping other people, endangered species, the planet, or some other worthy endeavour, without mention of personal benefit.

Adolescence is also a time of confusion, as youth are becoming their own persons, as distinct from family: a time when order and disorder commingle. Violent gangs are formed. Yet, there are unnumbered instances where youth have sacrificed themselves for the benefit of others.

In a passage under the intriguing heading 'The Challenging Requirements of the Present Hour', Shoghi Effendi asked the Bahá'í community in North America (United States and Canada),

> How could it forfeit its birthright or mar its heritage, when the country from which the vast majority of its members have sprung, the great republic of the West, government and people alike, is itself, through experiment and trial, slowly, painfully, unwittingly and irresistibly advancing towards the goal destined for it by both Bahá'u'lláh and 'Abdu'l-Bahá? Indeed if we would read aright the signs of the times, and appraise correctly the significances of contemporaneous events that are impelling forward both the American Bahá'í

TWO PROCESSES

Community and the nation of which it forms a part on the road leading them to their ultimate destiny, we cannot fail to perceive the workings of two simultaneous processes, generated as far back as the concluding years of the Heroic Age of our Faith, each clearly defined, each distinctly separate, yet closely related and destined to culminate, in the fullness of time, in a single glorious consummation.

One of these processes is associated with the mission of the American Bahá'í Community, the other with the destiny of the American nation. The one serves directly the interests of the Administrative Order of the Faith of Bahá'u'lláh, the other promotes indirectly the institutions that are to be associated with the establishment of His World Order. The first process dates back to the revelation of those stupendous Tablets constituting the Charter of 'Abdu'l-Bahá's Divine Plan . . .

The other process dates back to the outbreak of the first World War that threw the great republic of the West into the vortex of the first stage of a world upheaval. It received its initial impetus through the formulation of President Wilson›s Fourteen Points, closely associating for the first time that republic with the fortunes of the Old World.[7]

There is a striking similarity to the two processes Bahá'u'lláh mentioned to Professor Browne during His interview in April of 1890: 'these fruitless strifes, these ruinous wars shall pass away and the 'Most Great Peace' shall come.'[8]

In the *Messages to the Bahá'í World* Shoghi Effendi clearly outlined the two opposing forces developing simultaneously, writing in April 1957 that the world Spiritual Crusade had

> accelerated, to a notable extent, the two parallel processes of integration and disintegration associated respectively with the rising fortunes of God's infant Faith and the sinking fortunes of the institutions of a declining civilization.[9]

More than three-quarters of a century ago, the Guardian wrote words that equally serve as a commentary on today's world:

> The recrudescence of religious intolerance, of racial animosity, and of patriotic arrogance; the increasing evidences of selfishness, of suspicion, of fear and of fraud; the spread of terrorism, of lawlessness, of drunkenness and of crime; the unquenchable thirst for, and the feverish pursuit after, earthly vanities, riches and pleasures; the weakening of family solidarity; the laxity in parental control; the lapse into luxurious indulgence; the irresponsible attitude towards marriage and the consequent rising tide of divorce; the degeneracy of art and music, the infection of literature, and the corruption of the press; the extension of the influence and activities of those 'prophets of decadence' who advocate companionate marriage, who preach the philosophy of nudism, who call modesty an intellectual fiction, who refuse to regard the procreation of children as the sacred and primary purpose of marriage, who denounce religion as an opiate of the people, who would, if given free rein, lead back the human race to barbarism, chaos, and ultimate extinction – these appear as the outstanding characteristics of a decadent society, a society that must either be reborn or perish.[10]

Contrast the above with his vision of the future:

> National rivalries, hatreds, and intrigues will cease, and racial animosity and prejudice will be replaced by racial amity, understanding and cooperation. The causes of religious strife will be permanently removed, economic barriers and restrictions will be completely abolished, and the inordinate distinction between classes will be obliterated. Destitution on the one hand, and gross accumulation of ownership on the other, will disappear. The enormous energy dissipated and wasted on war, whether economic or political, will be

consecrated to such ends as will extend the range of human inventions and technical development, to the increase of the productivity of mankind, to the extermination of disease, to the extension of scientific research, to the raising of the standard of physical health, to the sharpening and refinement of the human brain, to the exploitation of the unused and unsuspected resources of the planet, to the prolongation of human life, and to the furtherance of any other agency that can stimulate the intellectual, the moral, and spiritual life of the entire human race.[11]

It is the transition from one to the other that promises to be long, thorny, treacherous and filled with setbacks. Standing at the crux, knowing the Faith will be victorious, is a major challenge during this time of protracted transition. Assurance is galvanized when the focus is on ultimate victory.

In 1987 the Bahá'í International Community prepared a statement in which it highlighted the junction of these two processes:

> We witness around us an accelerating two-fold process of disintegration and integration. There is a breakdown of exhausted and inappropriate ideals, of archaic institutions and ideas, of empty customs and beliefs, while at the same time there is a burgeoning of new ideas, fresh discoveries in science, insights into human behaviour, innovations in the management of human affairs. These perturbations and crises could give birth to new hope and promise and must be seen as opportunities for greater measures of creative human effort. The real enemies are not other nation-states, but ignorance, prejudice, greed, poverty, and disease. Such adversaries are far more worthy of our human and natural resources.[12]

The following table shows some issues in a state of transition. Thinking people throughout the world have accepted the value of the teachings of Bahá'u'lláh. What they lack is acceptance of His authority. Consider the gains made in these areas since first proposed over a century ago. Granted, all are still works in process.

Issues in transition	From	Toward
gender bias	subordination of women	partnership
ethnicity	racial dominance	equality and integration
religious differences	violent intolerance	acceptance and tolerance
science and religion	antagonistic	complementary
literacy	the privileged few	universal
formal education	learning what is known	creativity and citizenship
cultural foundation	materialistic	material & moral balance
medicine	curative	preventative
natural resources	unrestrained exploitation	sustainable development
material wealth	acquisition	contentment
profit	limitless gain	tool for service
economics	personal increases	benefits for all
authority	domination	inspiration and guidance
decision-making	confrontational	consultative

The processes can be illustrated by the intersection of declining and ascending arcs. Mankind is getting perilously close to the point of intersection, a tipping point in which colossal, albeit unpredictable, events will occur, forever altering the course of history.

TWO PROCESSES

Old world order

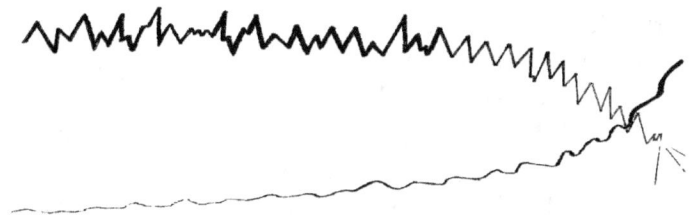

Emerging civilization

One feature of both arcs is that they are irregular. That is, each has short periods of decline followed by times when events appear to be improving. These normal variations are often misinterpreted as having greater long-range implications than they do. In our materialistic civilization, the variations of the declining arc are often interpreted as extremes concerning the never-ending cycles such as financial ups and downs – personal, local, national and global. For people who are not aware of greater trends, looking at minor variations is misleading. Temporary variations can alternately be depressing or pleasing. It is an article of faith to look beyond the chaos and be aware of the broad sweep of the two processes and conscious of the approaching chaotic time of intersection.

A large number of secular analysts have given serious thought to trying to figure out the significance of the fast-moving events of this age, with its obvious signs of both decay and progress. They all fall short.

The Universal House of Justice has recently clarified the interaction of the two processes: 'the forces of disintegration tend to sweep away barriers that block humanity's progress, opening space for the process of integration to draw diverse groups together and disclosing new opportunities for cooperation and collaboration'.[13] While this letter was addressed to the Bahá'ís of Iran, it has global implications.

A burning question is: what can Bahá'ís do about it? There

are two specific actions: one addresses immediate needs and the other involves long-term solutions.

Concerning immediate needs, in the letter quoted above the House of Justice gave advice for global application. It said the Bahá'í community should 'contribute to the advancement of civilization: its involvement in the society at large'. In a Tablet that Bahá'u'lláh considered as part of the *Kitáb-i-Aqdas*, Bahá'u'lláh instructed members of the House of Justice: 'for each day there is a new problem and for every problem an expedient solution . . . act according to the needs and requirements of the time'.[14] This has general application.

At a time when dysfunctional political, social and economic institutions are incapable of solving the urgent global issues, Bahá'ís, especially youth, guided by the Bahá'í Writings whether or not it is appropriate to disclose their sources, should work with like-minded groups in seeking solutions. As they do that, they are also honing problem-solving skills that will be crucial for cleaning up the mess left in the wake of 'the ruins of a tottering civilization'.[15]

A feature of the gradually strengthening ascending arc, representing the emerging Bahá'í community, is that it is barely visible on the world scene. Only an inconspicuous minority of people today is even aware of it. The Guardian pointed out that the Faith had to go

> through the stages of obscurity, of proscription, of emancipation, and of recognition – stages that must needs culminate in the course of succeeding centuries, in the establishment of the Faith, and the founding, in the plenitude of its power and authority, of the world-embracing Bahá'í Commonwealth.[16]

The current stage of relative obscurity enables the Faith to develop internally. While there is ferocious opposition in some parts of the world, in most places the Faith is either ignored or trivialized as both overly idealistic and irrelevant.

One example was seen during the dedication of the Baháʼí terraces on Mount Carmel in Haifa. For a short time in 1992, they attracted world attention. One well-known television commentator obviously missed its significance when he trivialized it by saying, 'It will take more than pretty gardens to bring peace to the Middle East.'

The point he missed was articulated in a statement from an Israeli director of tourism. He was talking to the Baháʼí in charge of tours at the gardens when he said, 'You Baháʼís don't know what you are doing. You think people come here because the gardens are beautiful or entrance is free. That's not why they come.' She told me that he went on with other misperceptions when the Baháʼí finally asked why he thought people came. He replied, 'They come here because it is the only place where they can find hope.' That is what the pretty gardens offer!

I was once on an extended international teaching trip followed by an International Convention in Haifa. It had been physically and mentally exhausting. When it was over, I craved nothing but peace, quiet and solitude. On an extra day before my flight home, I went by myself to the old city of Jerusalem. In the Church of the Holy Sepulchre, while standing in the long, slow-moving line to the tomb, absorbed in my own private thoughts, there was an overly friendly tour guide who tried to make conversation. I was not inclined to talk. He persisted. He finally asked what I was doing in Israel. I told him I had been attending a Baháʼí Convention in Haifa. His face lit up and he exclaimed, 'Baháʼí! Haifa! That's where the peace is. Here (Jerusalem) everything is money, money, money (he said while rubbing his fingers together). But, Haifa! That's where the tranquillity is. That's where the beauty is. That's where I go when I want peace and quiet, and to meditate. I go to Haifa, to the Baháʼí gardens to find hope.' He ruined my self-absorption. For the rest of my time in that long line we had a continuing, smiling relationship as he paced back and forth astride the line, making a positive comment when he would pass me.

Hope is a priceless but often ignored and vastly underrated characteristic! How many significant tragedies have been salvaged by the power of hope? How many crises have been endured because people clung to hope? Hope is one real and tangible thing that Bahá'ís can give to their family, friends, neighbours, co-workers, indeed to the world. It has an immediate effect of uplifting spirits. The impact on future events is incalculable. People have often said to Bahá'ís, 'I feel better when you are around.' This is not because Bahá'ís are Pollyannas who cannot see what is wrong. It is largely because Bahá'ís still have a positive attitude, in spite of all that is wrong during these days of turmoil and confusion. Hope is infectious.

At this point in the deterioration of the world it is easy to lose sight of the power of hope. Perhaps the greatest gift Bahá'ís can offer to the multitudes who are not yet ready to embrace Bahá'u'lláh is their world-view and infectious conviction that mankind is on the cusp of the transition to a better world.

Slowly, as the ascending arc gains more recognition, greater hope will be induced – partly because of the increasing number of Bahá'ís radiating hope and confidence. As more people become aware of Bahá'u'lláh's teachings, the positive outlook will increase.

When the tipping point is reached there will be a dramatic change. Even then, not everyone will understand what is happening. Future generations will look back and mark the time and unravel the dynamics of transition. Those who will live through it may well miss much of its significance as it unfolds.

John Able, who is not a Bahá'í, in his book *Apocalypse Secrets: Bahá'í Interpretation of the Book of Revelation,* sees today's conflicts as fulfilling the prophecies of the 17th chapter of the Book of Revelation. On one hand are the 'Militant Muslims'. In his view they are fighting against what he called the 'Malignant Materialism' of the West. He claimed that this is referred to as the whore of Babylon in the Book of Revelation. The tumultuous events of the 16th and 17th chapters are today's headlines. He likens the balance of that Book to the emerging World Order foretold by Bahá'u'lláh. In his view, the global economic collapse, narrated in the book is very close at hand – not decades away, but years.[17]

In its Riḍván Message of 2006, the Universal House of Justice called attention to the declining world conditions:

> One need only consider the deepening moral crisis engulfing humanity to appreciate the extent to which the forces of disintegration have rent the fabric of society. Have not the evidences of selfishness, of suspicion, of fear and of fraud, which the Guardian perceived with such clarity, become so widespread as to be readily apparent to even the casual observer? Does not the threat of terrorism of which he spoke loom so large on the international scene as to preoccupy the minds of young and old alike in every corner of the globe? Have not the unquenchable thirst for, and the feverish pursuit after, earthly vanities, riches and pleasures so consolidated their power and influence as to assume authority over such human values as happiness, fidelity and love? Have not the weakening of family solidarity and the irresponsible attitude towards marriage reached such proportions as to endanger the existence of this fundamental unit of society? 'The perversion of human nature, the degradation of human conduct, the corruption and dissolution of human institutions,' about which Shoghi Effendi forewarned, are sadly revealing themselves in their worst and most revolting aspects.

The Guardian lays the greatest share of the blame for humanity's moral downfall on the decline of religion as a social force. *Should the lamp of religion be obscured* he draws our attention to the words of Bahá'u'lláh, *chaos and confusion will ensue, and the lights of fairness, of justice, of tranquillity and peace cease to shine.* The decades that followed the writing of his letters have seen not only a continued deterioration in the ability of religion to exercise moral influence, but also the betrayal of the masses through the unseemly conduct of religious institutions. Attempts at reinvigorating it have only given rise to a fanaticism that, if left unchecked, could destroy the foundation of civilized relationships among people. The persecution of the Bahá'ís in Iran, recently intensified, is ample evidence alone of the determination of the forces of darkness to quench the flame of faith wherever it burns brightly. Though confident in the ultimate triumph of the Cause, we dare not forget the warning of the Guardian that the Faith will have to contend with enemies more powerful and more insidious than those who have afflicted it in the past.[18]

Many people are concerned by what is happening, but don't know what to do about it. Other people seem to be in a state of denial or indifference, concentrating on personal diversions of entertainments, material advancement, or other private concerns. Oblivious to what is going on they are, as Bahá'u'lláh suggested, mesmerized by 'vain and trivial pursuits', seeing the 'facts' through seriously distorted lenses. Nowhere is this more apparent than on issues concerning the environment, economics or public safety and policy.

There are those who are preaching their own form of gloom and doom, offering dire warnings and/or pat solutions that offer simplistic, black and white answers that are unrealistic. Religious revival is apparent among fundamentalist circles of all faiths. The theme frequently includes an end of the physical world.

There are many people of goodwill and good intentions who seek solutions to the dilemmas of the day. Many have excellent ideas, but often they are mired in a materialistic view of the world and their well-meaning schemes for repair cannot break out of that mold. Rather than understanding that there are spiritual solutions to economic problems, with great sincerity

TWO PROCESSES

and fervour they apply economic solutions to spiritual problems (see Chapter 16 below). It doesn't work. They lack a clear appreciation of the colossal, underlying, cataclysmic upheaval that will become obvious with the tipping point.

Bahá'u'lláh gave this eloquent appraisal:

> A new life is, in this age, stirring within all the peoples of the earth; and yet none hath discovered its cause or perceived its motive. Consider the peoples of the West. Witness how, in their pursuit of that which is vain and trivial, they have sacrificed, and are still sacrificing, countless lives for the sake of its establishment and promotion.[19]

Only with the vision of Bahá'u'lláh is it possible to see that mankind is on an exodus through the modern-day desert of materialism, on its way to the 'promised land' of the New World Order. Shoghi Effendi explained:

> As we view the world around us, we are compelled to observe the manifold evidences of that universal fermentation which, in every continent of the globe and in every department of human life, be it religious, social, economic or political, is purging and reshaping humanity in anticipation of the Day when the wholeness of the human race will have been recognized and its unity established. A twofold process, however, can be distinguished, each tending, in its own way and with an accelerated momentum, to bring to a climax the forces that are transforming the face of our planet. The first is essentially an integrating process, while the second is fundamentally disruptive. The former, as it steadily evolves, unfolds a System which may well serve as a pattern for that world polity towards which a strangely-disordered world is continually advancing; while the latter, as its disintegrating influence deepens, tends to tear down, with increasing violence, the antiquated barriers that seek

to block humanity's progress towards its destined goal. The constructive process stands associated with the nascent Faith of Bahá'u'lláh, and is the harbinger of the New World Order that Faith must erelong establish. The destructive forces that characterize the other should be identified with a civilization that has refused to answer to the expectation of a new age, and is consequently falling into chaos and decline.

A titanic, a spiritual struggle, unparalleled in its magnitude yet unspeakably glorious in its ultimate consequences, is being waged as a result of these opposing tendencies, in this age of transition through which the organized community of the followers of Bahá'u'lláh and mankind as a whole are passing.[20]

Viewing these turbulent times as a necessary, unstable, though temporary, period of transition can bring calm and contentment to Bahá'ís. Disturbing events, whether personal or worldwide, can be seen as a fleeting but intrinsic part of the emergence of a new world civilization. At the same time, Bahá'ís have the twin challenge of using the guidance of the Bahá'í Writings to minimize the current problems, whether personal or global. Emphasis needs to be placed on building the spiritual foundation for the future.

How will this be done? In this two-fold process Bahá'ís work on the emergence of the new. At the same time they are developing the skills needed for the reformation of this tottering world civilization as its institutions collapse.

This monumental task will be carried out by the three protagonists.

10

Three Protagonists

> ... the relationships among the individual, the institutions,
> and the local community – the Plan's three protagonists
> – are evolving soundly.
> The Universal House of Justice[1]

During a meeting with the Bahá'í Boards of Counsellors of the world in 1995, the Universal House of Justice called attention to these three separate entities. It said:

> At Riḍván 1996, the Bahá'ís of the world will embark on a global enterprise aimed at one major accomplishment: a significant advance in the process of entry by troops. This is to be achieved through marked progress in the activity and development of the individual believer, of the institutions, and of the local community. That an advance in this process depends on the progress of all three of these intimately connected participants is abundantly clear. The next four years must witness a dramatic upsurge in effective teaching activities undertaken at the initiative of the individual. Thousands upon thousands of believers will need to be aided to express the vitality of their faith through constancy in teaching the Cause and by supporting the plans of their institutions and the endeavours of their communities. They should be helped to realize that their efforts will be sustained by the degree to which their inner life and private character 'mirror forth in their manifold aspects the splendour of those eternal principles proclaimed by Bahá'u'lláh'.[2]

The individual

In His monumental final address to the Letters of the Living, the Báb gave an early indication that the development of the Cause rests with individual believers and not people in positions of authority. He said.

> O My beloved friends! You are the bearers of the name of God in this Day. You have been chosen as the repositories of His mystery. It behoves each one of you to manifest the attributes of God, and to exemplify by your deeds and words the signs of His righteousness, His power and glory. The very members of your body must bear witness to the loftiness of your purpose, the integrity of your life, the reality of your faith, and the exalted character of your devotion . . . Such must be the purity of your character and the degree of your renunciation, that the people of the earth may through you recognise and be drawn closer to the heavenly Father who is the Source of purity and grace . . . Verily I say, immensely exalted is this Day above the days of the Apostles of old. Nay, immeasurable is the difference! You are the witnesses of the Dawn of the promised Day of God. You are the partakers of the mystic chalice of His Revelation. Gird up the loins of endeavour, and be mindful of the words of God as revealed in His Book . . . Arise in His name, put your trust wholly in Him, and be assured of ultimate victory.[3]

This placed divine responsibility squarely on the shoulders of people who had little status in the power structure of the day. What they had was utter devotion to the Voice of God for this age and unshakable confidence that whatever He said would work.

In days gone by few people could read and write. The clergy informed people of spiritual realities and were to teach the right way to live. Among other things, this created what might be called a congregational mentality. That is, religious leaders were viewed as shepherds, and individuals the flock that was to follow.

Bahá'u'lláh eliminated the clergy. That started the colossal change from the congregational mentality to individual responsibility. The nature, transition and consequence of this profound difference, although not always obvious, is slowly being realized.

But, what should the individual do? For many Bahá'ís the mental shift is not complete. Too often both the institutions and its members are viewed as a substitute or replacement for the clergy. When looking for teachers for summer schools and other programmes, it is natural to look for well-known members of institutions because of their position, not because of their expertise on a particular subject.

The Covenant established administrative institutions. By design, they were not to function as clergy. The Guardian defined their purpose as follows. 'Now that they [the American believers] have erected the administrative machinery of the Cause they must put it to its real use – *serving only as an instrument to facilitate the flow of the spirit of the Faith out into the world*' (emphasis mine).[4] Rúhíyyih Khánum wrote:

> Over and over in the letters of these early years Shoghi Effendi mentions the need to 'arise to offer your share of service to this heedless and suffering world'. In a letter to one of the friends he makes a highly revealing distinction: 'The time has come for the friends . . . to think not as to how they should serve the Cause, but how the Cause should be served.' We might well continue to this day to ponder these words. What are its needs, what its direction, what its goals?[5]

Action comes from individuals. They do things. Being a passive believer is not enough. Not only is the individual responsible for her or his own spiritual development, but the collective growth and progress of the Cause are dependent on individual believers taking the initiative. This leaves no room for the congregational mentality. Institutions facilitate the flow of the spirit generated. But people make things happen.

The Fire Tablet is a dialogue between the Manifestation and God. Its last paragraph includes the instruction that all believers should ponder or think about this Tablet.[6] The word champion is used three times. The first is in the 28th verse, where Bahá'u'lláh laments, 'Canst Thou see any who have championed Thy Self, or who ponder on what hath befallen Him in the pathway of Thy love? Now doth My pen halt, O Beloved of the worlds.' Imagine that! Divine Revelation interrupted because there are not enough champions. Today, progress still depends on those who will arise as champions. In the very next verse the term is used as an attribute of God.

Further in that Tablet, in God's final response to the Manifestation, He states His own grief: 'Dost Thou wail, or shall I wail? Rather shall I weep at the fewness of Thy champions.' It stretches the imagination to realize that the slow transition from a passive, congregational mentality, to becoming champions, causes God to weep!

In my thinking there are four kinds of champions:

1. Of course, dedicated enrolled Bahá'ís are the main champions of the Cause when they do their utmost to promote its interests. The Guardian made a distinction: 'There are two kinds of Bahá'ís, one might say: those whose religion is Bahá'í and those who live for the Faith. Needless to say if we can belong to the latter category, if we can be in the vanguard of heroes, martyrs and saints, it is more praiseworthy in the sight of God.'[7] These are champions of the first order.
2. There are also many people who are not Bahá'ís who further the interests of the Faith for this day. They may never even hear of the Cause. They are in the vanguard

of working for the elimination of prejudice, women's rights, social justice, the harmony of science and religion, and so on.
3. Many people are defenders of the Faith from the outside. There was a Muslim in Persia whose wife and children were Bahá'ís. At the time of the Islamic Revolution, the children were in America going to school, but the parents remained in Iran. She would hold Bahá'í meetings in their home and he, as a Muslim, would not attend. Several times the authorities came to the house saying they heard there was a Bahá'í meeting being held there. He would say, 'I'm a Muslim. What are you doing in my house?' That would be the end of it and the meetings would go on. Eventually, they moved to the United States. Three years later, when he no longer needed to defend his wife, he enrolled as a Bahá'í. Tears flowed for three days. He, indeed, as a Muslim, was a champion of the Faith.
4. There are many who have enrolled in the Faith but don't show up at meetings. There are others who became Bahá'ís and, for some reason, resigned from the Faith. These are reserve troops. They just don't happen to be on active duty at the moment. Many of them will step forward when needed. My wife and I applied for a teaching position in a remote village in order to pioneer. The Episcopal Priest from the village learned of it and wrote a letter of protest to the Department of Education. I was called to the regional office. The director had been a Bahá'í, but had left the Faith because he felt it was too idealistic and did not actively address the pressing social problems of the day. He told me that he had been at the meeting where the letter was read and he had been able to assure the others that Bahá'ís do not act in the way the priest feared. He said, 'They will "live the life", but not abuse their positions as teachers.' He told me our

application had been accepted. Then, he looked me in the eye and said, 'It is up to you to be sure I was telling the truth.' He was an essential champion for our pioneering plans.

Suffice it to say, this is a grass-roots religion and every believer has both the capability and responsibility to become a champion. The following words of the Guardian speak to this point:

> Neither the local nor national representatives of the community, no matter how elaborate their plans, or persistent their appeals, or sagacious their counsels, nor even the Guardian himself, however much he may yearn for this consummation, can decide where the duty of the individual lies, or supplant him in the discharge of that task. The individual alone must assess its character, consult his conscience, prayerfully consider all its aspects, manfully struggle against the natural inertia that weighs him down in his effort to arise, shed, heroically and irrevocably, the trivial and superfluous attachments which hold him back, empty himself of every thought that may tend to obstruct his path, mix, in obedience to the counsels of the Author of His Faith, and in imitation of the One Who is its true Exemplar, with men and women, in all walks of life, seek to touch their hearts, through the distinction which characterizes his thoughts, his words and his acts, and win them over tactfully, lovingly, prayerfully and persistently, to the Faith he himself has espoused.

He goes on to list obstacles that are guaranteed to get in the way:

> The gross materialism that engulfs the entire nation at the present hour; the attachment to worldly things that enshrouds the souls of men; the fears and anxieties that

distract their minds; the pleasure and dissipations that fill their time, the prejudices and animosities that darken their outlook, the apathy and lethargy that paralyze their spiritual faculties – these are among the formidable obstacles that stand in the path of every would-be warrior in the service of Bahá'u'lláh, obstacles which he must battle against and surmount in his crusade for the redemption of his own countrymen.[8]

The Bahá'í Writings are filled with encouragement for each one to arise and serve. Speaking specifically of religious fanaticism and the fierce opposition that it unleashes, Bahá'u'lláh made a comment about what to do in the face of any opposition. He wrote:

> Gird up the loins of your endeavour, O people of Bahá, that haply the tumult of religious dissension and strife that agitateth the peoples of the earth may be stilled, that every trace of it may be completely obliterated. For the love of God, and them that serve Him, arise to aid this most sublime and momentous Revelation.[9]

Part of girding up the loins is proceeding even when you are not certain of what to do. Shoghi Effendi wrote, 'If the friends always waited until they were fully qualified to do any particular task, the work of the Cause would be almost at a standstill! But the very act of striving to serve, however unworthy one may feel, attracts the blessings of God and enables one to become more fitted for the task.'[10]

Who is competent to serve? No one! With the Guardian's assurance that the act of striving attracts blessing, why should anyone hesitate? Skill comes from doing. Mistakes are guaranteed, but mistakes are a marvellous tool for learning. Hand of the Cause John Robarts was fond of saying, 'Do it! Find out you were wrong later.'

That means using individual initiative, creativity and enterprise to serve the Faith and making a lot of mistakes along the way.

Many Bahá'ís have inspirations or ideas for worthwhile projects. That is wonderful. Problems arise when they expect the Spiritual Assembly or someone else to carry out their ideas. That doesn't work very well. The thought, no matter how worthy, becomes a 'vain' or useless imagining. Becoming aware of something carries a responsibility. The one who has the inspiration has an obligation to do something about it. Generally, the Bahá'í institutions have enough to do without pursuing every great idea individuals have. However, if the one with the idea follows through, that is different. Guidance or permission of the Spiritual Assembly is sometimes, but not always, appropriate. If the one with the idea does not have the needed motivation to push it forward, there is little chance of success.

This brings up the question of leadership. In order for any project to be carried out, it is necessary to have a leader or leaders who can work together. When the Covenant is carefully considered, it will be seen that the role of leadership is important, but shifts.

William was to compete in a dance competition. He wrote a song that illustrated a Bahá'í principle and enlisted some of the friends to help him. He was definitely the leader when it came to the music and dancing. However, Rachel had experience in stage management and she was the boss for that. Sequine knew costumes and clothing and that was her domain. Arthur had organizational skills and he was the overall producer. The team worked superbly well because no one tried to be boss, but all respected the leadership roles that were exercised by others in each area of expertise.

Most projects start with one or more people taking the initiative. There are several possible outcomes. When it shows promise, and assistance is needed for further development, institutions may become involved. The Ruhi series of deepening booklets started when some Bahá'ís discussed the need for deepening new believers. Many Bahá'í-inspired projects, including Bahá'í schools throughout the world, are the result of individual and small group initiatives.

A marvel of the spirit of the Cause is the enormous accomplishments by people who had ideas and the initiative to proceed. Wonders have resulted, even when people were inexperienced and unsure of what they were doing. They went ahead, relying on guidance from on high.

Never before in all of history has so much been accomplished by so many people with such meagre resources, experience and skills. This happens when there is an eagerness to work together, a willingness to let leadership flow and, most essentially, reliance on the Concourse on High. The Guardian proclaimed the readiness of the Heavenly Concourse when he quoted 'Abdu'l-Bahá:

> The triumphant hosts of the Celestial Concourse, arrayed and marshalled in the Realms above, stand ready and expectant to assist and assure victory to that valiant horseman who with confidence spurs on his charger into the arena of service.[11]

Bahá'ís use a variety of resources, but there are some things that are tragically underused. We have an abundance of ignorance and incompetence, but neglect to use them creatively.

Martha Root was an outstanding example of the skilful use of ignorance. She would travel alone when women did not usually travel alone – especially not internationally. She knew her own shortcomings, but that never stopped her. She would develop networks of resources to do those things she could not do. Without knowing the local language, she would find someone who would translate Bahá'í literature and help her get material printed. Through these skills, she would gain audiences with people of prominence, including the dowager Queen Marie of Romania.

With full confidence in the Concourse on High, she would proceed. However, she did not just wing it. She prepared by first learning as much as she could about where she was going. When she arrived in a new location, after finding a place to stay, her first activity would be to say the Tablet of Aḥmad, not just once, but nine times. Then, she would venture forth, knowing that divine assistance would be with her to find ways to do things she could not do.

The Guardian said of her and her unparalleled accomplishments: 'To Martha Root, that archetype of Baháʼí itinerant teachers and the foremost Hand raised by Baháʼu'lláh since ʻAbdu'l-Bahá's passing, must be awarded, if her manifold services and the supreme act of her life are to be correctly appraised, the title of Leading Ambassadress of His Faith and Pride of Baháʼí teachers, whether men or women, in both the East and the West.'[12]

This praise came from the Guardian because she ventured forth, unfazed by the fact that the seas on which she sailed were seas she did not have charts for. She was not always aware of what she was getting into, but with full confidence of assistance from on high, she used even her lack of knowledge and expertise to serve the Cause. What an example to follow!

Here is to more creative uses of ignorance!

However, barging ahead without preparation is not a good idea. In pioneering to a country where one does not know the language, it is best to learn the language first, when possible. That cannot always be done, and there have been many successful pioneers who did not know the local language. Some learned it after arriving at their pioneering post and some never learned it. Yet they carried on, many with great success.

During the 1992 World Congress in New York, Rúḥíyyih Khánum remarked that the only thing Baháʼís lacked was imagination. Lack of confidence hinders many people from venturing into the unknown. With imagination and confidence in the support of the Supreme Concourse, astounding things have been accomplished, even by Bahá'ís who really did not know what they were doing.

Mistakes will be made, but most of them will not be nearly as serious as the value of what is accomplished when the only motivation is to serve the Cause.

In this way anyone can add to the number of champions mentioned above that the Fire Tablet lamented as lacking.

Institutions

There are a number of institutions in the Faith to assist individual believers in their activities. Two significant groups are the rulers and the learned. These were described briefly in Chapter 3.

In the secular world the priorities of those who are in authority often take precedence over ordinary citizens. It is as if people are to support the system, not that the system is for the benefit of the people. This is another dramatic shift caused by the Covenant. However, it is a change that is not easy to grasp.

The following description from the Guardian is starkly different from existing systems:

> Let us also bear in mind that the keynote of the Cause of God is not dictatorial authority but humble fellowship, not arbitrary power, but the spirit of frank and loving consultation. Nothing short of the spirit of a true Bahá'í can hope to reconcile the principles of mercy and justice, of freedom and submission, of the sanctity of the right of the individual and of self-surrender, of vigilance, discretion and prudence on the one hand, and fellowship, candor, and courage on the other.[13]

In His Will and Testament Bahá'u'lláh specifically warned:

> Say: O servants! Let not the means of order be made the cause of confusion and the instrument of union an occasion for discord. We fain would hope that the people of Bahá may be guided by the blessed words: 'Say: all things are of God.' This exalted utterance is like unto water for quenching the fire of hate and enmity which smouldereth within the hearts and breasts of men. By this single utterance contending peoples and kindreds will attain the light of true unity. Verily He speaketh the truth and leadeth the way. He is the All-Powerful, the Exalted, the Gracious.[14]

This quotation was used as part of the devotions at a Feast I once attended. There was a young man, who came in late. He had been responsible for a lot of agonizing consultation at a recent Spiritual Assembly meeting. I looked at him, thinking of both that statement and the Assembly time he had consumed. How could his problems fit the notion that *all things are of God*, I asked myself? The thought struck me that he had brought serious growth and deepening to the Assembly that might not have happened without him. As these thoughts were going through my head, his physical features seemed to soften. At the same time, he seemed to relax. The relationship between the two of us dramatically improved after that insight.

That statement from Bahá'u'lláh gives assurance that through obedience to the Covenant, everything will work out in the final analysis, despite temporary glitches, provided the institutions – that is, 'the means of order' – do not get in the way and become the means of disorder. That is an ongoing challenge. Attitudes are key.

In most of the world today, people in authority tell others what to do. Within the Faith, it is not up to the institutions to dictate, but 'to facilitate the flow of the spirit of the Faith out into the world'.[15] The energy needed for all activity is a vital

THREE PROTAGONISTS

and integral part of both individuals and the community. The institutions may originate plans or approve them. But nothing gets done without the creativity, initiative and power of the individuals and the community.

Even though the following was written for Spiritual Assembly members, it applies to all institutions of the Faith:

> Their function is not to dictate, but to consult, and consult not only among themselves, but as much as possible with the friends whom they represent. They must regard themselves in no other light but that of chosen instruments for a more efficient and dignified presentation of the Cause of God. They should never be led to suppose that they are the central ornaments of the body of the Cause, intrinsically superior to others in capacity or merit, and sole promoters of its teachings and principles. They should approach their task with extreme humility, and endeavor, by their open-mindedness, their high sense of justice and duty, their candor, their modesty, their entire devotion to the welfare and interests of the friends, the Cause, and humanity, to win, not only the confidence and the genuine support and respect of those whom they serve, but also their esteem and real affection. They must, at all times, avoid the spirit of exclusiveness, the atmosphere of secrecy, free themselves from a domineering attitude, and banish all forms of prejudice and passion from their deliberations. They should, within the limits of wise discretion, take the friends into their confidence, acquaint them with their plans, share with them their problems and anxieties, and seek their advice and counsel.[16]

The Guardian's secretary, writing on his behalf, put it this way:

> The first quality for leadership, both among individuals and Assemblies, is the capacity to use the energy and competence that exists in the rank and file of its followers. Otherwise the

more competent members of the group will go at a tangent and try to find elsewhere a field of work and where they could use their energy.¹⁷

In many national Bahá'í communities, National Conventions are open. That is, Bahá'ís who are not delegates, National Spiritual Assembly members or other specially invited guests can also attend. In those situations it seems there are two Conventions going on simultaneously. One is inside the conference hall with an official programme. The informal consultation in the corridors, coffee shops or other casual settings is also important. Many collaborative projects and exciting teaching plans have had their origin in those informal gatherings. Frequently, non-Convention members hear about what is going on in the hall, and find creative ways to achieve the goals as they are still being discussed in the Convention hall. Furthermore, they do it with great enthusiasm. A sense of ownership gets things done.

A major challenge for institutions is to create the environment in which both the initiation and ownerships of projects become natural while remaining under the guidance of the institutions.

The community

Anyone who has tried to build a fire learns that one log does not burn by itself. Two logs, near each other, are needed to sustain fire. In putting out a fire, the first thing to do is to separate the logs. People aflame with love of Bahá'u'lláh are much the same. Two or more believers working together are much more effective than one.

It takes an enormous amount of personal strength for a Bahá'í to remain strong when there are no other Bahá'ís around. Unfortunately, some people drift away when there is no one in the community with whom they can relate and feel comfortable.

The most wonderful plans are useless without the enthusiasm and energy of the community. As communities grow, it is easier for like-minded Bahá'ís to find others with whom they can share interests and activities and more effectively invest their energy. There is a group of motorcycle enthusiasts who call themselves the 'BOBs' – 'Bahá'ís on bikes'. Not only do personal relationships like that have a powerful bonding effect on believers with similar interests, they often help believers to come up with imaginative ways for serving the Faith. Spontaneous team teaching works.

In one large community, Bahá'ís acquired a church facility that had both a gymnasium and a sizeable education building. It became a magnet, attracting Bahá'ís and their friends with a variety of interests. Bahá'ís who had not been seen for some time because they had little tolerance for long meetings, suddenly appeared because there were things they could do with like-minded community members. Activities were plentiful, from a community garden to a magnificent choir that sang during weekly devotionals. The facility was located in a high-traffic area. Often people would walk in off the street, attracted by the activity, just to see what was going on. They would have one or more enrolments each month from intrigued walk-ins.

One devoted Bahá'í, who did not care for long meetings, organized gym activities. School kids would come in the evening. For one hour one group would play basketball while another group did homework. After an hour, the two groups switched.

When I visited the community, the Secretary told me there were 50 activities going on that were authorized but not sponsored by the Spiritual Assembly. Groups for gardening, knitting, crafts, AA, expectant mothers and other groups including both Bahá'ís and non-Bahá'ís were formed because of individual or joint initiatives that were encouraged by the Spiritual Assembly.

One man, who grew up in Tehran before the Revolution,

was asked when it was that he became a Bahá'í in his own right and not because of his family. He explained that he really did not know. There was a Bahá'í centre and it was the place to go after school to hang out with his friends. This community within a community contributed greatly to a strong dynamic adult Bahá'í. As an adult, he was a motive force in his community to make sure that youth had healthy activities to keep them together, busy and oriented.

Community building is a major challenge in these early days of the Faith. It is the arena in which Bahá'ís practise getting along with people who are not always that easy to get along with. It is easy to talk about the oneness of mankind and unity in diversity when talking about race, nationhood and gender issues. It is harder when talking about not only the lovable, but the obnoxious; not only the friendly, but the suspicious; not only the idealistic, but the cynical. Tolerance for a range of personalities can be a challenge, but living with the entire human family is essential. Bahá'u'lláh writes, 'Nothing whatever can, in this Day, inflict a greater harm upon this Cause than dissension and strife, contention, estrangement and apathy, among the loved ones of God.'[18]

The Institute process with its core activities has done more than anything else since the Ten Year Crusade to energize believers. In cluster after cluster people feel empowered to implement core and other activities with vigour and imagination.

When communities are large, strong and diverse enough, they attract the masses. A vibrant community life may well be a stimulus for entry by troops. When the masses see the transforming power of Bahá'u'lláh, they will embrace it.

The question, however, remains: what can the individual Bahá'í do during these chaotic times?

11

Living the Life

To be a Bahá'í simply means to love all the world; to love humanity and try to serve it; to work for universal peace and universal brotherhood.
'Abdu'l-Bahá[1]

Many people like to celebrate the anniversaries of their birth. That is all right. However, it is more important to know WHY you were born than when.

Some people stumble through life from one thing to another. Chance events determine futures. Other people live in the moment with little thought beyond that, or meander from interest to interest, or have such flights of ideas that they do not focus on anything.

Then, there are some people who find something that grabs their attention like a magnet. They become enthusiastic about some specific interest, ranging from extreme self-indulgence to sacrificial service to mankind. These interests can include elements of sports, science, making money, philanthropy, sensual pleasures, the environment, commerce, the arts, entertainment, food, debauchery, humanitarian work, or anything else that captures their passion. They can become so focused that their zeal becomes an obsession. Subcultures are formed by people with common interests in some specific hobby or activity. Some of these pursuits are worthy and some are not.

Bahá'u'lláh summarized how Westerners select their pathways as follows:

> Consider the peoples of the West. Witness how, in their pursuit of that which is vain and trivial, they have sacrificed,

and are still sacrificing, countless lives for the sake of its establishment and promotion.[2]

Bahá'ís are told the reason they were born is to know and worship God. That means a life based on the Covenant, enabling them to remain focused in a meaningful and productive way while going about the business of living. Obedience to the Writings, even when not well understood, is a balm for healing the wounds inflicted by a culture of self-absorption. This chapter offers a glimpse of the guidance available. It remains a daunting challenge just to pay attention to that guidance. Applying its wise counsel is an even greater challenge.

The quotation at the beginning of this chapter was 'Abdu'l-Bahá's response when asked, 'What is a Bahá'í?' He was also quoted as saying, 'A Bahá'í is one who has all the human perfections in full activity.'[3] In one of His London talks He said: 'The man who lives the life according to the teachings of Bahá'u'lláh is already a Bahá'í. On the other hand, a man may call himself a Bahá'í for fifty years, and if he does not live the life he is not a Bahá'í. An ugly man may call himself handsome, but he deceives no one . . .'[4]

Being a Bahá'í implies the spiritual level as described above. There is also the question of who is registered administratively. The Guardian's secretary wrote in his behalf, 'those responsible for accepting new enrolments must just be sure of one thing – that the heart of the applicant has been touched with the spirit of the Faith. Everything also can be built on this foundation gradually.'[5]

On another occasion, his secretary wrote:

> the Guardian fully shares your view that it would be most unwise, and unfair to those who apply for membership in the Community to require that they should at first accept all the laws of the Faith. Such a requirement would be impossible to carry out as there are many laws in the 'Aqdas' with which

even the well-confirmed and long-standing believers are not yet familiar. As you rightly point out the process of becoming a Bahá'í is an evolutionary one, and requires considerable time, and sustained effort on the part of the new believer.[6]

There are two Bahá'í lists. One is the record kept by the administrative institutions. Then, there is the list that Bahá'u'lláh has. It is likely that names appear on each that are not on the other. I know I am on the institutional list. And, hope I am also on Bahá'u'lláh's list.

There are people of goodwill everywhere who applaud and practise many beneficial features of life on earth. Wonderful as these are in themselves, Bahá'u'lláh asks us to look deeper into His Writings for the 'essential prerequisites of concord, of understanding, of complete and enduring unity'.[7] Following are a few areas in which the Bahá'í teachings overlap with the good from all walks of life, but add another dimension.

Purpose of life

All religions give guidance for this life, while providing for the development of those qualities needed for the next world. These involve freeing the individual from baser instincts. This is sometimes referred to as salvation – going from a lower form of self to a higher form: enlightenment, nirvana, rapture, ultimate reality and so on. Bahá'u'lláh added a third dimension. In addition to the personal experience of salvation or enlightenment while preparing for the life to come, there is the collective salvation: building the *Kingdom of God on earth*.

In the West, where materialism is king, the purpose of life often circles around, 'What can I achieve?' In places with less emphasis on materialism the question is, 'How can I serve?' In those cultures, service to the family, tribe or mother earth is far more important than anything an individual may gain for himself.

A related area concerns how we interpret the statement in the Book of Genesis:

> And God said, Let us make man in our image, after our likeness: and let them have dominion over the fish of the sea, and over the fowl of the air, and over the cattle, and over all the earth, and over every creeping thing that creepeth upon the earth.[8]

At the materialistic extreme, this gives people the right to exploit the earth with wild abandon. From another view it is a custodial responsibility. Even being given the right and responsibility to name the other creatures of the earth (a responsibility God gave Adam, according to the Book of Genesis) implies a protective custodianship.

That difference is a major source of frustration for many aboriginal people for whom the good of the family or tribe and respect for nature are greater than personal achievement. This is a commitment that even well-meaning Westerners have difficulty in fully comprehending.

In Israel, before the Six Day War, some young Palestinian youths saw a couple of us Westerners as a chance to practise their English, so they politely approached us for conversation. I asked one of the boys what he wanted to do after secondary school. The answer of this Palestinian youth in Israel still resonates. He said, 'I want to be chemist.' That was not so extraordinary, but what he said next really caught my attention. He said, 'because Israel needs chemists'. Political leaders have made it very difficult for modern-day Palestinian youth to have that motivation.

A young girl from India attended university in England. She told me that when she first talked to her fellow students, she could not understand what they were talking about. They viewed their education as a means to better themselves personally. That was incomprehensible to her. She came to university so she could better serve her people.

Part of worship involves fostering the well-being of fellow humans and the environment. Rúḥíyyih Khánum was fond of reminding believers that it has always been the job of the strong to look after and carry the weak. This statement was often followed by a story of how, as a young girl, her mother would send her off to help someone in need. Caring for the less able is part of two overarching principles of this Revelation: promoting the oneness of mankind and world peace.

On one occasion 'Abdu'l-Bahá said, 'every one has the right to a happy, comfortable life.'[9] On another occasion He said what seems like the opposite:

> . . . look at me, follow me, be as I am; take no thought for yourselves or your lives, whether ye eat or whether ye sleep, whether ye are comfortable, whether ye are well or ill, whether ye are with friends or foes, whether ye receive praise or blame; for all these things ye must care not at all.[10]

These statements are not contradictory, but state priorities. Wanting to be happy and comfortable is all right. However, it should never overshadow the larger purposes.

While a prisoner in Akka, Bahá'u'lláh yearned for the beauty and composure of the country. The Guardian explained,

> The garden of Na'mayn, a small island, situated in the middle of a river to the east of the city, honored with the appellation of Riḍván, and designated by Him the '*New Jerusalem*' and '*Our Verdant Isle*', had, together with [Mazra'ih] become by now the favorite retreats of One Who, for almost a decade, had not set foot beyond the city walls, and Whose sole exercise had been to pace, in monotonous repetition, the floor of His bed-chamber.[11]

Bahá'u'lláh often went to the pleasant surroundings of that 'Verdant Isle'.

In the early days of His life, 'Abdu'l-Bahá endured all manner of physical hardships, including in the caravanserai in Akka where he had to turn the bedding every half an hour to avoid being bitten by the fleas. During His last decades, His was one of the first houses in Haifa to have electricity and plumbing. He had an adequate bed complete with a mosquito net. Yet, He would sometimes sleep on the floor in His room, as a reminder of how some people had to live. During hot summer months, He would travel to Tiberias on the Sea of Galilee for its milder climate and air that was easier to breathe.*

He was also a master of dual purpose and the essence of a balanced life. He would swim in the Bay of Haifa for recreation. By so doing He was building up His strength and endurance for His gruelling travel to the West in later years. Material relaxation and delights can be beneficial. It is a matter of balance and priorities.

The lesson, for me, is that comfort is all right. It just should not become too important. My home has modern amenities and is kept at a pleasant temperature, both summer and winter. My recliner chair is prized and I sleep on a comfortable bed. But I have also pioneered in the extremes of the Arctic and the tropics, lived in log houses without plumbing and had to cut my own wood for heat. I've slept in the open, usually in a tent, sometimes in a car; in cold and wet forbidding environments; on floors and in a hut with a cow-dung floor; all while doing various things in service to the Faith. I cherished all those situations, as well as my comfortable home. Which do I prefer? That depends on the needs of the moment.

Seeking comfort and sacrificing for a greater good are not a conflict between a material and spiritual path. Bahá'u'lláh writes:

---

*   It was a thrill for me one night in Tiberias, when reading David Ruhe's book *Door of Hope*, I realized I was staying at the same hostel 'Abdu'l-Bahá had used. There was a picture showing His room and I ran outside fondly gazing at His window, envisioning Him looking out, basking in the beauty of the Sea of Galilee.

O My Servants! Ye are the trees of My garden; ye must give forth goodly and wondrous fruits, that ye yourselves and others may profit therefrom. Thus it is incumbent on every one to engage in crafts and professions, for therein lies the secret of wealth, O men of understanding! For results depend upon means, and the grace of God shall be all-sufficient unto you. Trees that yield no fruit have been and will ever be for the fire.[12]

There is nothing wrong with material comfort and means. They are laudable when they serve, rather than impede the ultimate reality, as stated in the short obligatory prayer to know and worship God. The reverse is the 'What's in it for me?' mentality.

Prayer

There is no end to the motivations for prayer: praise, thanksgiving, petitions, personal salvation, help in solving problems, better health for yourself or someone else, guidance, the weather, achieving a material benefit and so on. These are all worthy motives.

The ways to pray are likewise limitless. One Bahá'í, while losing control of his car on an icy road, yelled out perhaps the shortest prayer of desperation: 'Alláh-u-Help!' Help can be sought from a vast array in the realms above. Asking a departed soul for assistance is acceptable. But it is important to have a clear idea whom you are addressing.

Whether prayer is a revealed prayer or made up by the one praying is also secondary. An advantage of the revealed prayers is that the Manifestation or Centre of the Covenant know our true selves and our real needs better than we do ourselves – not just what we think we need or want. Besides, their words are invested with greater power.

Another question without a simple, clear answer is when and where to pray. Many people find the clearest channel when just getting up in the morning or before going to bed, or while walking. Some people can go into a deep level of prayer, no matter the noise and chaos going around them. Other people prefer silence and solitude. Each one needs to figure out the best way to enter the atmosphere of prayer.

There is also a vast range in the intensity of prayer, all the way from mindlessly mouthing words while thinking of other things, to complete absorption in the presence of God. That intense level of prayer is extremely rare. It is illustrated by a story told about 'Alí – called the Defender of the Faithful, the son-in-law of the Prophet Muḥammad. It was said that during a battle, an arrow pierced the calf of his leg. Attempts to remove it created intolerable pain. Muḥammad was asked what to do. He recommended waiting until 'Alí was enrapt in his midday prayer. The intensity of his prayer would be such that the arrow could be removed and 'Alí would not even know it.

While praying out loud when alone seems strange to many people, it has a powerful effect. It helps to get more connected with the prayer. There is much to think about in Bahá'u'lláh's statement:

> Intone, O My servant, the verses of God that have been received by thee, as intoned by them who have drawn nigh unto Him, that the sweetness of thy melody may kindle thine own soul, and attract the hearts of all men. Whoso reciteth, in the privacy of his chamber, the verses revealed by God, the scattering angels of the Almighty shall scatter abroad the fragrance of the words uttered by his mouth, and shall cause the heart of every righteous man to throb. Though he may, at first, remain unaware of its effect, yet the virtue of the grace vouchsafed unto him must needs sooner or later exercise its influence upon his soul. Thus have the mysteries of the Revelation of God been decreed by virtue of the Will of Him Who is the Source of power and wisdom.[13]

The idea that 'the scattering angels . . . shall scatter abroad the fragrance of the words' brings to mind stringed instruments. If two instruments are close to each other and the string of one is plucked, the string similarly tuned in the other instrument will start to vibrate. When reciting the verses of God out loud, even when alone, there is no way to tell what other hearts might be vibrating as a result. The key elements are sincerity and purity of motive, not method, length, language or fervour.

In recent years there has been serious research into the power of prayer. Most studies centre on personal benefits such as healing, peace of mind or longevity. There is verifiable evidence that prayer does make a difference in these areas. There are also anecdotal testimonials to the power of prayer. But they all seem to focus on getting God to do something in the service of man.

The Bahá'í Writings take prayer beyond personal benefit, valued though that may be. The Guardian pointed out:

> These daily obligatory prayers, together with a few other specific ones, such as the Healing Prayer, the Tablet of Aḥmad, have been invested by Bahá'u'lláh with a special potency and significance, and should therefore be accepted as such and be recited by the believers with unquestioned faith and confidence, that through them they may enter into a much closer communion with God, and identify themselves more fully with His Laws and precepts.[14]

Even some Bahá'ís interpret the words 'special potency' as having greater power for personal benefit or to solve some problem. A more important use of that power is stated in the last part of the quotation: 'that through them they may enter into a much closer communion with God, and identify themselves more fully with His Laws and precepts'.

How does that happen? It is possible that a significant portion of the special potency is delivered by thinking deeply about the names and attributes of God listed in them. In the long healing prayer, 139 different names and attributes of God are 'called' before the three requests are made: protection, healing and guidance. Superficially, some of the names and attributes even seem contradictory, such as 'known to all' and 'hidden from all'. The Tablet of Aḥmad starts with God's supreme Station as King, followed by the attributes of knowledge and wisdom – not just knowledge but 'All-Knowing'. It can be inferred that the wisdom is also universal rather than limited. Those are potent things to think about.

In the Fire Tablet, 41 names and attributes, each relating to the entire world, are sprinkled throughout, placed at the end of each passage. Then the final sentence states that pondering those words kindles in one's very blood 'a fire that shall set aflame the worlds'.

It strikes me that thinking seriously about the names and attributes of God may well be a factor in helping the believer gain both a closer communion with God and more readily identify with His laws and precepts.

At the higher levels of prayer, a believer can experience:

Reveal then Thyself, O Lord, by Thy merciful utterance and the mystery of Thy divine being, that the holy ecstasy of prayer may fill our souls – a prayer that shall rise above words and letters and transcend the murmur of syllables and sounds – that all things may be merged into nothingness before the revelation of Thy splendour.[15]

Stated another way, rather than using the prayers to get God to serve ME, the emphasis should be on better aligning me with the will of God. As one Bahá'í likes to say about this aspect of prayer, 'Don't tell God what to do. Just report for duty.'

In one of the prayers for the Fast, Bahá'u'lláh redefines blessings. The prayer reads, 'I beseech Thee to grant that I may be assisted to observe the fast wholly for Thy sake.'[16] Another prayer for the Fast asks 'Grant that they may be filled with the treasures of Thy munificence and bountiful favour.'[17] And in the same prayer he defines those treasures:

> Help Thou Thy loved ones, O my Lord, them that have forsaken their all, that they may obtain the things Thou dost possess, whom trials and tribulations have encompassed for having renounced the world and set their affections on Thy realm of glory.[18]

While everyone wants good health, and there are many prayers for health and healing, physical healing should not be an end in and of itself. 'Abdu'l-Bahá explained it this way:

> If the health and well-being of the body be expended in the path of the Kingdom, this is very acceptable and praiseworthy; and if it is expended to the benefit of the human world in general – even though it be to their material (or bodily) benefit and be a means of doing good – that is also acceptable. But if the health and welfare of man be spent in sensual desires, in a life on the animal plane, and in devilish pursuits – then disease is better than such health; nay, death itself is preferable to such a life. If thou art desirous of health, wish thou health for serving the Kingdom.[19]

(The world would have been better off if the terrorists had called in sick on 11 September 2001.)

More important than physical health is spiritual well-being. Getting over a cold is good and desirable, but overcoming the twisted sickness of jealousy is even better. Even those with incurable diseases can attain health and healing on the more important spiritual level, even if there is little apparent benefit on the physical.

There is still another dimension to prayer. In addition to getting assistance for whatever is requested, something else is happening. In prayers for healing, teaching, for the Universal House of Justice, or other objectives, the prayer shapes positive mental attitudes. Prayers for healing create expectations of health within us; prayers for teaching make us more mindful to look for teaching opportunities; prayers for other people strengthen a bonding with that person; prayers for the Universal House of Justice stimulate love for that body and make us more engaged in its guidance. The change the prayers can make within us may be more important than the help from on high that is being requested.

Adib Taherzadeh reported that once when he was in intense prayer for a personal problem, he got the strong impression that Bahá'u'lláh was before him saying, 'Shame on you! Every time you have a problem you come to me . . . Do you ever come to me saying, "Please help me to spread your Faith"? No, you only come to me when you have a problem. Shame!' Adib said he stopped praying about his personal problem.[20]

I had a similar experience one day when facing the most wrenching problem of my life. I was home alone and got out the heavy artillery. I read through an entire book of Bahá'í prayers, all the Hidden Words, the Tablet of Aḥmad, said five hundred times the 'Remover of Difficulties', and the Long Obligatory Prayer. Being a slow learner, it wasn't until the middle of the Long Obligatory Prayer that my body began to shake as if hit with a bolt of lightning. I heard a voice echoing the Arabic Hidden Word No. 18, 'Ask not of Me that which We desire not for thee'. My plea immediately changed from 'Fix my problem,' to 'Help me use this problem in a way that serves You.'

It wasn't until later that I read,

> Whosoever hath recognized Thee will turn to none save Thee, and will seek from Thee naught else except Thyself. Thou art the sole Desire of the heart of him whose thoughts are fixed on Thee, and the highest Aspiration of whosoever is wholly devoted unto Thee.[21]

The Guardian mentioned different sensations that come through prayer, 'For the core of religious faith is that mystic feeling which unites Man with God.'[22] This is also suggested by No. 16 of the Arabic Hidden Words, 'Forget all save Me and commune with My spirit.'

That 'mystic feeling' can be found during times of deep, concentrated prayer and meditation. When that does happen, the world, time and circumstances seem to vanish. There is almost a trance-like state, a taste of the eternal. It can be so intense that even the ringing of a telephone may not be heard. Few people are capable of that level of prayer, but when that intensity is experienced, it is a treasured respite that makes the trials and tribulations of life seem insignificant. Unparalleled inspirations have also occurred during those precious moments.

'Abdu'l-Bahá said, 'God will answer the prayer of every servant if that prayer is urgent.'[23] Many people have prayed for better weather, to get a job, improved health, win a lottery, pass a test or some other material benefit. There is nothing wrong with those petitions. However, there is so much more. It is a significant advance when one aspires to the higher levels of prayer: to attain 'that mystic feeling' and 'identify . . . more fully with His Laws and precepts'.

Children ask for all kinds of things, from wanting a new toy to permission to go next door to help a neighbour. We, older children, continue to ask God for all kinds of things and occasionally forget that the best use of prayer is for assistance in efforts to be of service. Of this higher form of prayer Bahá'u'lláh writes,

> I beseech Thee, therefore, O Thou Who art the Possessor of the entire creation and the King of the realm of Thine invention, graciously to aid Thy creatures to accomplish that which is pleasing and acceptable unto Thee, that they may arise to serve Thy Cause amidst Thy creatures, and to speak forth Thy praise before all who are in heaven and on earth.[24]

Reading the Writings

There are an endless number of reasons for reading Sacred Writings – inspiration, study, meditation, relaxation, seeking specific information and so forth.

In these days of electronic search engines and use of the Ruhi booklets, the Writings are often used in reference to specific themes or questions. Intensive study on a specific topic is hard to beat. That has made an important impact in the lives of many believers. However, there is ever so much more.

Naturally, searching the Writings for insight on a specific question can lead to profound joy. There is also a special joy in just picking up something and reading from beginning to end, letting the flow of divine Words lead you on a journey through a variety of unanticipated of thoughts and insights. Abu'l-Faḍl, the premier scholar of the Faith, made scores of marks in his copy of the *Kitáb-i-Íqán*, one for every time he read it. I've forgotten the number of marks he was said to have made, but I recall it was well over a hundred.

In the process of memorizing either prayers or other Writings, deeper and clearer understandings are often discovered. Many nuanced meanings become apparent.

Just leafing through pages can be soothing. One blind Bahá'í mentioned loving to pick up *Gleanings* and just thumb through its divine pages. It can be refreshing to glance at a page, read a phrase or part of a sentence, then skip to another page. This allows the reader to bask in the rhythm, flow and spirit of the Creative Word without having to consider literal meanings. There is an open copy of the Arabic *Kitáb-i-Aqdas* on my desk, even though I don't read Arabic. It is a refreshing joy just to look at it.

The point is not to be limited in the ways of imbibing the Sacred Word. The Words of God help anyone gain access to divine realities in countless ways. After all, Bahá'u'lláh wrote that 'The Word is the master key for the whole world, inasmuch

LIVING THE LIFE

as through its potency the doors of the hearts of men, which in reality are the doors of heaven, are unlocked.'[25]

Those keys from many books fit many doors and work in many ways.

Religious observances

Over time, religious observances tend to become secularized. They often take on a party atmosphere that has nothing to do with the event they are to commemorate.

In India it is interesting to see the many different ways that the same Holy Day is celebrated in different Hindu villages, depending on local traditions. Traditionally, Hanukkah (the Festival of Lights) is a minor Jewish holiday. The eight-day festival commemorates the miracle of a one-day supply of olive oil that miraculously lasted eight days. Traditional celebrations tend to be informal and based on custom. The practice of giving presents is of recent, North American, origin. It is probably taken from the Christian gift-giving custom that is such a prominent feature of North American materialism.

Just as a secularized Christmas has nothing to do with the birth of Jesus, it has lured a minor Jewish celebration away from a focus on the miracle it was to commemorate to an indulgent form of materialism.

There may be some question as to whether or not the Emperor Constantine was a committed Christian, but there is no doubt he was a consummate politician. He realized the enormous political advantage of merging the Roman celebrations of the winter solstice with Christianity. He decreed that the birth of Jesus be celebrated on 25 December. Never mind that Jesus may have been born in September or October, but definitely not December. Most likely it was a few years earlier than the calendar indicates.

The party atmosphere came with Constantine's decree. While his actions had questionable spiritual significance, they did consolidate his political power and authority. At Easter, the relationship between a rabbit, chicken eggs and the resurrection of Christ is another example of combining a religious celebration with the secular.

For Muslims, Ramadan, their 9th month, is the most venerated month of the Hijri calendar. Muslims are expected to fast from dawn to dusk and to honour the poor. It is a time of personal, internal purification. Some fundamentalists have taken that as an excuse for *external* purification – that is, purging the community of anyone who does not believe as they do.

The Prophet Muhammad made special compassionate provisions for non-Muslims. Today, in many parts of the Islamic world, the days of Ramadan are feared by anyone who is considered an apostate. Horrible atrocities have been committed in the name of Islam in these otherwise sacred days of personal renewal.

This is another area in which the Bahá'í teachings add a new dimension. There are few, but clear and simple, provisions for 11 Holy Days. One interesting variation from the past has to do with some non-Holy Days. People like parties and have historically blended the sacred with the secular and turned holy events into a party atmosphere. Bahá'u'lláh gave people a time to party and kept it separate from Holy Days, reducing the temptation to dilute their sacred nature. The Badí' (Bahá'í) Calendar with its 19 days each with 19 months adds up to 361 days, a bit short of the solar cycle. In order to coincide with the time it takes for the earth to orbit the sun, there are four or five special days called Ayyám-i-Há. These are also called Intercalary Days – literally, 'days between the calendar'.

These are not Holy Days. It is as if Bahá'u'lláh is saying: You want a party? Here is the time to party, but leave the Holy Days alone. The notes accompanying the *Kitáb-i-Aqdas* contain the following explanation:

Bahá'u'lláh enjoined upon His followers to devote these

days to feasting, rejoicing and charity. In a letter written on Shoghi Effendi's behalf it is explained that: 'the intercalary days are specially set aside for hospitality, the giving of gifts, etc.'[26]

In the Western world there is a danger of these days becoming a sort of 'Bahá'í Christmas'. The rampant gross materialism has created a climate of over-indulgence for children, as characterized by lavishing presents on birthdays, graduations, Christmas and other celebrations. It corrupted the Jewish Hanukkah and can happen to Intercalary Days. This tendency is contrary to 'Abdu'l-Bahá's explicit advice:

> While the children are yet in their infancy feed them from the breast of heavenly grace, foster them in the cradle of all excellence, rear them in the embrace of bounty . . . Bring them up to work and strive, and accustom them to hardship. Teach them to dedicate their lives to matters of great import, and inspire them to undertake studies that will benefit mankind.[27]

Some Bahá'ís have taken deliberate steps to emphasize the 'charity' aspect as well as keeping the 'giving of gifts' from becoming an exercise in indulgence. One 10-year-old Bahá'í child went door to door in his non-Bahá'í neighbourhood, collecting food for the community food bank, all in the name of Ayyám-i-Há. The next year, he enlisted some of his non-Bahá'í friends to join him. It became a major annual community event. Another variation is giving children money with the instructions, 'Use this money to do something nice that you would not otherwise do, for someone who is not a member of the family.' Fascinating and touching stories have resulted.

Among my favourite Holy Days are the commemorations of the Ascensions of Bahá'u'lláh and 'Abdu'l-Bahá respectively. And the *times* of their observance. Who, other than Bahá'ís, gets up in the middle on the night, and sometimes travels long distances at such a time of day, for a religious observance?

I remember an unforgettable occurrence once during the memorial for the Ascension of 'Abdu'l-Bahá. An elderly believer who had been in the presence of 'Abdu'l-Bahá was there. About 1:30 in the morning, while she was reading about the Ascension from *God Passes By*, she put down the book and said, 'I can remember it as if it were yesterday.' She went on describe how the news was spread among the believers and the reaction it had. The emotions she shared continue to give me a taste of what it must have been like.

In addition to the commemorative aspect of Holy Days, it is especially nice when the friends go together to museums or other places of local interest. Family interactions during those outings have been highly memorable.

One Holy Day is especially appropriate in the context of this book – the Day of the Covenant. After the Ascension of Bahá'u'lláh, many Bahá'ís asked 'Abdu'l-Bahá for permission to celebrate the day of His birth. He refused. In the cultural context of Persia, it was considered inappropriate for people to celebrate their own birth. The only birth date to celebrate was that of 'Grandfather' – the Prophet Muhammad. No one else's birth was worthy of this recognition.

However, both the birth of the Báb and Bahá'u'lláh are Holy Days and many believers thought it would be appropriate to honour 'Abdu'l-Bahá as the Centre of the Covenant in this way. He disagreed. Among other things, His birth occurred at the very time the Báb declared His Mission to Mullá Ḥusayn. 'Abdu'l-Bahá would not permit anything to detract from that sacred event.

There were other traditions of the time that were significant. Because of the high rate of infant mortality, children were not usually given a name until about six months after they were born. Then, an event called fête day would be a time to name the new child. This was often a time of great celebration.

LIVING THE LIFE

Another tradition of the time was that instead of celebrating a person's birth, the date of death was remembered. In later years there would be joyous gatherings to extol the life of the departed one.

'Abdu'l-Bahá created a new Holy Day that combined some of those features. Instead of focusing on His birth, He selected a date 180 days after the Ascension of Bahá'u'lláh that He called the Day of the Covenant. The event was to celebrate not 'Abdu'l-Bahá's birth, but the birth of the Covenant – this incomparable legacy Bahá'u'lláh bequeathed to the world. It so happened that this was the last event 'Abdu'l-Bahá celebrated during His earthly life, occurring, as it did, just two days prior to His own Ascension. That Holy Day becomes a special occasion to celebrate the Covenant, followed two days later by a celebration of His life and mission.

In addition to the Holy Days, Bahá'ís are frequently asked how they worship. That can bring up a discussion of the unique occasion of the Nineteen Day Feast. In His Most Holy Book Bahá'u'lláh writes:

> Verily, it is enjoined upon you to offer a feast, once in every month, though only water be served; for God hath purposed to bind hearts together, albeit through both earthly and heavenly means.[28]

And these are the words of 'Abdu'l-Bahá:

> As to the Nineteen Day Feast, it rejoiceth mind and heart. If this feast be held in the proper fashion, the friends will, once in nineteen days, find themselves spiritually restored, and endued with a power that is not of this world.[29]

Some people have said that the Feast is a worship service. That is true in a limited way. The entire Feast is intended to be spiritual. However, it has three distinct parts that other forms of worship do not enjoy: the strictly devotional, community business and social. All three parts are to be conducted as if 'Abdu'l-Bahá were there and listening – which He is. The Feast also lacks a time for preaching or sermonizing, which is a major feature of some worship services in other Faiths.

Members of the Bahá'í community come together in a spirit of joy and friendliness. The Feast should be filled with the fire of the love of God and reflect the best tradition of family closeness, bonding and concern.

The Feast is also a metaphor for life, with a focus on balancing three of life's most important elements: devotion, practical matters and sociability. Each month there is an opportunity to readjust priorities for a proper balance. All three parts of the Feast are spiritual, just as these three elements of life should be built on a spiritual foundation and filled with joy and gladness. These elements get out of balance in everyday life. The Feast is readjustment time. The three components of life can be put back into proper perspective and the spiritual foundation of each reestablished.

The Feast starts with prayers and other selections from the Sacred Writings. These should primarily be the Writings of Bahá'u'lláh. If the devotional readings seem tedious and boring, it may indicate how far out of balance that part of life is.

A discussion of the practical affairs of the community follows. Hand of the Cause Mr Furútan called that part of the Feast the 'parliament of the future'. In the secular world, there are relatively few people who concern themselves in civic matters or become a part of the political process. This is one reason why politics can so easily get corrupted. That corruption seems to increase the further it goes from the local level. Among Bahá'ís, everyone becomes involved with community affairs as a part of religious life. Suggestions go to the local Spiritual Assembly for action. These can be sent to the National Spiritual Assembly, and even to the Universal House of Justice. The Feast, therefore, is a direct link between every believer,

LIVING THE LIFE

including small children, and all the institutions of the Faith.

The Universal House of Justice gave guidance on what to do if non-Bahá'ís are present. Just as you don't discuss family business when non-family members are present, so, too, it is a good idea to skip the business portion when non-Bahá'ís are present.

The last portion of the Feast blends two important features of life, refreshment and fellowship. It is both an experience and a reminder that our vital nutritional needs and social interactions are to be maintained on a spiritual and uplifting level. One of my fondest memories was a Feast in a remote village where the only refreshment was sharing water from a 5-gallon container.

'Abdu'l-Bahá compared the Feast to the Lord's Supper. He wrote:

> You must continue to keep the Nineteen Day Feast. It is very important; it is very good. But when you present yourselves in the meetings, before entering them, free yourselves from all that you have in your heart, free your thoughts and your minds from all else save God, and speak to your heart. That all may make this a gathering of love, make it the cause of illumination, make it a gathering of attraction of the hearts, surround this gathering with the Lights of the Supreme Concourse, so that you may be gathered together with the utmost love.[30]

He then gave a prayer, especially designed for the Feast:

> O God! Dispel all those elements which are the cause of discord, and prepare for us all those things which are the cause of unity and accord! O God! Descend upon us Heavenly Fragrance and change this gathering into a gathering of Heaven! Grant to us every benefit and every food. Prepare for us the Food of Love! Give to us the Food of Knowledge!

Bestow upon us the Food of Heavenly Illumination! In your hearts remember these things, and then enter the Unity Feast.³¹

Just think of that! The attitude He described is actually an invitation for 'Abdu'l-Bahá not only to attend, but to attend as a Servant. He went on to say:

Each one of you must think how to make happy and pleased the other members of your Assembly,* and each one must consider all those who are present as better and greater than himself, and each one must consider himself less than the rest. Know their station as high, and think of your own station as low.† Should you act and live according to these behests, know verily, of a certainty, that that Feast is the Heavenly Food. That Supper is the 'Lord's Supper'! I am the Servant of that gathering.³²

In a real sense, the Nineteen Day Feast is a celebration. It commemorates the unity, love, and fellowship within the community. It is a monthly reminder of the fact that God has once again spoken to man. It is a celebration of the survival of the Faith despite all kinds of oppressions and conflicts. It is a

---

* 'Abdu'l-Bahá often used the word 'assembly' for a general gathering of friends. The word was not used in the institutional sense of Spiritual Assembly until the Guardian's letter to North American believers of 5 March 1922.

† Superficially, this seems like false humility. There are at least two things to consider in addition to being 'created from the same dust'. Everyone's primary duty is to know and worship God. Everyone has unique capacities and challenges, so a valid comparison of how people are using their respective talents is impossible. Even on the level of comparison, everyone else knows something that you don't know, can do something that you cannot do as well, has skills you don't have and has had experiences you can only imagine. In short, there is no realistic basis for considering yourself better than anyone else and ample reason to consider 'your own station as low'.

festival of joy and hope for the future. It is a celebration because once again, there is an opportunity to get together with fellow Bahá'ís. It is a time to glory in the fact that only the power of the Covenant is capable of bringing a diversity of humanity together. It is a joyous reminder of the fact that Bahá'ís are engaged in a divine enterprise that is humanly impossible, but divinely certain: uniting the world.

In essence, the Nineteen Day Feast reminds us of who we are as members of the community of the Greatest Name of Bahá'u'lláh: the Army of Light.

Moral ideals

Following Bahá'í standards is not easy. Almost everyone faces some degree of difficulty in adopting a Bahá'í lifestyle. If it were easy, where would the challenge be? What would be the opportunity for growth and development? For some people, following divine teachings is a monumental struggle. The excuse has been heard that they would follow a particular law, if only they knew its purpose. The irony is that the value of any law is best understood *only* once the law is followed. Then, the purpose and importance generally become self-evident.

The tasks of changing individual hearts and making cultures more conducive to spiritual development are hard and persistent work. History describes a long parade of cultures reluctant to change. Even when difficult, Bahá'í standards are the best possible route for an individual's spiritual development and the *only* means of building the new world civilization.

Bahá'u'lláh highlighted the dilemma when He wrote:

> The fears and agitation which the revelation of this law provokes in men's hearts should indeed be likened to the cries of the suckling babe weaned from his mother's milk, if ye be of them that perceive. Were men to discover the motivating purpose of God's Revelation, they would assuredly

cast away their fears, and, with hearts filled with gratitude, rejoice with exceeding gladness.[33]

Among the bigger challenges people face are tendencies to addictions of various kinds, an inclination to be judgmental of people who are different, or to gossiping and backbiting. Confrontation is the customary way to settle differences. Western cultures glorify violence and sex in entertainment; the news media, video games and advertising increasing the appetite for both.

The cultural mores of the day are the environment in which all activities are carried out. This background makes it hard for people to control the normal challenges of life and live according to Bahá'u'lláh's teachings.

In *The Advent of Divine Justice*, the Guardian elaborated on proper morality. He wrote:

> A rectitude of conduct, an abiding sense of undeviating justice, unobscured by the demoralizing influences which a corruption-ridden political life so strikingly manifests; a chaste, pure, and holy life, unsullied and unclouded by the indecencies, the vices, the false standards, which an inherently deficient moral code tolerates, perpetuates, and fosters; a fraternity freed from that cancerous growth of racial prejudice, which is eating into the vitals of an already debilitated society – these are the ideals which the American believers must, from now on, individually and through concerted action, strive to promote, in both their private and public lives, ideals which are the chief propelling forces that can most effectively accelerate the march of their institutions, plans, and enterprises, that can guard the honor and integrity of their Faith, and subdue any obstacles that may confront it in the future.[34]

This quotation focuses on the attitudes Bahá'ís should cultivate, without dwelling on what is forbidden. Undeviating justice, a chaste, pure, holy life and freedom from prejudice are all matters of putting the best foot forward with integrity. The statement also implies that prevailing standards of the culture have a major and negative influence on individual values.

The Guardian went on to say:

> A chaste and holy life must be made the controlling principle in the behavior and conduct of all Bahá'ís, both in their social relations with the members of their own community, and in their contact with the world at large. It must adorn and reinforce the ceaseless labors and meritorious exertions of those whose enviable position is to propagate the Message, and to administer the affairs, of the Faith of Bahá'u'lláh. It must be upheld, in all its integrity and implications, in every phase of the life of those who fill the ranks of that Faith, whether in their homes, their travels, their clubs, their societies, their entertainments, their schools, and their universities. It must be accorded special consideration in the conduct of the social activities of every Bahá'í summer school and any other occasions on which Bahá'í community life is organized and fostered. It must be closely and continually identified with the mission of the Bahá'í youth, both as an element in the life of the Bahá'í community, and as a factor in the future progress and orientation of the youth of their own country.[35]

According to *Webster's New World Dictionary*, chastity involves being 'pure, decent, modest in nature and behavior; restrained and simple in style; not ornate'.[36] This broad concept seems to be the principle the Guardian was conveying.

It is only natural to wonder how to incorporate these noble thoughts into everyday life. Most Bahá'ís live in a world in which moral laxity and low standards are the norm. Contemporary values put Bahá'ís in the role of fish swimming upstream, against the social current.

Historically, emphasis on sensual pleasures – including

sports, entertainment, sex, foods, etc. – is an early sign of a deteriorating culture. Examples are described in many narratives of the Old Testament; the fall of the Athenian and Roman civilizations are others. In Rome, for example, the world's best-known sports arena – the Colosseum – was built as the Roman Empire was declining. Roman festivals became increasingly lascivious at the same time.

The Guardian writes:

> Such a chaste and holy life, with its implications of modesty, purity, temperance, decency, and clean-mindedness, involves no less than the exercise of moderation in all that pertains to dress, language, amusements, and all artistic and literary avocations. It demands daily vigilance in the control of one's carnal desires and corrupt inclinations. It calls for the abandonment of a frivolous conduct, with its excessive attachment to trivial and often misdirected pleasures. It requires total abstinence from all alcoholic drinks, from opium, and from similar habit-forming drugs. It condemns the prostitution of art and of literature, the practices of nudism and of companionate marriage, infidelity in marital relationships, and all manner of promiscuity, of easy familiarity, and of sexual vices. It can tolerate no compromise with the theories, the standards, the habits, and the excesses of a decadent age. Nay rather it seeks to demonstrate, through the dynamic force of its example, the pernicious character of such theories, the falsity of such standards, the hollowness of such claims, the perversity of such habits, and the sacrilegious character of such excesses.[37]

The Guardian was specific about the sexual aspect of chastity. He explained:

> Chastity implies both before and after marriage an unsullied, chaste sex life. Before marriage absolutely chaste, after

marriage absolutely faithful to one's chosen companion. Faithful in all sexual acts, faithful in word and in deed.[38]

In healthy societies, it has been common and acceptable for both men and women to live fulfilling celibate lives. Bachelors and spinsters have made significant contributions to the stability of society in general and extended families in particular. The Western world promotes behaviours that diminish the value and importance of the celibate option.

At another time, in a letter written in his behalf the Guardian explained:

> Concerning your question whether there are any legitimate forms of expression of the sex instinct outside of marriage; according to the Bahá'í Teachings no sexual act can be considered lawful unless performed between lawfully married persons. Outside of marital life there can be no lawful or healthy use of the sex impulse.[39]

It should come as no surprise that among Bahá'ís, like followers of any other religion, there are enrolled believers who, for reasons of their own, choose not to follow the divine teachings. It is hard to know what to do when other Bahá'ís are not living according to Bahá'í principles. The Universal House of Justice gave this guidance to a Spiritual Assembly. When the 'conduct has no significant bearing on the good name of the Faith, the Assembly may decide to leave the individual to go his or her own way . . .'[40]

In the *Kitáb-i-Íqán*, Bahá'u'lláh explained that under Mosaic law the punishment for adultery was death. Enforcement was later stopped because, according to one well-regarded rabbi, 'considering the extremely limited number of the Jews . . . every survivor who hath been delivered from the hand of Nebuchadnezzar would have to be put to death according to the verdict of the Book.'[41] Stoning is still the punishment for adultery in some cultures. If the death penalty were enforced today among the Abrahamic religions of Judaism, Christianity, Islam and the Bahá'í Faith, it would have a big impact on world population.

In Bahá'í law, instead of stoning, there is a fine for adultery. It is 9 mithqals of gold for the first infraction.[42] (In 2015 that is approximately €900, £750 or US$1,200.) The penalty doubles with each subsequent infraction (I'm not aware of any other punishment in Bahá'í law that increases with subsequent offences). The second time, it is approximately €1,800, £1,500, or $2,400, and the third infraction about €3,600, £3,000 or $4,800, and so on. Adultery quickly becomes exceedingly expensive.

Harsh though that is, there is more. The infraction affects more than life on earth. A letter written in behalf of the Guardian states, 'Bahá'u'lláh says adultery retards the progress of the soul in the afterlife...'[43]

Sexual indiscretion is an obvious and often singled out sign of the disintegrating moral standards. But it is just one of the slipping morals that include integrity, honesty, courtesy, generosity, personal responsibility and general trustworthiness.

There is no doubt that chastity, though trivialized today, is a major factor that can benefit both the individual and society. The Western world is so saturated with sex – in entertainment, advertising, literature, news reporting, etc. – that it is hard to maintain proper perspective. It gives rise to easy familiarity that has the added problem of exciting appetites for which there is no outlet or expression that is consistent with Bahá'í standards.

The cultural preoccupation with sex arouses and stimulates latent sexual urges toward members of the same sex as well as those of the opposite sex. Bahá'ís have clear guidance concerning the attitude toward homosexuality in the following letter written in behalf of the Universal House of Justice, dated 27 October 2010:

With respect to your question concerning the position Baháʼís are to take regarding homosexuality and civil rights, we have been asked to convey the following.

The purpose of the Faith of Baháʼuʼlláh is the realization of the organic unity of the entire human race, and Baháʼís are enjoined to eliminate from their lives all forms of prejudice and to manifest respect towards all. Therefore, to regard those with a homosexual orientation with prejudice or disdain would be against the spirit of the Faith. Furthermore, a Baháʼí is exhorted to be 'an upholder and defender of the victim of oppression,' and it would be entirely appropriate for a believer to come to the defence of those whose fundamental rights are being denied or violated.

At the same time, you are no doubt aware of the relevant teachings of the Faith that govern the personal conduct of Baháʼís. The Baháʼí Writings state that marriage is a union between a man and a woman and that sexual relations are restricted to a couple who are married to each other . . . The teachings of Baháʼuʼlláh on personal morality are binding on Baháʼís, who strive, as best they can, to live up to the high standards He has established.

In attempting to reconcile what may appear to be conflicting obligations, it is important to understand that the Baháʼí community does not seek to impose its values on others, nor does it pass judgment on others on the basis of its own moral standards.[44]

Baháʼís have been accused of being homophobic because they do not embrace homosexual behaviour. In countering that misconception, it is helpful to remember three themes mentioned in the letter:

1. Baháʼís are to defend oppressed people whether or not they have similar values.

2. Bahá'u'lláh equally forbids all sex acts – heterosexual or homosexual – outside of marriage.
3. Bahá'ís are not to impose their standards on other people.

Bahá'ís have a massive challenge in resisting the standards of the day. It starts with what each one chooses to see and read. As Bahá'u'lláh wrote, 'Let your eye be chaste.'[45]

Transforming all aspects of society's moral climate is a monumental challenge. It is no wonder that some people find specific parts of it hard to follow. Yet, Bahá'ís are to take the lead in this major shift. The cumulative application of Bahá'í laws cleanses social norms.

Marriage, family life and divorce

Every culture places a high premium on the family as the basic structure for nurturing and raising young, so that new generations can carry on the culture. There are great variations among cultures, starting with marriage. There are two traditional forms, arranged marriages and partners selecting each other. In addition to traditional forms of marriage, in many cultures cohabitation, without formal marriage, is common. This arrangement is increasing in industrialized nations.

Self-selection, which is the most common in the Western world, is the system in which the couple decides to get married – generally after some form of courtship. Other members of the family may or may not be involved.

Arranged marriages are connections between families. Loyalty and relationships are more about the families than the individuals. In some cases, children are selected to marry each other even before they are born. Families that want to merge will negotiate so that when one has a boy and the other a girl, the children are pledged to be married as a means of uniting the families.

There are other situations in which the family seeks a partner after the boy or girl reaches a certain age. One girl from such a culture commented, 'My father loves me so much, that he would only find a husband who would be good for me.' In another example, there was a young man who was going home to be married. He was so excited. He could hardly wait to see whom his family had selected to be his bride. For both these youngsters, the thought of having to select a marriage mate on their own was frightening, if not incomprehensible. They feared they might make the wrong choice. They were also spared from the Western style of dating that focuses on superficial qualities and prematurely arouses strong sexual urges.

Interpersonal emotional relationships are important. However, in the West, these have loomed larger than their fundamental purpose as the major and primary social institution. Often, family members are not even consulted. There are even marriages to protest concern from other family members. It is increasingly common for couples to just start living together. When the initial appeal wanes, the relationship is in danger. Attraction alone is not sufficient to withstand the tests that are bound to come with any long-term relationship, nor is it the best environment for nurturing the next generation.

In terms of family stability, endurance and happiness, none of the current systems of arranged marriages, self-selection, or just living together have proved superior. Both arranged marriages and self-selection have strengths and both have weaknesses. Both produce more stability and long-term contentment than simply living together, even though living together is sometimes justified as 'trying it out to see if it will work'. Unions are increasingly abandoned when relationships are based on initial attraction only. The language reflects this in the use of the terms 'significant other' or 'partner'. One man surprised his wife one morning at breakfast by casually saying he wanted a divorce because, he said, 'the chemistry is no longer there'.

The Bahá'í system blends the advantages of both the arranged and self-selected marriage and prohibits co-habitation. It is clear from the Bahá'í Writings that the family unit is the basic institution of society. In addition to strengthening the relationship between families and the individuals, the system elevates marriage to an institution that is sufficiently strong and enduring to serve as the very foundation of society itself.

In 1982 the Universal House of Justice published a compilation of Bahá'í Writings it called *Family Life*. This included a segment on marriage.[46] Following are some of the points stressed in that compilation.

> ➢ The couple makes the selection without interference from the family. The basic requirement is to know each other's character.
> ➢ Consent of living parents is required. This cements family relationships in the very beginning – circumventing future in-law problems. It has also prevented some potentially disastrous unions from taking place.
> ➢ The primary purpose for marriage is procreation with a caring, protective and nurturing environment for the next generation.
> ➢ Daily prayers and reading from the Writings are strongly encouraged, especially when there are children.
> ➢ Special prayers have been revealed for parents, children and spouses.
> ➢ There is great emphasis on educating the children, with priority being given to girls since they are the first educators of the next generation.

'Abdu'l-Bahá described Bahá'í marriage as follows:

> Marriage, among the mass of the people, is a physical bond, and this union can only be temporary, since it is foredoomed to a physical separation at the close.
>
> Among the people of Bahá, however, marriage must be a union of the body and of the spirit as well, for here

both husband and wife are aglow with the same wine, both are enamoured of the same matchless Face, both live and move through the same spirit, both are illumined by the same glory. This connection between them is a spiritual one, hence it is a bond that will abide forever.[47]

Procreation is a primary, though not the only, function of marriage. It should be recalled that Bahá'u'lláh wrote:

> And when He desired to manifest grace and beneficence to men, and to set the world in order, He revealed observances and created laws; among them He established the law of marriage, made it as a fortress for well-being and salvation, and enjoined it upon us in that which was sent down out of the heaven of sanctity in His Most Holy Book. He saith, great is His glory: 'Marry, O people, that from you may appear he who will remember Me amongst My servants; this is one of My commandments unto you; obey it as an assistance to yourselves.'[48]

This 'fortress for well-being' is the basic social institution for rearing, training and orienting the next generation. There have also been many strong, stable, productive marriages in which there have been no children. The Guardian gave the following description:

> The institution of marriage, as established by Bahá'u'lláh, while giving due importance to the physical aspect of marital union, considers it as subordinate to the moral and spiritual purposes and functions with which it has been invested by an all-wise and loving Providence. Only when these different values are given each their due importance, and only on the basis of the subordination of the physical to the moral, and the carnal to the spiritual, can such excesses and laxity in marital relations as our decadent age is so sadly witnessing

be avoided, and family life be restored to its original purity, and fulfill the true function for which it has been instituted by God.[49]

Sex is a wonderful and exciting activity. Why then, as noted in the previous section, is emphasis placed on refraining from sex outside of marriage? Isn't it great under any circumstances? There are two extremes of the sex act. On the one hand it is a basic animal drive – motivated by both physical and psychological impulses. At the other extreme, it is a profound physical expression of a spiritual connection. Sex on the strictly animal or physiological level lessens its significance as a spiritual connection.

In addition to the spiritual component, there are several practical considerations for sex being restricted to a male and female who are married to each other.

- ❖ First and foremost is obedience to the law of God and living the life.
- ❖ In seeking a marriage partner, 'Abdu'l-Bahá wrote, 'Each must, however, exercise the utmost care to become thoroughly acquainted with the character of the other. . .'[50]
- ❖ Judging someone else's character for a potential mate requires dispassionate, cool and objective thought. That is almost impossible when the excitement of sexual activity is involved.
- ❖ Pre-marital sex robs intimacy of some of the power that helps sustain a healthy marriage.

A couple that met at the World Centre desired to marry. First they wanted to know each other better, so they arranged take part in a teaching campaign in a country that was unfamiliar to both of them. Each wanted to see how the other responded under stressful conditions in foreign surroundings, to better assess each other's character.

It is reasonable for someone seeking a spouse to ask 'Is that the person I want as a partner for raising children?' That judgement is hard enough to make with a clear head and almost impossible from the bedroom.

Does that mean there is no room for romance? Of course not! But, romance should not be allowed to get in the way of sound judgement.

When two people get married there is a precarious time of adjustment. The excitement of sexual activity is an enormous help in enabling the couple to get used to one another and accept each other's peculiarities. Sex before marriage dilutes the ability of sex to be of assistance during this crucial adjustment period. Sex is also a healing balm to help a couple re-bond and restore a healthy relationship after inevitable disagreements and differences. The ability of sex to repair damaged relationships is most powerful when there has been absolute fidelity.

Hormones flow and the sex urge is strong when people reach adolescence. This may be one of the reasons why 'Abdu'l-Bahá strongly encouraged people to marry when young. According to the *Kitáb-i-Aqdas*, the age of 15 is the age when people have the right to marry. However, no one is under any obligation to marry. Then, or ever!

A history of casual or recreational sex with multiple partners before marriage can be a difficult habit to break, no matter how much a person might love the spouse and wish to remain faithful. During unavoidable times of stress, the temptation can be overwhelming for someone with an active pre-marital sex history to revert to previous habits.

Once a family is established, the greatest effort should go into its strengthening and development. No activity, no matter how important, should interfere with the well-being of the family. The Guardian's secretary, writing on his behalf, stated it this way:

> Surely Shoghi Effendi would like to see you and the other friends give their whole time and energy to the Cause, for

we are in great need for competent workers, but the home is an institution that Bahá'u'lláh has come to strengthen and not to weaken. Many unfortunate things have happened in Bahá'í homes just for neglecting this point. Serve the Cause but also remember your duties towards your home. It is for you to find the balance and see that neither makes you neglect the other.[51]

Many valued workers at the Bahá'í World Centre have been counselled to return home when there have been problems involving one or more of their parents, children or siblings. Care of the family was considered the higher priority.

One of the great ways to strengthen the family is through consultation. The Universal House of Justice quoted the Guardian as follows: 'Family consultation employing full and frank discussion, and animated by awareness of the need for moderation and balance, can be the panacea for domestic conflict . . .'[52]

Even small children can be brought into consultation in some matters. A Bahá'í psychologist stated it this way:

> Children should be granted full citizenship in the family, with its privileges and responsibilities. They should be informed about matters which affect them and gradually be incorporated as full-fledged members of the family council. Furthermore, the parents must exercise considerable wisdom in preparing items for family consultation, even as the children grow up and develop new capabilities . . .
>
> Children should participate particularly in those decisions which directly affect them. Their participation should neither be a token involvement nor an all-consuming participation. It should be a genuine activity aimed at allowing everyone's views to be considered and reaching the soundest decision. Decisions reached by all members prevent family disunity, have greater chance for implementation, and are

consistent with ideals of love, respect and consideration for all.⁵³

There are, however, subjects about which the husband and wife must have private discussions. The Universal House of Justice gave this advice:

> In any group, however loving the consultation, there are nevertheless points on which, from time to time, agreement cannot be reached. In a Spiritual Assembly this dilemma is resolved by a majority vote. There can, however, be no majority where only two parties are involved, as in the case of a husband and wife. There are, therefore, times when a wife should defer to her husband, and times when a husband should defer to his wife, but neither should ever unjustly dominate the other.⁵⁴

When marriage is based solely on personal attraction and relationships, breakdowns come easily and frequently. 'Abdu'l-Bahá wrote:

> Among the people of the past Dispensations a trifling matter would cause divorce. However, as the light of the Kingdom shone forth, souls were quickened by the spirit of Bahá'u'lláh, then they totally eschewed divorce . . . They must strictly refrain from divorce unless something ariseth which compelleth them to separate because of their aversion for each other, in that case with the knowledge of the Spiritual Assembly they may decide to separate. They must then be patient and wait one complete year. If during this year, harmony is not re-established between them, then their divorce may be realized . . . In short, the foundation of the Kingdom of God is based upon harmony and love, oneness, relationship and union, not upon differences, especially between husband and wife. If one of these two becomes the

cause of divorce, that one will unquestionably fall into great difficulties, will become the victim of formidable calamities and experience deep remorse.[55]

The spiritual nature and consequences of both marriage and divorce have not yet permeated the consciousness of many Bahá'ís who view both marriage and divorce as casually as the rest of society does. One devoted Bahá'í, while contemplating a marriage proposal, was heard to remark, 'Well, if it doesn't work out, there is always divorce.' This attitude reflected the culture, not her commitment to the Faith (and as it turned out, the marriage did not last).

As greater understanding of the spiritual station of marriage and aversion to divorce as described by Bahá'u'lláh emerges, and as believers mature and become naturalized in elements of the Covenant, divorce is bound to become more and more rare. Marriage will assume its rightful role in the development of human souls.

No matter how anyone tries to live, life is brimming with tests and difficulties, trials and tribulations. It is the individual's time of challenge and response.

12

Tests, Difficulties and a Radiant Life

Know ye that trials and tribulations have, from time immemorial, been the lot of the chosen Ones of God and His beloved, and such of His servants as are detached from all else but Him, they whom neither merchandise nor traffic beguile from the remembrance of the Almighty . . . Blessed are the steadfastly enduring, they that are patient under ills and hardships, who lament not over anything that befalleth them, and who tread the path of resignation.
Bahá'u'lláh[1]

Life is a time of challenge and response. All the world's great religious scriptures refer to good times and bad. Counsels are often stated as the dynamic tension between good and evil, right and wrong, reward and punishment, yin and yang, hope and fear or heaven and hell. How people respond is an enduring part of who each of us is.

Challenges mean problems: woes, tests, trials and tribulations. These are the most universal of human experiences. No one is immune. No one escapes. They are the lot of rich men and beggars, commoners and kings, the learned and illiterate, the fool and the sage. Everyone has his or her story. Woes are the stuff of life.

'Abdu'l-Bahá said, 'Life is a load which must be carried on while we are on earth, but the cares of the lower things of life should not be allowed to monopolize all the thoughts and aspirations of a human being.'[2]

Personal spiritual development

The Master tells us that there are two kinds of problems:

> One kind is for trial [to test the soul] and the other is punishment for actions. 'As a man soweth so shall he also reap.' That which is for testing is educational and developmental and that which is the punishment of deeds is severe retribution.³

These are parts of the 'twin pillars of reward and punishment'⁴ that Baháʼuʼlláh said are essential for stability and order.

When things go wrong, how do you know if it is a punishment or for your spiritual education, an obstacle to overcome in the path of service, a chance happening, or a sign to do something different? In one sense, it doesn't make any difference whether a problem is a test or a punishment or a sign from God; whether self-inflicted or from an external source; whether of malicious intent or a random event. It is possible to grow spiritually from any of those situations regardless of source, depending on how it is handled.

A Christian friend commented that God did not cause difficulties for our spiritual growth. She went on to say, 'He is so clever that He can make the most of any situation we get ourselves into.'

An atheist friend complained, 'How can a loving God allow so much suffering?' That's the wrong question. The question should be, 'Why does mankind allow terrible things to happen?'

The Divine Revelators have given ample guidance for most of the unsettling messes that have plagued mankind. Collectively, mankind has not done a good job of applying advice like the Golden Rule, a form of which is found in all religions. That universal teaching is often quoted but generally ignored, with great dedication.

TESTS, DIFFICULTIES AND A RADIANT LIFE

While in Paris, 'Abdu'l-Bahá said, 'The Heavenly Father gave the priceless gift of intelligence to man so that he might become a spiritual light, piercing the darkness of materiality, and bringing goodness and truth into the world.'[5]

No restrictions have been placed on the use of 'the priceless gift of intelligence'. Man has free will, so the gift has been used as intended and also for less worthy pursuits. The human species has developed an outstanding talent for distorting and corrupting any and all blessings for self-serving purposes.

The problem is not the absence or passivity of God, it is the misapplication of God-given intelligence. Whether for good or ill, the brilliance of the human mind is seen everywhere:

- For good: The scope of sciences and arts has widened, wonderful technical advances have been made, marvellous research centres, charities and public service organizations have formed throughout the world.
- For evil: Gas chambers, weapons of mass destruction; clever schemes of brutality, deception and/or corruption have sprung up like weeds.
- For frivolous pursuits: The world has an endless array of electronic games and gadgets, elaborate sports arenas, entertainment facilities and grand elegant resorts.
- For leisure: This can be a time for idleness and/or sensual recreation. Or, it can be a time of freedom to pursue inventive, purposeful and uplifting activity in the arts, science and technology.

It's a matter of choice and priorities. What would happen if the force of human creative energy were focused as intended: 'a spiritual light, piercing the darkness of materiality, and bringing goodness and truth into the world'? Think of the impact on preventing and/or healing mental, physical or congenital abnormalities, world hunger, crime, tyranny, and the burgeoning refugee problem?

Pain is part of life. Entrance into this world starts with 'birth pangs'. The mother experiences excruciating pain which is never fully forgotten, and the newborn usually enters this world crying.

Pain is part of the changes in every stage of life. But that is not all bad. As tests appear they bring some marvellous, if unwelcome, opportunities for detachment and clarity of vision.

Dr Ward, a highly regarded professional friend of my father's, was bedridden with a debilitating disease. As the two of them were talking about his situation, Dr Ward said, 'Something like this can be the best thing for you, if it doesn't get the best of you.' Another person crudely expressed the same idea when an extremely bad turn of events entered his life. He said, 'It must be character building because it is so damn unpleasant.'

How one reacts to tests tells much about a person. While meeting with an older brother at a restaurant, I encountered a minor cash problem. My loving brother laconically commented, 'Good. I wanted to see how you handle a crisis situation.'

In a prayer, the Báb revealed: 'Thou wilt never cause tribulations to befall any soul unless Thou desirest to exalt his station in Thy celestial Paradise and to buttress his heart in this earthly life . . .'[6] 'Abdu'l-Bahá elaborated on this idea:

> Tests are benefits from God, for which we should thank Him. Grief and sorrow do not come to us by chance, they are sent to us by the Divine Mercy for our own perfecting.
>
> While a man is happy he may forget his God; but when grief comes and sorrows overwhelm him, then will he remember his Father who is in Heaven, and who is able to deliver him from his humiliations.
>
> Men who suffer not, attain no perfection. The plant most pruned by the gardeners is that one which, when the summer comes, will have the most beautiful blossoms and the most abundant fruit.
>
> The labourer cuts up the earth with his plough, and from

that earth comes the rich and plentiful harvest. The more a man is chastened, the greater is the harvest of spiritual virtues shown forth by him. A soldier is no good General until he has been in the front of the fiercest battle and has received the deepest wounds.⁷

The highest level of suffering is experienced by the Manifestations of God. The Crucifixion of Christ, the wars waged against Muhammad, the martyrdom of the Báb, the afflictions heaped upon Bahá'u'lláh are the enormous prices the Divine Revelators willingly paid to bring the Word of God to man. Bahá'u'lláh wrote:

> The Ancient Beauty hath consented to be bound with chains that mankind may be released from its bondage, and hath accepted to be made a prisoner within this most mighty Stronghold that the whole world may attain unto true liberty. He hath drained to its dregs the cup of sorrow, that all the peoples of the earth may attain unto abiding joy, and be filled with gladness.⁸

The value of every problem may be measured against this standard. The Blessed Beauty shared His agonies with us to help us keep perspective: 'We disclosed to thee a glimmer of the woes that have come upon us, that thou mayest be made aware of Our sufferings, and patiently endure thy sorrows.'⁹

Two things stand out about that statement. First, it is a guarantee that we will all have *sorrows*. Second, it is an aid to placing our problems in perspective.

Some insight can be gained by looking at difficulties beyond time and circumstance. Think of a child in the teething process. It is an early and major experience of pain. What in the name of justice has that child done to deserve the pain?

What the child cannot know is that, not only is growing teeth a painful process, but there is more going on. The great bonding between mother and child is heightened during difficult times. An important lesson is that a gentle, concerned, nurturing hand can give support and security even when it cannot 'fix' the problem. The child experiences bad things ending; it will recover; life will go on. To deprive the child of these lessons would be an injustice, even though it appears to be an injustice to have so much pain that is not deserved. At the same time, the child's pain makes the mother even more sensitive to the well-being of the child. That concern lasts even when the child is an adult. Maternal instincts are at their peak when a child is suffering.

Crises not only clear the head of trivia, they have an unparalleled ability to change priorities. Many things that seemed essential become unimportant. Many other things, especially relationships that may have been neglected or taken for granted, suddenly assume a higher place in personal priorities. Some family feuds have been healed with the death of a family member – but others are intensified.

A Bahá'í who ran a conflict resolution service had an appointment to meet with two neighbours who had a difficult dispute over a dog. The appointment was for the afternoon of 11 September 2001 – the day the Twin Towers in New York City were destroyed. Late that morning he got a call from one of the people he was to meet with, cancelling the appointment. They figured that in the wake of the terrorist attack, their problem was not that important.

Petty grievances and resentments, that are so common and develop so easily, can vanish in the shadow of greater concerns.

People rarely think of the strong link between good and evil. In the Fire Tablet, immediately following Bahá'u'lláh's list of complaints, God's first two responses are: 'Were it not for the cold, how would the heat of Thy words prevail?' And: 'Were it not for calamity, how would the sun of Thy patience shine?' That suggests that both good and evil are needed: good is known by its contrast with evil. Later, God gives this advice for dealing with adversity – which implies inevitability: 'When the swords flash, go forward! When the shafts fly, press onward!'

Still later in that same Tablet comes the clearest of statements that the turmoil of the world is part of the divine plan. That includes problems and injustices, ranging from individual problems to global catastrophes. God refers to the Manifestation as, 'O Thou Who hast caused the wailing of the worlds.'[10] This suggests that the worldwide upheavals and turmoil of today were the result of the spirit of this age as a necessary, transitional step in building a better world – even though the process is chaotic and unpleasant.

In his thought-provoking monograph *The Metropolis of Satan*, Gary Matthews makes a compelling case, based on his understanding of the Bible, for the necessity for the 'Devil' – not as a negative deity, but as part of the divine scheme. Combatting a negative force is a stimulus for salvation – it implies going from a lower form of self to a higher form of self. The spectre of darkness creates a desire for light.

Bad things happening can be viewed either as a curse or an opportunity. Those who choose to view negative events as an opportunity are not only fortunate; they create their own good fortune, even as the pain lingers. The 20th-century theologian John K. Hick stated a similar view in his book *Evil and the God of Love*. Hick saw the evils of pain and suffering as serving God's good purpose of bringing 'imperfect and immature' humanity to itself 'in uncompelled faith and love'.*

While it is far beyond the scope of this book to consider the vast range of benefits available from tests and difficulties, here are a few items to consider.[11]

> ➤ A measure of a person is shown by what upsets instead of being taken in stride.
> ➤ Crises have a way of clearing the head of trivia.

---

*   This is an extension of Irenaean theodicy, named for the second-century CE philosopher and theologian, Irenaeus. See for example Davis, *Encountering Evil: Live Options in Theodicy*, pp. 40–42.

- Priorities are re-evaluated; old assumptions are tested and either validated or revised.
- Many people are forced into different ways of understanding and looking at things because of a crisis in which old reliable ways failed.
- Tests are reminders of limitations and mortality.
- They help reassess the sense of self.
- Nothing can bond hearts together like sharing mutual hardships. There is an Arab saying that we remember people we cry with longer than those we laugh with.
- They can link us to the bounties of God and prepare us for new forms of service.

Good people suffering bad things

'Why did this have to happen? Where is the justice? Why me? Why now, of all times? What did I do to deserve this?' These questions are all likely in the wake of undesirable events that are unexpected, immediate, illogical, severe and/or prolonged. People may ask 'Why?' But the real, passionate desire is for relief from the strong emotional impact and deep anguish. Answers are secondary.

A sense of fairness is violated and understanding is hard to come by. There are no simple answers. Accepting whatever happens as the will of God may be sufficient for some people. However, especially among Westerners, that is far from adequate. The questions for most Westerners are: how to stop the horrible, unforeseen ordeal; whom to blame; how to fix it; and how to prevent a repeat.

It is hard to find a reasonable explanation because:

- The problem is immediate, obvious and emotional.
- Answers, if any, are delayed, not easily seen, and based on reason.
- Reason and logic are no match for aching emotions.

Many people lash out in frustration and anger at friends, relatives, strangers, events, even God for allowing undeserved things to happen. They need to vent their anguish.

Being wrapped in a heavy cloud of emotion makes it nearly impossible to look past raw pain. This intense weight not only looms large, it leaves little appetite for rational reflection.

It is natural to want to ease the grief of those going through such tests. That is a major challenge. The real need is to wipe away the emotional pain that leaves little room for reason.

People want immediate relief and understanding and that is hard to provide. There is no magic formula to undo the damage, dry the tears, or make the pain go away. Simply showing compassion and loving support is usually best, and maintaining support as they go through the painful process that comes with the ordeal.

Avoid the temptation of assuring someone that it will pass, or that something is for the better, or that good will come out of the ordeal. That may be counterproductive. Rather than calming, such assurances can make the anguish worse. It tells the person that you really do not understand what they are going through. That may increase their frustration and anger.

Good people who are blameless victims of bad things are unwitting, unwilling, often tortured, yet essential heroes in the forward movement of civilization. That is little consolation for the good people facing the problem.

Bahá'u'lláh states, 'Were the mysteries, that are known to none except God, to be unravelled, the whole of mankind would witness the evidences of perfect and consummate justice.'[12]

Perfect justice? This potent statement may be a little hard to digest, especially when facing seemingly irrational ordeals that inflict nearly intolerable pain. It is an enormous challenge to find insight, let alone justice, in the face of an ordeal with no apparent rhyme or reason.

The dilemma is one-sided. The pain, anguish and frustration are intense and NOW! Any good to come out of the situation, when recognized at all, is usually understood much later. Even when there is insight, it is usually during clear-headed reflection. It is a calm and delayed blessing, without the powerful emotional passion that marked the crisis.

To get a sense of possible benefits when bad things happen to good people, the potential that can result from different situations is worth a look.

- ❖ The victim: An unexpected and undeserved crisis may bring out some hidden talent or quality in a person in the struggle to cope with the unwelcome event. Many important prosthetic devices were invented by people with an unexpected need and focused intensity, born of their condition.
- ❖ Caregivers: Suddenly having responsibility for someone else has been a life-saver for many people. One irresponsible young man suddenly became a model father when his estranged wife died and he had sole responsibility for their children.
- ❖ Mankind: Enormous benefits to mankind have developed in the wake of disastrous events. Communities destroyed by earthquakes, hurricanes, wars, tornadoes or other devastating events often rebuild better than ever. The city of Enterprise, Alabama is famous for a large monument of a woman holding a boll weevil. The destruction of cotton crops by the boll weevil led to agricultural diversity and greater prosperity than had ever been provided by cotton. It is said to be the only statue in the world honouring a pesky insect.
- ❖ Spiritual: No one can tell the impact that responding to problems in this world may have on the individual's ultimate spiritual destiny.

Attitudes are changing. The two major features for redirecting creative energy are the growing consciousness of the oneness of mankind and the quest for world peace. These are incrementally gaining prominence and creating an atmosphere in which human creativity increasingly focuses on the greater good.

This is not a sudden change. Yet, there are gratifying signs that these essential remedies are gaining prominence. News media focus on deteriorating events. The slowly emerging features that transform the world are less exciting, therefore generally ignored, but they are unstoppable.

Among the harmful features of materialism are a focus on predictable outcomes and an expectation of immediate understanding and gratification without glitches.

Children are asked what they want to be when they grow up. When enrolling in college, the student is expected to declare a major area of study. Both of these presuppose that a defined goal or destination is the object of life. In fact, the journey is usually more important than the goal. Admittedly, I am among those who need a goal, challenge or deadline that is pressing enough to motivate me. The problem is realizing that these are only a means to the more important ends of a rewarding journey. Life itself is a pilgrimage, the course of which cannot be foreseen. At best, goals can more or less chart a preliminary and general, desired route.

In terms of immediate gratification, the faster the reward the better – reward delayed is considered bad! Buying some new gadget to be delivered later is no longer sufficient. There is growing demand for 'same day delivery'. Patience is in short supply among Westerners.

There are many other obstacles to clear perspectives. Here are a few.

- Not everything has an obvious simple cause. Sometimes a person just gets in the way of random chance. Searching for an explanation is often futile.
- In our materialistic world, 'bad' is a knee-jerk label for anything unpleasant or disturbing. Money or benefits

that bring immediate satisfaction are considered good. When people get an unexpected material advantage someone may say, 'The heavens were smiling on you,' as if so-called good fortune is a reward, implying that unpleasant things are a punishment.

- Drastic, unexpected and unwarranted problems are disorienting. Most people act as if life were stable and predictable. Careers, holidays, celebrations and retirement plans are based on predictability. Serious and unwarranted problems throw people off balance into deep and prolonged grieving, giving rise to confusion, uncertainty and irrational thought.
- Emergencies intensify the immediate. If a cow is standing on your foot, the reaction is: 'Get off RIGHT NOW!' It is not a time for philosophical reflection on the wisdom of suffering.

Problems – challenge and response – bring out the best and the worst in people. Some people become bitter; others become more tolerant and humane. Some of the most creative artists suffered greatly through no fault of their own, leaving the world the rich treasures they produced either because of or in spite of their pain. Beethoven and Van Gogh are two examples.

Parents of children with special needs face a range of issues. In addition to caring for the child, there are often prolonged financial, social, emotional and fatigue issues that have no simple answers. People of means can and often do hire assistants to deal with the issues at hand. People of modest means and the impoverished face the same issues, but with insufficient resources. They are left frantically searching for ways to cope. Some people place the child in an institution, others abandon it or collapse under the imposed weight. There are still others who have found the special needs child the best thing that ever happened to them. Many have been heard to rave about the enrichment of life and insights gained because of the special needs child.

The following story has been a source of comfort for many parents with difficult children. 'Abdu'l-Bahá stayed at the summer residence of Arthur and Agnes Parsons in New Hampshire. Their son Royall was mentally handicapped, and was often hard to manage. One day Agnes recorded the following in her diary: 'I asked how He ('Abdu'l-Bahá) could be pleased when R(oyall) had behaved so badly, and He answered that such people as R. are pure, clearsighted, inspirational, even prophetic. That I must not be troubled. All are in God's hands. That there is a wisdom in this experience.'[13]

By nature, people are compassionate and caring. One person's ordeal often brings out the best in others. Consider the number of people who rush to aid strangers who are victims of disasters such as floods, illnesses, earthquakes, criminal attacks, accidents, storms or other calamities.

Concern over the problems of someone else can have enormous social benefits. The common household zipper – which we could hardly do without – was the result of an unfair problem. Whitcomb Judson came up with the idea to help a friend who could not buckle his own boots.[14] We are the beneficiaries of the fact that Judson used his God-given talents to help a friend who had a problem.

Sensitive people have an additional problem. Many are keenly affected by the problems of others. Some are weighed down by the problems of others. Other caregivers are besieged with feelings of inadequacy when they cannot 'fix' someone else's problem. A physician friend plunged into despair because he could not 'cure' his wife's dementia. Caregivers experience clinical depression more often than those receiving care.

At the same time, callous and indifferent people simply go about their business painlessly. That really seems unfair unless you look closely at the many bounties they deprive themselves of.

Before I accepted Bahá'u'lláh, I believed in social engineering: eugenics, euthanasia and sterilization of the physically and/or mentally unfit – essentially, the elimination of people who did not have the capacity to be what I considered productive! That was utilitarian; not a spiritual life-view. Bahá'u'lláh explained that my job as a person was to know and worship God. It dawned on me that a major part of the gift of worship was the challenge of bettering the world in which we live.

In order to better the world, it has to have problems worth the effort. When you look at history without romanticizing the past, that process has been going on since a human struggled and stumbled to walk upright. This, most likely, inspired others to embark on their own learning curve of walking upright. Improvements have continued ever since, through challenges, trial and error, reversals, successes and failures. Each step had its special problems. We are recipients of a much better world than our forefathers knew in so many ways, because of the troubles they faced. Still, there are plenty of issues calling for attention.

High on that list is concern and care for others – especially the less able. If there were no one in need of help, we would all lose an important part of our job as human beings! Problems and people in need are crucial parts of productivity and progress.

This has many paradoxes. One is that part of the excellence of this world, during the short, terrestrial stage of spiritual development, is the world's imperfections – giving the likes of you and me something worth our efforts to improve, thereby giving us a chance to exercise our spiritual muscles. 'Abdu'l-Bahá expressed it this way:

> If the world of nature were perfect and complete in itself, there would be no need of such training and cultivation in the human world – no need of teachers, schools and universities, arts and crafts. The revelations of the Prophets of God would not have been necessary, and the heavenly Books would have been superfluous.[15]

TESTS, DIFFICULTIES AND A RADIANT LIFE

A related irony is that in order for the compassionate nature of people to come out, there must be someone in distress. Otherwise, the caring one has no one to help. That would be a real injustice. Without someone or something to help, there is a double-edged danger: 1) some people become self-absorbed, thinking only about their own immediate and personal benefit; 2) other people see no purpose and give up on life.

People gain a better perspective of their own situations when they reach out to others. When they do that, they themselves are improved. Companion animals have become popular because of the healing value they impart to the one giving care, helping them to better maintain their own emotional balance. How many scatter-brained teenagers have become responsible parents when they had children of their own? A woman who had given comfort during someone's grief was thanked for her thoughtfulness. Her response was, 'Thanks for letting me help.'

There are some people who have difficulty learning to accept help graciously, no matter how much they need it. Everyone has a special challenge. Learning to accept help is a challenge for many people. Some distressed individuals have committed suicide rather than depend on others – never realizing that their dependency was, in fact, a bounty for the caregiver.

One way to view this life is as a school, laboratory or workshop for the soul. Problems are needed in both school and life for individuals to progress. Only, in life the tests are not scheduled and they have consequences that are far more severe. Schools are to prepare people for life after school. Life experiences prepare people for the future, both in this world and hereafter. The effectiveness of both depends on how immediate issues are managed.

All the Divine Revelators bring teachings for both the here and now and hereafter. For the here and now, we are enlightened on three levels of relationships: 1) How to get along with our God – including nature and the universe; 2) How to get along with other people; and 3) the trickiest of all – how to get along with ourselves.

No matter what anyone claims, no one knows much about the next world. It doesn't even matter much whether or not the individual believes it exists. All Divine Revelators affirm that trying to get a better place for yourself in the next world is self-defeating. While it may seem strange, all of them indicate that progress comes from being forgetful of self and conscious of the needs of others – doing something about people in need, provided it is done with purity of motive without any self-serving interest.

There is no way to prepare adequately for a trip to an unknown world. The best thing to do is follow the instructions freely and abundantly given by the Messengers of God. That is the only valid guidance there is.

There is a relationship between reward and punishment in this world and the next. 'Abdu'l-Bahá replied to an individual who had asked:

> As to the question regarding the soul of a murderer, and what his punishment would be. The answer given was that the murderer must expiate his crime: that is, if they put the murderer to death, his death is his atonement for his crime, and following the death, God in His justice will impose no second penalty upon him, for divine justice would not allow this.[16]

It stands to reason that same principle applies in a broader sense: no penalty in this world equals penalty in the next; no justice in this world equals justice in the next. This gives rise to a realistic hope: people suffering from disasters – natural, from the hands of other people, or even self-inflicted – may well be compensated in the next world.

Much of the value lies in a realm beyond human comprehension. The lack of understanding of the relationship between the two worlds limits our ability to appreciate the value of bad things happening to good people. At the same time, horrendous injustices galvanize the hearts and minds of caring people, creating a commitment to put an end to gross atrocities. The term 'crimes against humanity' was an outgrowth of the horrors of the Second World War. 'Abdu'l-Bahá made this point about the First World War in His *Tablets of the Divine Plan*: 'The wisdom of this war is this: That it may become proven to all that the fire of war is world-consuming, whereas the rays of peace are world-enlightening,'[17]

Unfortunately, that was insufficient for avoiding the next 'great war' which Winston Churchill dubbed 'the unnecessary war' because the means to prevent it – the League of Nations – had been established, but the political will was insufficient for enforcement. Collectively, people continue to be slow learners.

The Balfour Declaration of 1917 stated: 'His Majesty's government view with favour the establishment in Palestine of a national home for the Jewish people . . .'[18] That was a hollow pledge. Nothing was done to make it happen. The sacrifice of six million Jews during the Holocaust was crucial for the favourable vote in the United Nations establishing the State of Israel, turning the earlier noble but empty assurance into reality. Justice demands recompense in the next world for those millions of victims whose sacrifice proved essential.

Not that the Jews were the only ones to suffer from the 'cleansing' of National Socialism. Many others were slaughtered: the mentally, emotionally or physically handicapped, the Roma people (Gypsies), homosexuals, many members of the clergy and anyone else accused of being contrary to the warped concept of an ideal State.

The treaties of Westphalia in 1648 spawned an attitude toward national sovereignty that whatever a government did within its own borders was no one else's business. While the treaties were a major step away from the abusive hegemonies of the Holy Roman Empire and the House of Hapsburg, they gave rulers licence to do whatever they wanted within their borders.

The world was informed of what was happening in the Holocaust, but people were indifferent because: 1) it wasn't happening to them; and 2) it was behind the insulated wall of national sovereignty.

That wall began to crumble with the founding of the United Nations following the end of the Second World War and the Universal Declaration of Human Rights in 1948. Amnesty International, founded in London in 1961, and Human Rights Watch, founded in 1978 – are international non-governmental organizations that conduct research and advocacy on human rights. Neither organization would have been possible had the mentality from Westphalia not been replaced by international concern.

Horrendous atrocities continue. Old tribal rivalries have reappeared with newer weapons of aggression such as between Hutu/Tutsi and other disputes in Africa; there are territorial problems, as with the Balkans, Crimea and the disenfranchisement of the Palestinians; sectarian animosities and oppressions continue to flare up, as between Sunni and Shi'ih in parts of the Middle East, the persecution of Bahá'ís in Iran and between Muslims and Buddhists in Myanmar; extremist Islamic fringe groups throughout the Middle East and western Africa are wreaking havoc; totalitarianisms still hold forth, as in Syria and North Vietnam. These discords have created a refugee problem such as the world has never seen before. So far, efforts to deal with the issues have proved insufficient.

However, hope looms, for two reasons. Unlike during the abuses in Europe in the 1930s, news is broadcast and large numbers of people care. An element of self-righteousness remains; for instance, the American press makes a big issue of human rights abuses in China, Russia, Cuba, Venezuela and other places. Less reported are the well-documented abuses within the United States – it is easier to point fingers at others. But at least the issue of human rights is no longer ignored.

Another major reasons for hope is that for the first time,

world leaders are not indifferent to problems within other sovereign borders. They are attempting to work together to stem the tide of abuse. Cooperation is limited; self-interest continues to interfere with collective action. But it is nevertheless a significant first step to curb a gigantic human problem.

Atrocities remain a major motivator for people of good conscience to do something. Action, fuelled by indignation over the suffering of innocent people, while incomplete, awkward and halting, has started and is propelling civilization forward.

Bad things happen to both good and bad people. That is part of the mix needed for development, both for civilization and individuals. They sacrifice, in the highest sense of 'making sacred', to the path of progress.

While I was writing this, my wife, Janet, was in a memory loss facility in the advanced stages of Alzheimer's. Stuff happens. Someone might have a heart attack. Someone else might be in a severe accident, have cancer, or be the innocent victim of someone else's evil intent. You can't control everything that happens. You have some choice how to deal with it. Janet's condition provided rich insights for me.

Comfort was found in the words of the Báb quoted earlier in this chapter about 'tribulations' actually being a means 'to exalt' the individual's 'station'.[19] Bahá'u'lláh took it further in a prayer, 'Thou wilt send down upon Thy servants only what is good for them . . .'[20]* The facts that no spiritual harm can come to the loved ones and that mental disorders do not affect the soul are indeed comforting – mental illness is but a veil between the soul and the personality.

These insights motivated me to look for some hidden value in Janet's debility, even though there was no way for me to know what was going on in her heart during this ordeal that was necessary for her spiritual development.

---

*   As mentioned earlier, 'Abdu'l-Bahá made a clear distinction between the tests sent by God for our benefit and the problems we bring upon ourselves.

Janet set the tone. Early on, when she knew she was losing her memory, some kind, well-meaning friend tried to console her. Janet's comment was, 'It has to happen to someone. Why not me? I'm someone.'

There have been difficult days. When she was aware of her failing memory, she once burst into tears, saying, 'I just hate what is happening to me.' A few times she lashed out in frustration. She progressed past that stage to one primarily marked by acceptance, tranquillity and contentment.

A dear friend wrote, 'Life would be so wonderful without these particular challenges.' What he said showed compassion and caring. However, life would also be incomplete without these challenges. Public concern over Alzheimer's is sharply increasing. People are energetically trying to end the suffering. Money for research to find its cause and a cure is on the rise. Individuals and groups are expending ever more effort to reach out and comfort the distressed. Good people who are not afflicted are agonizing over this disease and resolved to do something about it. While focused on this issue, their personal lives are improved and they are likely to discover some things that will prove beneficial for humanity on an even broader scale.

The challenge of improving health is a much better use of time, energy and genius than developing more sophisticated ways to kill, abuse or steal from other people.

Janet got wonderful care in the facility where she was a resident. Many staff members confided that she was a favourite resident. One young caregiver called Janet, 'my best friend'. Several things have been mentioned. Unlike many of the other residents, she didn't swear or lash out. Also, unlike many other residents, she did not start fights. She maintained her pleasant disposition, would willingly go wherever a staff member took her, and said, 'Thank you' for services rendered.

It didn't stop there. Sally, a friend of Janet's, asked her if she still thought about things, but just couldn't find the words to express it. She said, 'Oh, yes.' When asked what she thought about, she said, 'We need more birdies.' Since Sally would frequently read the 'broken-winged bird' prayer – a prayer for the Western states – to Janet, Sally asked if she was thinking that we need more Bahá'ís. Janet replied, 'Oh, yes!' Her final stage opened up marvellous teaching opportunities among people who were caring for her. Her passing and funeral turned out to be significant proclamations for the Faith, which was the strongest desire of her life.*

Two other Bahá'ís with whom I have had close and loving relations have had Alzheimer's. Howard Brown had been an Auxiliary Board member. The last time I saw him he gave me that warm, loving embrace that was his way of greeting people. Even though we had spent much time together over the years, I wasn't altogether sure that he knew who I was. The thought struck me that if unconditional love is the last thing left, it is a sign of a life well lived.

When I last saw Blaine Reed, the glowing smile that was his seemed to light up the whole room. Conversation was not possible, but he radiated a heart full of joy to be with friends. Again, he may or may not have had specific knowledge of who I was, but that did not matter. There, as with Janet, many of the staff members considered Blaine their favourite resident.

Janet, Howard and Blaine all recognized Bahá'u'lláh and devoted their lives to living under His Covenant. That included rising above countless tests and being happy, regardless of situations. When rational thought was no longer available to them and they were incapable of façade, their inner radiance remained, enhanced over the years by the vicissitudes of life. They have been great examples of 'Abandon not the incorruptible benefits, and be not content with that which perisheth.'[21]

Detachment, contentment and radiance are highly prized virtues in the Faith. All three of these believers continued to reflect these qualities. It was all they had left, demonstrating

---

*   She was unshackled from the prison of Alzheimer's on 17 May 2014.

who they really were. When incapable of speaking or putting on false fronts, they still showed what it means to be a Baháʼí. Janet would softly hum a tune that has been used for the Greatest Name. It showed both her continued spiritual connection and contentment as she hovered between two worlds.

These three were fortunate in that none of them suffered much damage to that part of the brain that alters personality. Becoming negative and lashing out is common among people suffering from various forms of dementia. Many wonderful people have experienced changes that make them different from their former selves. It is a blessing that for these three, their true natures were tarnished only to a small degree by that additional burden. They retained their basically positive dispositions.

Prayers for the departed are said for all of them. However, when I consider their spiritual station compared to mine, I feel like a child who is trying to master adding and subtracting attempting to help those already doing advanced algebra!

I was discussing the Faith over breakfast with someone whose life had been transformed because of an aneurism several years earlier that brought him close to death. Many strangers had come forward to help him during his time of need. He has since dedicated his life to giving others the kindness that was shown him. He helped me move Janet's personal items into her new facility and was well aware of her situation. We were talking about the Baháʼí Faith in general and the value of tests and difficulties in particular when he looked me straight in the eye and said, 'If it wasn't for Janet, we wouldn't be having this conversation.' I stared back at him and said, 'If it wasn't for your aneurism we wouldn't be having this conversation.' He agreed, and we went on with our joy-filled breakfast.

Do I miss the Janet I used to know? Of course! I feel robbed of my best and dearest friend and confidant with whom I could share both innermost thoughts and wildest ideas. That is my problem. On a trip I had an experience that I was eager to share with her. Then I realized there was no way she could manage a telephone or even know what I was talking about. Just as quickly it struck me that it was not a problem for her; it was a problem for me. It hurt, prompting self-pity. Alzheimer's interfered with my ability to communicate with her. That upset me. Grieving is a natural and normal, but irregular process that is highly individualistic. It is not easy.

I also learned that in addition to kind words of concern, there is great solace for the anguish of a grieving soul in the quality of listening. Silently listening, with sincerity, interest and compassion, has an enormous therapeutic effect for the one in grief.

A short time before her death I was in a discussion group with some men. One of them had gone to school with Janet. During a time of socializing, he asked how she was doing. As I was describing her condition, other members of the group gathered around and quietly listened with keen interest. It was surprisingly therapeutic for me to share details of her declining situation with concerned friends who said nothing, but listened compassionately.

While life goes on, grieving is not something that one can 'just get over', as people are so often ill advised. While it is awkward and many people are reluctant to ask, it is highly therapeutic to share feelings with sympathetic listeners.

God gave me a test, so there must be wisdom in it. Whether or not I see the wisdom is beside the point. It is up to me to deal with the situation without violating the first counsel: to have 'a pure, kindly and radiant heart'. Someday I may discover a deeper insight, but then, maybe not. It doesn't matter.

In the *Seven Valleys*, Bahá'u'lláh writes of the beneficial outcome of a perceived terrible event: 'those who journey in the garden-land of knowledge, because they see the end in the beginning, see peace in war and friendliness in anger.'[22] While it is difficult to see the logic of this, it is even harder to apply its reality in the heat of the moment. 'Abdu'l-Bahá expanded that idea when He said, 'Let them see no one as their enemy, or as wishing them ill, but think of all humankind as their friends.'[23]

How can that be? Enemies who lash out in anger strive to hurt us. Friends try to protect us. There are several ways to consider the above quotations. One is that hate and anger are conditions and not the essence of the individual. It is helpful to separate them. It is possible to look past the rage. Anger has resulted from something or things – it is not the person. The next, harder step is to focus on the spiritual reality of the individual.

Another point is that love and hate are so not much opposites as different positions on a continuum of an emotional relationship. The opposite of both is indifference.

It is interesting that responding to the anger of an 'enemy' can make us reach inside ourselves to find some unknown qualities. In that way we are forced to find insights that friends would be happy to see, but never pressure us to do.

One time I was to meet with some Bahá'ís who were causing difficulties within their Bahá'í community. Working with these people before had been a challenge, so I was not looking forward to the meeting. En route, while reading the above words, it dawned on me that while my friends would never want to hurt me, these folks were not so constrained.

We each have within us some hidden gems. Ordeals can bring out these nuggets, like kneading bread with jewels hidden within. The dough has to be punched and kneaded hard for those gems to surface. It made me wonder if this encounter might reveal some quality that lay hidden within myself – if so, these 'enemies' were true friends. Instead of dreading our meeting, I became eager to see them and all went well.

There is this wonderful story from the Middle East: A certain ruler wished to appoint one of his subjects to a high office; so, in order to train him, he cast the man into prison and caused him to suffer much. The man was surprised at this, for he had expected great favours. The ruler had him taken from prison and beaten with sticks. This greatly astonished the man, for he had thought the ruler loved him. After this he was hanged on the gallows until he was nearly dead. After he recovered he asked the ruler, 'If you love me, why did you do these things?' The ruler replied: 'I wish to make you prime minister. By having gone through these ordeals you are better fitted for that office. I wish you to know how it is yourself. When you are obliged to punish, you will know how it feels to endure these things. I love you so I wish you to become perfect.' [24]

Whether a problem is a test for our growth or punishment for bad deeds, whether deserved or undeserved, whether 'fair' or 'unfair', whether accidental or deliberate, whether natural or someone's dumb mistake, whether a vicious attack or an unfortunate mishap, whether caused by others or self-inflicted, whether or not any underlying wisdom is obvious – all problems are best dealt with as opportunities for human progress. They are also necessary, if unpleasant obstacles for the individual to conquer in order to become happy, content and radiant, not just when things are going well, but under all circumstances.

For society, much has been gained from the suffering and sacrifice when bad things happen to good people.

As individuals deal with adversities – whether or not deserved – they build strength and virtues, steeled through hard, often painful experience, rather than passive and naïve innocence.

Contention

> Nothing whatsoever can, in this Day, inflict a greater harm upon this Cause than dissension and strife, contention, estrangement and apathy, among the loved ones of God. Flee them, through the power of God and His sovereign aid, and strive ye to knit together the hearts of men, in His Name, the Unifier, the All-Knowing, the All-Wise. [25]

It is fun to be around people who are easy to get along with. However, a difficult personality in the community can be a real test. It is easy to get consumed in a conflict and have priorities distorted. The Writings are filled with warnings about contention. The Book of the Covenant of Bahá'u'lláh and the Will and Testament of 'Abdu'l-Bahá both have strong, direct statements concerning this odious characteristic. Avoiding contention is part of being firm in the Covenant.

When I was studying to become a Bahá'í, all the believers I encountered impressed me. One day I met a woman who caused me to reexamine whether or not I wanted to be part of this group. There was one Bahá'í with whom I felt comfortable enough to share my concern. I asked him about her. He laughed, threw his arms around me and said, 'We have always regarded her as a kind of a test.' In that instant, I recognized that it was commitment to Bahá'u'lláh that was the essence of faith; not the Bahá'ís, not the sense of community, not even its sublime Message. Attachment has to be connected to the reality of Bahá'u'lláh. The man who calmed my concern demonstrated that when the focus is on Bahá'u'lláh and priorities are in order, it is possible to have acceptance and tolerance for someone with whom it is not easy to get along.

Withstanding attacks from enemies is one thing, but enduring the criticisms of fellow believers or even the institutions of the Faith can be even harder. Yet they must be endured with patience. It is not appropriate to withdraw from activity, brood over criticism or do anything in retaliation. We are admonished to endure patiently, no matter the tests or from whom.

There is a way to rise above the difficulties caused by other believers. 'Abdu'l-Bahá spoke of twin responsibilities – neither offending others nor allowing yourself to be offended:

> Let not your heart be offended with anyone. If some one commits an error and wrong toward you, you must instantly forgive him. Do not complain of others. Refrain from

reprimanding them, and if you wish to give admonition or advice, let it be offered in such a way that it will not burden the hearer. Turn all your thoughts toward bringing joy to hearts. Beware! Beware! lest ye offend any heart. Assist the world of humanity as much as possible. Be the source of consolation to every sad one, assist every weak one, be helpful to every indigent one, care for every sick one, be the cause of glorification to every lowly one, and shelter those who are overshadowed by fear.[26]

Mary Hanford Ford reported that when 'Abdu'l-Bahá was asked how He could endure difficult people, He said, 'in all those upon whom I look I see only my Father's Face'.[27]

There is a mistaken notion among some Bahá'ís that the Faith is a great leveller. People may be equal in some respects, but they are not at all equal in physical, mental or spiritual characteristics. Some have a greater capacity for service than others. Sometimes the intensity of a devoted and energetic Bahá'í can cause antagonism and jealousy. These are grave dangers. 'Abdu'l-Bahá warned:

> Some even use the affairs of the Cause and its activities as a means of revenge on account of some personal spite, or fancied injury, interfering with the work of another, or seeking its failure. Such only destroy their own success, did they know the truth.[28]

Speaking of the persecutions he endured, 'Abdu'l-Bahá said,

> But there was a third kind of persecution which brought 'Abdu'l-Bahá sorrow and unhappiness, a persecution difficult to bear: the bitter words and criticisms of the friends. Where love was expected, hatred and jealousy was found; instead of friendship and kindness, envy and discord were manifested; instead of harmony there appeared dissension

and ill wishing in place of assistance and appreciation, calumny, falsehood and slander. This is hard to bear.[29]

Both Bahá'u'lláh and 'Abdu'l-Bahá endured with great patience not only onslaughts from enemies, but the strife of believers, who should have known better. Bahá'u'lláh lamented,

> My captivity cannot harm Me. That which can harm Me is the conduct of those who love Me, who claim to be related to Me, and yet perpetrate what causeth My heart and My pen to groan.[30]

Even to those who eventually were declared Covenant-breakers great restraint was shown, and their actions were endured with patience until the situation became so extreme that these contentious individuals had to be expelled from the Cause.

Responding to tests

During a dinner at which there was much laughter, Abdu'l-Bahá said that 'laughter is a spiritual relaxation'. He spoke of His years in prison, explaining that,

> Life was hard . . . tribulations were never far away, and yet, at the end of the day, they would sit together and recall events that had been fantastic, and laugh over them. Funny situations could not be abundant, but still they probed and sought them, and laughed. Joy was not . . . a by-product of material comfort and affluence. Were it so, dejection would have ruled every hour of their lives in those days, whereas their souls were joyful.[31]

In London, 'Abdu'l-Bahá said,

Unless one accepts dire vicissitudes, he will not attain. To me prison is freedom, troubles rest me, death is life, and to be despised is honour. Therefore, I was happy all that time in prison. When one is released from the prison of self, that is indeed release, for that is the greater prison. When this release takes place, then one cannot be outwardly imprisoned.[32]

On a long international flight, there was one passenger who was confused and disruptive. An exceptionally patient steward sat next to this belligerent passenger, calming and soothing him. His patience and gentleness was a marvel to witness. Later, I complimented the steward for the way he handled that difficult situation. He said, 'Oh that poor man! He has to live with himself all the time, at least I can put up with him for eight hours.'

People who are hard to deal with may not be very happy with their own lives. Why add to their burden? When someone offends you, you might consider that he may be carrying around a lot of garbage. You just happened by when he needed to dump some of it. Don't take it personally.

There is always a danger that ill feelings can influence your relationship to the Faith. If you allow someone else to turn you away from Bahá'í activity, you are giving that person power over your spiritual life. As one dear soul who had faced a lot of prejudice, even within the Bahá'í community, said, 'No one can make me stay away from a Nineteen Day Feast!'

One strong Bahá'í was facing extreme difficulties from other believers because of some things he was doing for the Faith. His wife asked him, 'Why do you keep doing so much for people who treat you so badly?' He responded that he was not trying to please them, but trying to serve Bahá'u'lláh. Another believer who served energetically and had received both praise and criticism said, 'When someone says something I say, "Yá Bahá'u'l-Abhá", throw it over my shoulder and give it to

Bahá'u'lláh. Whether they like it or don't like it, what do I care? I do it for Him, so I give Him both praise and blame.' One Bahá'í explained: 'A Bahá'í is a Bahá'í who has met all the other Bahá'ís and is still a Bahá'í.'

No matter what happens, the most important thing is maintaining a healthy relationship with the Covenant. 'Abdu'l-Bahá wrote, 'Be ye assured with the greatest assurance that, verily, God will help those who are firm in His Covenant in every matter . . .'[33]

This was used daily by me during a prolonged difficult time. Problems were both personal and financial. The repeated use of this Tablet from 'Abdu'l-Bahá did not magically solve my problems. It made me wonder if the fact that problems persisted meant I was not firm in the Covenant. Then, it occurred to me that His words were telling me that no matter how things turned out, firmness in the Covenant was most important and assurance was given for that protection. I was assured that it was possible to remain firm in the Covenant regardless of what happens in the problems of life. There was no quick fix and it took years for the problems to abate.

'Abdu'l-Bahá wrote, 'Grieve thou not over the troubles and hardships of this nether world, nor be thou glad in times of ease and comfort, for both shall pass away.'[34]

Finally, Bahá'u'lláh gives this emphatic command:

> If any differences arise amongst you, behold Me standing before your face, and overlook the faults of one another for My name's sake and as a token of your love for My manifest and resplendent Cause.[35]

Forgiveness

This complex question has two major components: one is the responsibility of society and the other is personal. 'Abdu'l-Bahá explained the difference this way:

> An individual has no right to seek revenge, but the body politic has the right to punish the criminal. Such punishment is intended to dissuade and deter others from committing similar crimes. It is for the protection of the rights of man and does not constitute revenge, for revenge is that inner gratification that results from returning like for like. This is not permissible, for no one has been given the right to seek revenge.[36]

This is a highly significant but subtle distinction. Society, or the body politic, has the obligation to punish wrongs. It is not up to the individual to 'get even' or seek vengeance. If someone hits you and you hit back, that doesn't even things out – it is simply two misdeeds rather than one. Besides, it is counterproductive. How many small infractions have escalated into major events because of a desire to 'get even'? Conflicts and wars continue to be waged around the world in misguided attempts to get even.

The Bahá'í Writings make it clear that any violation not adequately punished in this life interferes with spiritual development in the next. Leave it to God. The individual should seek to forgive.

It is impossible to overstate the importance of forgiveness. Holding on to a wrong – no matter how grievous and superficially justified – generally does no harm to the one who did the wrong, but can do enormous damage to the one holding on to ill feelings. There is an American Indian saying, 'holding on to a hurt is like being shot a thousand times with a single arrow'. In a real sense, if someone is trying to hurt you and you do NOT forgive the person, you are helping that individual harm you. Lingering ill feelings can do more severe damage than the original event.

One of the most outstanding examples of human forgiveness concerns a death-camp survivor of the Holocaust. He had subsisted on a starvation diet living in a disease-ridden barracks for six years without the least trace of physical or mental deterioration. How did he do it? In telling his own story he said: 'We lived in the Jewish section of Warsaw, my wife, our two daughters, and our three little boys. When the Germans reached our street they lined everyone against a wall and opened up with machine guns. I begged to be allowed to die with my family, but because I spoke German they put me in a work group.

'I had to decide right then whether to let myself hate the soldiers who had done this. It was an easy decision, really. I was a lawyer. In my practice I had seen too often what hate could do to people's minds and bodies. Hate had just killed the six people who mattered most to me in the world. I decided then that I would spend the rest of my life —whether it is a few days of many years – loving every person I came in contact with.'[37] The power of forgiveness sustained him.

There are many prayers for forgiveness. Expecting God to forgive our transgressions implies that we are willing to forgive those who harm us. Christ said as much when He said, 'Forgive us our debts, as we forgive our debtors.'[38] Looking at it literally, God is asked to forgive us in the same way and to the same extent that we are willing to forgive those who wrong us. That is a big order.

There were many letters from the Guardian giving advice on how to deal with recurring strife among believers. In general, he encouraged patience and said to forgive and forget, regardless of who may be right. A typical reply to an individual was. 'Perhaps the greatest test Bahá'ís are ever subjected to is from each other; but for the sake of the Master they should be ever ready to overlook each other's mistakes, apologize for harsh words they have uttered, forgive and forget.'[39]

In response to a dispute between two Bahá'ís, the Guardian's secretary wrote in his behalf,

He does not want the friends to form the habit of taking up

a kind of Bahá'í litigation against each other. Their duties to humanity are too sacred and urgent in these days, when the Cause is struggling to spread and assert its independence, for them to spend their precious time, and his precious time, in this way. Ask them, therefore, to unite, forget the past, and serve as never before.[40]

Happiness, contentment and radiance

> If we are not happy and joyous at this season, for what other season shall we wait and for what other time shall we look?[41]

When meeting people for the first time, 'Abdu'l-Bahá would often disarm them with the simple question, 'Are you happy?' Where, other than in the Bahá'í Faith, is there such emphasis on being happy? The Bahá'í search engine 'Ocean' lists 2,227 entries for 'happy' or 'happiness'; 'Joy' or 'joyful' yields almost as many, 1,984. 'Radiant' or 'radiance' has another 1,328. Contrast those with 'sad' or 'sadness' that has 289, with 'depressed' lagging behind with 42 entries.

There is probably no human yearning more desired, yet more elusive, than happiness. The thirst for pleasure has been a central theme of the arts and literature since the beginning of recorded history.

But where are joy and contentment found? Bahá'u'lláh placed happiness in the realm of insight rather than circumstances when He wrote, 'Happy is the man that hath apprehended the Purpose of God in whatever He hath revealed from the Heaven of His Will that pervadeth all created things.'[42]

In the story cited earlier about 'Abdu'l-Bahá's view about His imprisonment, it is clear that attitudes do not depend on time, place, circumstances or things. It is a choice, a choice that anyone is free to make at any time, at any place under any conditions.

According to Hand of the Cause Mr Furútan, two of the

four special qualities that Bahá'u'lláh loved to see in people are: 'enthusiasm and courage'; and 'a face wreathed in smiles and a radiant countenance'.[43] Both of these suggest inner radiance, tranquillity and contentment without reference to circumstances. It is important to know that Bahá'u'lláh wants to see them. How to achieve these conditions was not mentioned; that is up to each person to figure out.

There may be no better example of the power of divine radiance than 'Abdu'l-Bahá's meeting with Dr Florian Krug, a prominent New York surgeon. Dr Krug had been a hardheaded warrior in his native Germany. He was proud of the scars on his face – remnants of his more than 40 sword fights. He was furious when his wife, Grace, became a Bahá'í.

'Abdu'l-Bahá was to go to the Krug home and Dr Krug shouted, 'If that old man comes into this house I'll have the doorman throw him out!' Later, he changed his mind. He had a more sinister idea. He decided to let 'Abdu'l-Bahá in the house because, 'Now I can get my hands on the *ringleader* of this bunch!'

The household atmosphere was extremely tense since everyone knew Dr Krug's attitude. His daughter, Louise, described 'Abdu'l-Bahá's arrival this way: 'He put His arms out with that wonderful gesture – you could feel the love pouring out. He walked right up to my father and looked him straight in the face. And he said, "Dr. Krug, are you happy?" . . . my father just *wilted*.'

Nine years later the Krugs were in Haifa at the time of the passing of 'Abdu'l-Bahá. Dr Krug did finally get his hands on 'the ringleader', but not as he had first imagined. Dr Krug's fingers closed the Master's earthly eyes for the last time.[44]

More than just a preferred state of being, happiness comes close to being a command. Many dire situations have been resolved because someone chose to be happy, could inject humour into a grim situation and was able, by a condition of inner radiance, to make the best of it.

Hand of the Cause John Robarts talked about the tragic days in Bahjí immediately following the passing of Shoghi Effendi. The Hands, except for Amelia (Millie) Collins, were all understandably overwhelmed with grief. Somehow, Millie seemed to rise above the sorrow that had engulfed everyone else. She remained radiant and wreathed in smiles. When asked how she could remain so happy under such dire circumstances, she explained that as Shoghi Effendi and Rúḥíyyih Khánum were leaving on what proved to be his last journey, he gathered the friends serving in the Holy Land to say goodbye. The last words Millie heard him say were, 'Millie, be happy.' She explained that if she were not happy, even under these tragic conditions, she would be disobedient to her Guardian. She could not abide that. Her good spirits were a healing balm for all the Hands as they set about the agonizing and serious business of dealing with issues left in the wake of Shoghi Effendi's sudden and unexpected passing.

'Abdu'l-Bahá gives a formula for abiding joy:

> Happy are those who spend their days in the pursuit of knowledge, in the discovery of the secrets of the universe, and in the meticulous investigation of truth! And woe to those who content themselves with ignorance, who delight in thoughtless imitation, who have fallen into the abyss of ignorance and unawareness, and who have thus wasted their lives![45]

Bahá'ís are recipients and bearers of the greatest news ever to come to planet Earth. It is easy to lose sight of this reality and get bogged down in the creature needs, the minutiae, and the trials and tribulations of life. Then, sight is lost of the enormous bounty of recognizing Bahá'u'lláh, Who said, 'O Son of Man! Rejoice in the gladness of thine heart, that thou mayest be worthy to meet Me and to mirror forth My beauty.'[46]

Gladness comes to the heart with the recognition of

Bahá'u'lláh. We are called upon to be happy and rejoice in that awareness, not just because it is a good thing to do and certainly not just for the moment of recognition. It goes beyond that. He affirms that gladness of the heart is the key to being worthy to meet Him and reflect divine attributes. It is part of radiating, or mirroring forth, His beauty for the redemption of the whole world.

Further to this point, in a talk in America 'Abdu'l-Bahá gave a long list of the bounties of recognizing Bahá'u'lláh. Then He said:

> You must live in the utmost happiness. If any trouble or vicissitude comes into your lives, if your heart is depressed on account of health, livelihood or vocation, let not these things affect you. They should not cause unhappiness, for Bahá'u'lláh has brought you divine happiness. He has prepared heavenly food for you; He has destined eternal bounty for you; He has bestowed everlasting glory upon you. Therefore, these glad tidings should cause you to soar in the atmosphere of joy forever and ever. Render continual thanks unto God so that the confirmations of God may encircle you all.[47]

In the Tablet of Ahmad – that most powerful of teaching prayers – soon after Bahá'u'lláh tells Ahmad that his responsibility is 'but to deliver this clear message', He reminds him: 'Remember My days during thy days, and My distress and banishment in this remote prison.' Since Ahmad had spent so much time of blissful joy in the presence of Bahá'u'lláh in Baghdad, he was told to think about both those happy times as well as the distress Bahá'u'lláh suffered: remembering the joy without overlooking suffering. It is counterproductive to think about dire adversity all the time. The Central Figures of the Faith were models of enduring difficulties and still being able to find rich elements of joy and happiness. Both are needed for balanced living.

TESTS, DIFFICULTIES AND A RADIANT LIFE

Many people confuse fleeting pleasures with happiness. The pleasure-seeking quest can be self-defeating, a distraction from our true selves, and can even have disastrous effects. Untold harm has come to mankind from those who seek joy in mind-altering substances; acquisition of things; sensual pleasures; excessive pursuit of sports, entertainment, and leisure-time activities; accumulation of wealth and so on. Those attempts for a blissful state can and do wreak long-term havoc on individuals, families and society as a whole.

Once a material goal is attained, short-lived pleasure is common, but it is often followed by a desire for more, and is easily abandoned when something newer and/or better comes along. The more vigorously someone pursues happiness the further it is pushed out of reach. Or, when something is attained that should bring joy, it proves not only temporary but can have severe unintended consequences.

It has been said that a luxury, once enjoyed, soon becomes a necessity. That reflects several things. It confirms how temporary and fragile material pleasure is. It is really just the beginning of an endless process. Once the luxury is accepted as normal, an appetite is created for more. This goes on and on in a process that is headed for disaster.

In the meantime, this works well for the advertising industry. Their pitches are based on the premise that life is incomplete. They promote the idea that people need the latest gadget, pill, experience or trip in order to attain the happiness and fulfilment each one deserves. Pretty faces, that smile and look radiant on camera, portray the joy that is supposed to be experienced from some sort of purchase. Yet, when people come out of stores with a pile of boxes designed to bring cheer, they rarely look as happy as the come-on smiles in the advertising.

A wisdom shared by many psychotherapists holds that the quest for 'happiness' is not only common, it is elusive and self-defeating. They subscribe to the idea presented by Victor

Frankl* in his book *Man's Search for Meaning*. Enduring happiness is the by-product of a strong sense of purpose and meaning in life, provided it is related to something bigger than self.

In addition to the fact that acquiring things brings, at best, a temporary and shallow satisfaction, there is an irony in that the pursuit of pleasure or short-lived happiness actually opposes a condition that is essential for true and enduring human satisfaction. Bahá'u'lláh wrote, 'Verily the most necessary thing is contentment under all circumstances; by this one is preserved from morbid conditions and from lassitude. Yield not to grief and sorrow: they cause the greatest misery.'[48]

No one can be content and crave more things at the same time. However, contentment should not be confused with being passive. 'Abdu'l-Bahá was the embodiment of contentment, but was hardly passive. His contentment came from doing what He felt needed to be done. It is a matter of priorities. In a prayer, Bahá'u'lláh asks us to pray,

> I beg of Thee, O my God . . . to ordain that my choice be conformed to Thy choice and my wish to Thy wish, that I may be entirely content with that which Thou didst desire, and be wholly satisfied with what Thou didst destine for me by Thy bounteousness and favor. Potent art Thou to do as Thou willest. Thou, in very truth, art the All-Glorious, the All-Wise.[49]

Contentment is a matter of choice, not circumstances. Who can be content at all times and under all circumstances? If that were possible, why would there be so many prayers for relief from tests and difficulties? Those prayers are needed to ease the ache of dire circumstances.

Wonderful stories have come out of the prisons in Iran, from the time of Bahá'u'lláh down to recent years. Prisoners who

---

* A survivor of the Holocaust, Frankl learned from his tortures that fulfilment was an inner quality, not dependent upon external circumstances.

TESTS, DIFFICULTIES AND A RADIANT LIFE

were not Bahá'ís frequently reported that the attitude and happiness of the Bahá'ís who were in prison with them gave them the strength and courage needed to face their own ordeals.

The degree to which Bahá'ís choose to be happy has a great bearing on the speed with which people will be attracted to the Faith. More than once I've heard staff members at rented summer school facilities say how glad they are to see the Bahá'ís because of the spirit of joy that comes with them.

Following a large Bahá'í conference at an upscale hotel, I once stayed for an extra day. Walking through the lobby with no Bahá'ís was a shocking revelation. Instead of the joyful, radiant faces of the previous days, there was stony-faced gloom.

Striving to walk in the light of the Covenant and live according to Bahá'í teachings does not erase all problems. What it does is increase both the frequency and stability of enduring joy, satisfaction and contentment.

It enables anyone to look past those problems that are a guaranteed part of life. When contentment and radiance become normal, default conditions, people are better able to balance words and deeds, as will be discussed next.

13

Words and Deeds

The essence of faith is fewness of words and abundance of deeds; he whose words exceed his deeds, know verily his death is better than his life.
Bahá'u'lláh[1]

All that are on earth shall pass away, while good deeds alone shall endure.
Bahá'u'lláh[2]

Advice from the Bahá'í Writings is clear:

> Beware, O people of Bahá, lest ye walk in the ways of them whose words differ from their deeds. Strive that ye may be enabled to manifest to the peoples of the earth the signs of God, and to mirror forth His commandments. Let your acts be a guide unto all mankind, for the professions of most men, be they high or low, differ from their conduct. It is through your deeds that ye can distinguish yourselves from others. Through them the brightness of your light can be shed upon the whole earth. Happy is the man that heedeth My counsel, and keepeth the precepts prescribed by Him Who is the All-Knowing, the All-Wise.[3]

> Should your words, O people, be at variance with your deeds, what then shall distinguish you from those who profess their faith in the Lord, their God, and yet, when He came down to them overshadowed with clouds, rejected Him and waxed proud before God, the Incomparable, the Omniscient?[4]

Application

While the importance of a balance between words and deeds is clear and its wisdom easy to see, the challenge in harmonizing them is staggering. The common expression, 'What you are speaks so loud I cannot hear what you say,' reflects the difficulty. It is not easy to have words and deeds mirror each other.

There is an analogy in a person's two legs – they have to work together in order to get anywhere. When they are not coordinated there are no end of problems.

The world is filled with lofty, pious and generally ignored words. The so-called Golden Rule is one example of a teaching that is commonly known, often solemnly quoted, but rarely followed. One cynic commented that Christianity intrigued him so much that he would like to see someone try it some day.

All cultures – whether or not they have a written language – have noble and lofty advice for right living, stated as principles, values or traditions. The New Age writer Don Miguel Ruiz recently resurrected ancient good words when he popularized the Toltec Four Agreements: Be Impeccable With Your Word; Don't Take Anything Personally; Don't Make Assumptions; Always Do Your Best. He added a fifth: Be Sceptical but Learn to Listen.[5]

How many organizations have lofty slogans and mission statements that bear little resemblance to what they actually do? One Bahá'í mediation specialist has parties to a dispute look at their common mission statement – if they have one – as a part of resolving their differences. The most common result is changing the statement to make it more accurately reflect reality.[6]

There are many challenges in integrating words and deeds:

❖ Compartmentalized thinking – few people see discrepancies in themselves when they hold mutually exclusive views.

- ❖ Denial – it is common to deny things that are painful or hard to deal with or conflict with a strongly held opinion.
- ❖ Self-deception – if someone claims not be a racist, it is a pretty clear indication that he has strong racially slanted views.
- ❖ The adage 'It's a wise man who knows himself' has survived the ages because it has the ring of truth.

Bahá'u'lláh gives a definition of what it really means to be human. He wrote, 'That one indeed is a man who, today, dedicateth himself to the service of the entire human race.'[7] It is easier to harmonize words and deeds when there is a clear and present reason for doing so.

Love and fear are probably the two most powerful forces in the universe for marrying words and having those two legs of activity work together. It is true that both love and fear can sometimes mask real problems. At the same time, when something is done because of love for someone or something, or fear of the consequences, words and deeds often become as one.

I have frequently done something or not done something because I wanted my actions to be consistent with my claim to be a follower of Bahá'u'lláh. These choices have been because of a desire to bring pleasure to Him and the fear of doing anything that might embarrass the Faith.

Chapter 8 discussed various aspects of the fear of God. Suffice to say that fear helps keep deeds consistent with words in a number of ways, both practical and spiritual. Fear of getting caught and no longer being trusted helps keep words and deeds in line. There are the extremes of fear: punishment, all the way from fear of a stern God; fear of not pleasing a loving God. Regardless of what a person fears, it can be a powerful motivator to do what is said.

The problem with love is a little more complex because it covers so much. 'Abdu'l-Bahá said, 'Love is the very cause of life . . . In the world of material creation, for instance, all things owe their actual life to unity. The elements which compose wood, mineral, or stone, are held together by the law of attraction.'8

When people speak of love it is hard to know what is meant because the word carries so many different meanings and connotations. Popular conceptions of love frequently focus on romantic elements, most often based on physical attraction or fascination. In today's Western culture, the flood of writing, movies, music and other expressions on the theme of love are generally reflections of what 'Abdu'l-Bahá dismissed by saying it 'is not in reality love'. He seems to be distinguishing between human or creature love and spiritual love.

That is not to trivialize the emotion of human love, or affection. It is a powerful driver of behaviour. The problem is that the human level of love is subject to change and is less resilient to the challenges, changes, chances and temptations of life. The courts are filled with people seeking divorce who once pledged their undying love for each other. How many crimes of passion are committed each day? When interests or job situations or stations in life change, the circle of friends often changes as well. How often have dear friends drifted apart, or even become bitter enemies?

'Abdu'l-Bahá's standard is rarely used: 'that men see the Divine Love reflected in the heart. Each sees in the other the Beauty of God reflected in the soul, and finding this point of similarity, they are attracted to one another in love.'9

When there is a group of people together that looks as if they don't belong together, they are most likely Bahá'ís. On a business trip to a medium-sized city, I informed the Bahá'ís that I would be available for the weekend. Since my plane was arriving late at night on a weekday, I did not tell them the flight I would be on. When the plane pulled up to the terminal on that warm summer night, I saw a group of people that was different. They varied by age, race, attire and even body language. I thought, 'They must be Bahá'ís.' They were. The Spiritual Assembly had been meeting. The meeting was over. They figured out when I would arrive and came out to greet me in their lovely diversity.

'Abdu'l-Bahá said: 'The lovers of mankind, these are the superior men, of whatever nation, creed, or colour they may be. For it is they to whom God will say these blessed words, 'Well done, My good and faithful servants.'[10] He further warned, 'Do not be content with showing friendship in words alone, let your heart burn with loving kindness for all who may cross your path.'[11] Love of that spiritual level helps match deeds to words.

The love for, and/or the fear of, disappointing God, the Central Figures of the Faith, fellow believers and the Faith itself make it possible for ordinary people to do the seemingly impossible. Legions of ordinary people became pioneers – often ill prepared for their challenges – to launch the Ten Year Crusade. They did this out of their love for the Faith and their Guardian and the refusal to let his Plan fail. Their love made them want to be part of that daring and exciting venture. Their feet echoed what their mouths said. After the passing of the Guardian, the Hands of the Cause, driven by love, overcame great obstacles to circle the globe in order that the beloved Shoghi Effendi's goals would be met. It was unthinkable for them that the Plan be marked with anything other than rousing success. Martha Root, in her many messages to the Guardian, would often sign her letters simply with 'love', and nothing would stop her from doing what she thought the Guardian wanted.

People are attracted to the Faith, launched on their own spiritual path, and sustained by the genuine love they feel from others. It is an extraordinary individual who can find Bahá'u'lláh and remain firm without a loving relationship with other believers. How many souls have left the Faith because of estrangement with fellow believers?

The story of the brilliant Bahá'í writer Stanwood Cobb

illustrates the point. He was a graduate from the Harvard School of Divinity, a student and scholar of religion. He knew the wisdom and value of great words, but his soul was uneasy. He was vacationing where a group of Baháʼís had gathered. He knew one member of the group, but was attracted by the unusual measure of love they showed to each other. Drawn to the group, the first words he heard about the Faith were, 'Our Lord has come!' Stanwood, overwhelmed by what he saw among the Baháʼís, replied, 'I believe!' And that was it.

In contrast to that, there was a couple from a large Baháʼí community who would sit on a park bench, praying that some seeking soul would stop by for a conversation. It worked. They met many people this way, told them about Baháʼu'lláh and presented several enrolment cards to the Spiritual Assembly each month. Unfortunately, some of these new enrollees did not remain in the Faith. A member of the Spiritual Assembly asked the couple why. The Assembly member reported that, with tears in their eyes, these dear friends answered that those who left the Faith did not find the same love from other members of the community as they had felt from them in their living-room.

Love cannot exist in the abstract. It must be focused. ʻAbdu'l-Bahá explained that there are many ways of expressing the love principle: love for family; for country; for race; political enthusiasm; community; common interests; even performing services. He said:

> These are all ways and means of showing the power of love. Without any such means, love would be unseen, unheard, unfelt – altogether unexpressed, unmanifested! Water shows its power in various ways, in quenching thirst, causing seed to grow, etc. Coal expresses one of its principles in gas-light, while one of the powers of electricity is shown in the electric light. If there were neither gas nor electricity, the nights of the world would be darkness! So, it is necessary to have an

instrument, a motive for love's manifestation, an object, a mode of expression.[12]

He was not vague about what he meant. He differentiated among four kinds of love:

The first is the love that flows from God to man . . .
> The second is the love that flows from man to God . . .

The third is the love of God towards the Self or Identity of God . . .

The fourth is the love of man for man. The love which exists between the hearts of believers is prompted by the ideal of the unity of spirits. This love is attained through the knowledge of God, so that men see the Divine Love reflected in the heart. Each sees in the other the Beauty of God reflected in the soul, and finding this point of similarity, they are attracted to one another in love. This love will make all men the waves of one sea, this love will make them all the stars of one heaven and the fruits of one tree. This love will bring the realization of true accord, the foundation of real unity.

But the love which sometimes exists between friends is not (true) love, because it is subject to transmutation; this is merely fascination. As the breeze blows, the slender trees yield. If the wind is in the East the tree leans to the West, and if the wind turns to the West the tree leans to the East. This kind of love is originated by the accidental conditions of life. This is not love, it is merely acquaintanceship; it is subject to change . . .

Love is only of the four kinds that I have explained. (a) The love of God towards the identity of God. Christ has said God is Love. (b) The love of God for His children – for His servants. (c) The love of man for God and (d) the love of man for man. These four kinds of love originate from God.

These are rays from the Sun of Reality; these are the Breathings of the Holy Spirit; these are the Signs of the Reality.[13]

All else is ephemeral. Don't be deceived. Love and fear are parts of the Divine Elixir. They provide the energy to bond deeds and words. They are primary drivers for consistency between word and deed.

Caution

Even when someone serves the Faith with nothing but the purist motives of love, and strives valiantly to be true in word and deed, others will not always appreciate their actions. 'Abdu'l-Bahá explained,

> When God calls a soul to a high station, it is because that soul has capacity for that station as a gift of God, and because that soul has supplicated to be taken into His service. No envies, jealousies, calumnies, slanders, plots, nor schemes, will ever move God to remove a soul from its intended place, for by the grace of God, such actions on the part of the people are the test of the servant, testing his strength, forbearance, endurance and sincerity under adversity. At the same time those who show forth envies, jealousies, etc. toward a servant, are depriving themselves of their own stations, and not another of his, for they prove by their own acts that they are not only unworthy of being called to any station awaiting them, but also prove that they cannot withstand the very first test, that of rejoicing over the success of their neighbor, at which God rejoices.[14]

At the conference of Badasht, about half the Bábís left the Faith when Ṭáhirih appeared unveiled. They did not understand or appreciate that history-making act, let alone grasp Ṭáhirih's enormous love and commitment to putting her words into deeds. Thank God she did not allow their disapproval to diminish her love and resolve to serve the Faith.

The important thing under all circumstances is to serve God for the love of God and for no expectation of praise or any selfish reason – either worldly or otherworldly. Then, His Words lead to proper deeds. Word and deed become so harmonized in the love and/or fear of God that they can give full expression in their balance and are the foundation for a culture of learning.

14

Culture of Learning

> *To strive to obtain a more adequate understanding of the significance of Bahá'u'lláh's stupendous Revelation must, it is my unalterable conviction, remain the first obligation and the object of the constant endeavour of each one of its loyal adherents. An exact and thorough comprehension of so vast a system, so sublime a revelation, so sacred a trust, is for obvious reasons beyond the reach and ken of our finite minds. We can, however, and it is our bounden duty to seek to derive fresh inspiration and added sustenance as we labour for the propagation of His Faith through a clearer apprehension of the truths it enshrines and the principles on which it is based.*
> Shoghi Effendi[1]

While Adib Taherzadeh was flying over the North Pole from London to Anchorage, Alaska – literally to the other side of the world – he recalled his youth in Yazd, Persia. He described Yazd as a place so backward that donkeys were the only means of transportation. Wagons were the only things with wheels – there was not so much as a bicycle. He was with his father among a group of believers when somebody mentioned that the Faith was to become a world religion. Someone raised the question: 'How can that be? How far can a man travel on a donkey in a day?' Someone else answered: 'God gives the challenge and God will provide the means.'

There he was, using a mechanism few could have even imagined when Bahá'u'lláh made His call to the nations. The means of travel, made possible by the creative energies released by Bahá'u'lláh, enable people to circle the globe in a matter of hours to spread the teachings for this age and stimulate a culture of learning. Bahá'u'lláh wrote,

> Bend your minds and wills to the education of the peoples and kindreds of the earth, that haply the dissensions that divide it may, through the power of the Most Great Name, be blotted out from its face, and all mankind become the upholders of one Order, and the inhabitants of one City.[2]

This was written at a time when much of the world was illiterate. Many people even considered learning to read and write as not just unnecessary and basically useless, but a frivolous luxury of the idle rich. Some even considered it an evil work of the Devil. Bahá'u'lláh gave the challenge of educating the world and provided the means of moving from a world wreathed in ignorance to a culture of learning. The Covenant provides both the necessary unity and the essential motivation to channel the changes made by greater education in a positive direction for mankind.

In the Western materialistic civilization, advanced education has created a culture of acquiring money and things. Bahá'u'lláh called for a deliberate, sustained, specific but difficult shift away from a culture of accumulating things to a culture of accumulating learning and wisdom.

What is a culture of learning? It is more than acquiring facts and information. It involves thinking seriously and deeply about what is known and has been discovered, while contemplating what is yet to be disclosed. Bahá'u'lláh quotes a well-known verse, 'One hour's reflection is preferable to seventy years of pious worship'.[3] For the first time, learning by the masses, and thinking deeply about what is learned, are now integral parts of religious life!

First and foremost, a culture of learning involves continuous study of the Sacred Words – that rich reservoir of the Creative Utterances given to mankind. The Universal House of Justice, through the Institute process, has launched Bahá'í communities on a systematic way to plunge into the ocean of the Creative Word. Private conversations with other believers and private study also remain important, and great stress is put on the study of arts and sciences. These are all valuable tools for the culture of learning and lead to the final step of applying what has been learned for the betterment of mankind.

Sharing views with one another enhances understanding. However, personal views, no matter how cogent, should never be confused with authoritative interpretation. The Universal House of Justice makes this clarification:

> The existence of authoritative interpretations in no way precludes the individual from engaging in his own study of the Teachings and thereby arriving at his own interpretation or understanding. Indeed, Bahá'u'lláh invites the believers to 'immerse' themselves in the 'ocean' of His 'words', that they 'may unravel its secrets, and discover all the pearls of wisdom that lie hid in its depths'.
>
> Bahá'u'lláh asserts that 'knowledge hath seventy meanings', and that the 'meaning' of the Word of God 'can never be exhausted' . . .
>
> Individual interpretations based on a person's understanding of the teachings constitute the fruit of man's rational power and may well contribute to a more complete understanding of the Faith.[4]

The Universal House of Justice mentions broad themes for areas of learning and reflection. These are the themes we must pursue in our efforts to deepen in the Cause.

- ➤ What is Bahá'u'lláh's purpose for the human race?
- ➤ For what ends did He submit to the appalling cruelties and indignities heaped upon Him?
- ➤ What does He mean by a 'new race of men'?
- ➤ What are the profound changes which He will bring about?[5]

What greater learning is there than delving into these questions? These are not questions with single or simple answers, nor do they suggest immediate, practical application. They are far more profound than that. The Universal House of Justice went on to assure us that

> The answers are to be found in the Sacred Writings of our Faith and in their interpretation by 'Abdu'l-Bahá and our beloved Guardian. Let the friends immerse themselves in this ocean, let them organize regular study classes for its constant consideration, and as reinforcements to their effort, let them remember conscientiously the requirements of daily prayers and reading of the Word of God enjoined upon all Bahá'ís by Bahá'u'lláh.[6]

This is more than collecting abstract information. What it does is create the proper framework of thinking within which beneficial applications can emerge.

In recent years, the Universal House of Justice has made learning part and parcel of the process of entry by troops.[7] It has further called upon the friends to hold 'reflection meetings' to give serious thought to actions being taken and to assess their effectiveness.

Bahá'u'lláh asked God to assist us in the path of knowledge, writing to an individual,

> We beseech God to aid thee to be just and fair-minded, and to acquaint thee with the things that were hidden from the eyes of men. He, in truth, is the Mighty, the Unconstrained. We ask thee to reflect upon that which hath been revealed, and to be fair and just in thy speech, that perchance the splendors of the daystar of truthfulness and sincerity may shine forth, and may deliver thee from the darkness of ignorance, and illumine the world with the light of knowledge.[8]

CULTURE OF LEARNING

The Báb specifically forbade His followers from asking any questions of 'He whom God will make manifest'. It was up to the new Messenger to determine what could or could not be asked of Him. Bahá'u'lláh answered this in His Most Holy Book. He not only opened the door to inquiry, He defined its purpose:

> In the Bayán it had been forbidden you to ask Us questions. The Lord hath now relieved you of this prohibition, that ye may be free to ask what you need to ask, but not such idle questions as those on which the men of former times were wont to dwell. Fear God, and be ye of the righteous! Ask ye that which shall be of profit to you in the Cause of God and His dominion, for the portals of His tender compassion have been opened before all who dwell in heaven and on earth.[9]

He also wrote:

> We have decreed, O people, that the highest and last end of all learning be the recognition of Him Who is the Object of all knowledge; and yet, behold how ye have allowed your learning to shut you out, as by a veil, from Him Who is the Dayspring of this Light, through Whom every hidden thing hath been revealed. Could ye but discover the source whence the splendour of this utterance is diffused, ye would cast away the peoples of the world and all that they possess, and would draw nigh unto this most blessed Seat of glory.[10]

In a Tablet sent to the Persian believers, 'Abdu'l-Bahá explained, 'Not all, however, will be able to engage in these advanced studies.' He suggested studies suited to the needs and capacity of the individual. He concluded:

> But the indispensable basis of all is that he should develop spiritual characteristics and the praiseworthy virtues of

humankind. This is the primary consideration. If a person be unlettered, and yet clothed with divine excellence, and alive in the breaths of the Spirit, that individual will contribute to the welfare of society, and his inability to read and write will do him no harm. And if a person be versed in the arts and every branch of knowledge, and not live a religious life, and not take on the characteristics of God, and not be directed by a pure intent, and be engrossed in the life of the flesh – then he is harm personified, and nothing will come of all his learning and intellectual accomplishments but scandal and torment.[11]

The news of the day is filled with the disastrous results of brilliant and well-educated people who lack 'spiritual characteristics and the praiseworthy virtues' and whose 'learning shut them out' and became 'veils'.

When the Universal House of Justice started using the term 'frontier of learning' in relation to the core activities of the Institute process, it highlighted a shift toward more intense 'praiseworthy virtues'. Obedience to the Covenant leads the way.

The spirit of inquiry is not just permitted, it is encouraged. It is also focused. The right kinds of questions need to be asked. As we saw in Chapter 12, Hand of the Cause Mr Furútan mentioned four things that brought special pleasure to Bahá'u'lláh. One of them was 'that they see all things with their own eyes and not through the eyes of others'.[12] Spiritual knowledge, insight and wisdom make this possible.

The importance of the spirit of inquiry is suggested in the names of the months in the Badí' (Bahá'í) calendar. The months are named after attributes that God has conferred upon man. One month is Masá'il (Questions). This may be the most important attribute because questions are the key to all knowledge. But, where is the month of Answers? That doesn't exist, suggesting that asking the right question is even more important than finding an answer. Answers change with time, circumstance and greater understanding. Relevant questions remain the key to continuous learning.

Bahá'u'lláh gave a problem-solving model in the Fire Tablet. The first 36 verses follow the pattern of stating a problem, followed by a question, then calling on a name of God. This is such a compelling example. First, get a clear idea of the problem or situation. Then, frame the appropriate question. Finally, call upon God.

In our fast-paced society and way of life it seems that people want answers before issues are understood. Furthermore, there is a desire for answers that are no more complex than will fit on a bumper sticker. The model from the Fire Tablet is to frame the question properly and ponder it. Then, meaningful answers can be found.

Wars and other acts of violence result when people ask the wrong questions. Lives have been sacrificed over where boundaries should be drawn and who should control certain territory. Those are the wrong questions. The issue should be, 'How can disparate people live together in harmony?' How can the right answer be found when the wrong question is asked?

Many of the Writings of Bahá'u'lláh were answers to questions, creating an enduring blessing for all mankind. Bahá'u'lláh used questions for clarification in the Most Holy Book. Many believers asked Bahá'u'lláh to reveal a book of laws and He eventually did. He asked one believer to review it and ask as many questions as he could think of. Those questions are the 'Questions and Answers' section of the *Kitáb-i-Aqdas*. More than 4,000 references to the word 'question' can be found in the computer search engine Ocean.

'Abdu'l-Bahá elevates the capacity and process of learning to the highest level:

> According to the words of the Old Testament God has said, 'Let us make man in our image, after our likeness.' This

indicates that man is of the image and likeness of God – that is to say, the perfections of God, the divine virtues, are reflected or revealed in the human reality.

He went on to say,

> The human kingdom is replete with the perfections of all the kingdoms below it with the addition of powers peculiar to man alone. Man is, therefore, superior to all the creatures below him . . . Therefore, it is said that man has been created in the image and likeness of God.[13]

Raising questions and seeking answers are fundamental parts of man's superiority over other creatures, according to 'Abdu'l-Bahá.

> All the powers and attributes of man are human and hereditary in origin – outcomes of nature's processes – except the intellect, which is supernatural. Through intellectual and intelligent inquiry science is the discoverer of all things. It unites present and past, reveals the history of bygone nations and events, and confers upon man today the essence of all human knowledge and attainment throughout the ages. By intellectual processes and logical deductions of reason this superpower in man can penetrate the mysteries of the future and anticipate its happenings.[14]

He also commented on the misuse of intellect:

> Is it not astonishing that although man has been created for the knowledge and love of God, for the virtues of the human world, for spirituality, heavenly illumination and eternal life, nevertheless, he continues ignorant and negligent of all this? Consider how he seeks knowledge of everything except knowledge of God.

'Abdu'l-Bahá went on to give several examples of misdirected intellectual inquiry, concluding:

> It is as if a kind and loving father had provided a library of wonderful books for his son in order that he might be informed of the mysteries of creation, at the same time surrounding him with every means of comfort and enjoyment, but the son amuses himself with pebbles and playthings, neglectful of all his father's gifts and provision.[15]

He gave learning a high priority:

> The first principle of Bahá'u'lláh is independent investigation of truth, that is, all the nations of the world have to investigate after truth independently and turn their eyes from the moribund blind imitations of the past ages entirely. Truth is one when it is independently investigated, it does not accept division. Therefore the independent investigation of truth will lead to the oneness of the world of humanity.[16]

Bahá'ís frequently speak of independent investigation of truth and generally use it to refer to people being free to find Bahá'u'lláh independently. This can be taken a step further. Acceptance of Bahá'u'lláh is an acknowledgement that He is the voice of God for this age. Therefore, He is truth. Then, independent investigation moves up a notch. Each one is to find the truth for herself or himself by investigating the Writings. The first step is investigation *for* truth. When the reality of Bahá'u'lláh has been discovered, studying His Writings is the investigation *of* truth.

Questions should all be for the sake of enlightenment and not a means of contention. In *Some Answered Questions* 'Abdu'l-Bahá described the way Bahá'u'lláh responded to a contentious request. He told of a situation in Baghdad, before Bahá'u'lláh's formal declaration. The religious authorities admitted that His wisdom and knowledge were generally acknowledged by all, but 'Abdu'l-Bahá quoted them as saying,

> 'But the divines say that they are not satisfied with this and cannot acknowledge the truth of your claim on the basis of your knowledge and attainments alone. They therefore ask you to produce a miracle in order to satisfy and assure their hearts.'

He continued,

> Bahá'u'lláh replied: 'Although they have no right to ask this, since it is for God to test His creatures and not for them to test God, yet their request is in this case accepted and allowed. But the Cause of God is not a theatrical stage where every hour a new performance may be offered and every day a new demand presented. For otherwise the Cause of God would become the plaything of children.
>
> 'Let the divines, therefore, assemble and choose unanimously one miracle, and let them stipulate in writing that once it has been performed they will no longer entertain any doubt, but will all acknowledge and confess the truth of this Cause.'

The clergy could not agree on what miracle to request. They feared Bahá'u'lláh would trick them and then they would have no basis to deny Him. So, they withdrew their demand. 'Abdu'l-Bahá explained that the man who delivered the message, 'reported this fact in many gatherings . . . he provided all with a detailed account of this episode and spoke of the fear and inaction of the divines.'[17]

Miracles

This is a good place to make a brief mention of miracles and how they fit into a culture of learning. Believing in God assumes a belief in miracles. It is inconceivable that the Intelligence that created the universe and established natural laws would be incapable of moderating those laws at will. But, what is a miracle? What role do they play? Of what importance are they? What do they have to do with a culture of learning?

The word miracle comes from the Latin '*miraculum*' which means 'an object of wonder'. It can be defined as, 'a surprising and welcome event that is not explicable by natural or scientific laws and is therefore considered to be the work of a divine agency', or 'a highly improbable or extraordinary event, development, or accomplishment that brings very welcome consequences, such as a miracle drug', or 'an amazing product or achievement, or an outstanding example of something'.[18]

Every major religion and every culture has a long list of events that the followers regard as miracles. 'Abdu'l-Bahá cautions:

> These accounts cannot be a decisive proof and testimony for all, since the hearer might say that they are not factually true . . . a miracle may be a proof for the eyewitness, but even then he might not be sure whether what he beheld was a true miracle or mere sorcery. Indeed, extraordinary feats have also been attributed to certain magicians.[19]

Creation is itself the greatest of miracles. The continuous guidance for mankind through the coming of each Manifestation is a recurring miracle. In this day, Bahá'u'lláh encouraged education, learning, and a culture of inquiry. That represents the spirit of this age, and the past century has seen an unprecedented and miraculous explosion of scientific and intellectual advancement. It is claimed by many people that this is a result of an infusion of the divine spirit of inquiry that comes with the Revelation of Bahá'u'lláh.

'Abdu'l-Bahá further explained: 'Moreover, most of the miracles attributed to the Prophets have an inner meaning.'[20] In a culture of learning, it is appropriate to probe for those inner meanings and not be content with a literal or surface explanation.

The first recorded miracle of Jesus, as the Christos, was at a wedding feast.[21] Literally, it makes an interesting story, but looking at it metaphorically is even more interesting. In those days, the weddings of prominent people would last for several days and feature a gathering of the most profound thinkers discussing philosophical matters. The fact that Jesus was invited indicates that He had been recognized as a profound thinker, despite His youth. In mystical language, wine, an extract from the grape that resembles the human brain, is frequently used to represent the highest level of thought or spirit. In this instance it can be inferred that Christ changed water (ordinary conversation) into wine or the most elevated and profound thoughts. In another passage He proclaimed: 'no man putteth new wine into old bottles; else the new wine will burst the bottles, and be spilled, and the bottles shall perish.'[22] This could be taken as indicating that the existing religious system and establishment would be incapable of containing the new spirit and truths He was bringing to mankind.

All four of the Gospels recount the story of the loaves and the fishes; it was indeed a profound miracle to feed so many with so little.[23] There may be another explanation. In those days it was common for people to carry a little food for themselves to eat when they were gone for the day. It is possible that an even greater miracle took place. When people saw how many people were there and how little food was available, each one opened his own heart to share the precious food he had carried for himself and the multitude was fed with food left over. Another miracle is that all over the world there are places inspired by that event, often called 'loaves and fishes', dedicated to feeding the hungry.

Many religious traditions have stories of raising the dead. Spectacular though that may be, the greater miracle is resurrecting someone from spiritual death.

These alternative explanations are not authoritative and are mentioned to illustrate that other meanings may be found that are different from and may even surpass the first and obvious explanation. All it takes is a little probing and looking beyond the literal. A major part of the foundation of a culture of learning is to look beyond the apparent and generally accepted explanation to find hidden realities.

Justice

One final thought here concerns the profound relationship between justice and a culture of learning. In the *Hidden Words* Bahá'u'lláh reveals:

> The best beloved of all things in My sight is Justice; turn not away therefrom if thou desirest Me, and neglect it not that I may confide in thee. By its aid thou shalt see with thine own eyes and not through the eyes of others, and shalt know of thine own knowledge and not through the knowledge of thy neighbour. Ponder this in thy heart; how it behooveth thee to be. Verily justice is My gift to thee and the sign of My loving-kindness. Set it then before thine eyes.[24]

What is more essential for a culture of learning than finding truth for yourself, with your own eyes? Furthermore, a culture of learning leads directly to its application in arts, science, work and leisure time activities. We will explore these in the next chapter.

15
Arts, Science, Work and Leisure

It is permissible to study sciences and arts, but such sciences as are useful and would redound to the progress and advancement of the people. Thus hath it been decreed by Him Who is the Ordainer, the All-Wise.
Bahá'u'lláh[1]

The word 'science' as used by both Bahá'u'lláh and 'Abdu'l-Bahá means any serious study. That would include history, economics, the so-called social sciences and philosophy. Both science and art are energized by inspiration and motivation. In general, science wells slightly more from rational thought and the arts spring slightly more from intuitive faculties. Obviously, both are important.

The relationship between religion and science has been a matter of controversy for ages. Perspectives from different geographical regions, cultures and historical epochs range from open conflict to harmony. Some people speculate that they are enquiries about different things; others say they are different perspectives of the same thing; still others say that while one deals with the nature of God, the other explores His handiwork, both of which can lead to a more profound worship of God or lead to severe scepticism. Both approaches are filled with acknowledged mysteries. There is a difference of opinion as to whether these mysteries should be explored, or accepted and left alone.

For Bahá'ís there is no question about the essential harmony of the two. 'Abdu'l-Bahá said, 'religion must reconcile and be in harmony with science and reason. If the religious beliefs of mankind are contrary to science and opposed to reason, they are none other than superstitions and without divine authority.'[2] Science, on the other hand, without the moral authority of religion can become a diabolical monster. It was Hitler's best educated, scientific minds that designed the gas chambers for the Holocaust. Atomic energy is probably the greatest single example of how scientific discoveries and developments can lead either to good or evil.

Science can show how things work, but without a moral dimension it can easily lead mankind astray. Some of the earliest records of a human presence on earth are through the arts. Visual and performing arts have been part of the human experience since before the dawn of recorded history. From paintings in caves to pottery with artistic designs and other artefacts, our ancestors left clear messages. Among other things, art stated: 'We were here. We had minds and spirits.' But it takes science to determine the significance of these artistic expressions.

One archeologist told me that the artefacts and carvings found in ancient Eskimo sites showed weather patterns. When there were few ivory carvings, this fact indicated severe weather conditions. During somewhat milder times, people could and did devote themselves to art.

'Abdu'l-Bahá states that the arts signify a major distinction between man and other creatures. He said, 'The arts we now enjoy are the expressions of that marvellous reality [discovering the reality of things]. The animal is bereft of them because these conscious realities are peculiar to the human spirit.'[3]

The arts have been at the forefront of religious expression at least as long as there has been organized religion. Sometimes, religious institutions encouraged art. At other times it ranged from being merely tolerated to being considered frivolous, to being denounced as the work of the Devil.

In this Dispensation there is clear and unambiguous affirmation of the value of the arts and sciences and definition of their proper use. In the *Kitáb-i-Aqdas*, Bahá'u'lláh wrote, 'We have permitted you to read such sciences as are profitable unto you, not such as end in idle disputation.' A note clarifying this passage states, 'The Bahá'í Writings enjoin the acquisition of knowledge and the study of the arts and sciences. Bahá'ís are admonished to respect people of learning and accomplishment, and are warned against the pursuit of studies that are productive only of futile wrangling.'[4]

Several things stand out. One is that equal weight is given to the arts and sciences. Both are not only permitted, but essential. Another is a matter of focus. They should be *useful* and lead to *progress* and *advancement*. This also suggests a level of maturity expected for this age. To a large extent, it is up to the discretion of the artists and scholars to determine what is of value and what is 'idle disputation'.

The importance of both for personal as well as cultural development was indicated by 'Abdu'l-Bahá when he spoke to some children: 'May you become learned in sciences, acquire the arts and crafts, prove to be useful members of human society and assist the progress of human civilization.'[5] Furthermore, their importance in education as a tool for civilization was specifically called to attention by Bahá'u'lláh:

> At the outset of every endeavour, it is incumbent to look to the end of it. Of all the arts and sciences, set the children to studying those which will result in advantage to man, will ensure his progress and elevate his rank. Thus the noisome odours of lawlessness will be dispelled, and thus through the high endeavours of the nation's leaders, all will live cradled, secure and in peace.[6]

'Abdu'l-Bahá even advocated the arts and sciences as a vehicle to advance gender equality:

> The realities of things have been revealed in this radiant

century, and that which is true must come to the surface. Among these realities is the principle of the equality of man and woman – equal rights and prerogatives in all things appertaining to humanity. Bahá'u'lláh declared this reality over fifty years ago. But while this principle of equality is true, it is likewise true that woman must prove her capacity and aptitude, must show forth the evidences of equality. She must become proficient in the arts and sciences and prove by her accomplishments that her abilities and powers have merely been latent.[7]

The art of music is one area that has been viewed differently in different cultures. 'Abdu'l-Bahá pointed out that 'Among certain nations of the East, music was considered reprehensible, but in this new age the Manifest Light hath, in His holy Tablets, specifically proclaimed that music, sung or played, is spiritual food for soul and heart.'[8]

A band director once commented, 'Teach a boy to blow a horn and he will never blow a bank.' Today, in many inner cities with high crime rates, music has proved to be a powerful agent helping youngsters rise above their negative surroundings.

In the *Kitáb-i-Aqdas*, Bahá'u'lláh gave a specific caution:

We have made it lawful for you to listen to music and singing. Take heed, however, lest listening thereto should cause you to overstep the bounds of propriety and dignity. Let your joy be the joy born of My Most Great Name, a Name that bringeth rapture to the heart, and filleth with ecstasy the minds of all who have drawn nigh unto God. We, verily, have made music as a ladder for your souls, a means whereby they may be lifted up unto the realm on high; make it not, therefore, as wings to self and passion. Truly, We are loath to see you numbered with the foolish.[9]

Morally, music is neither good nor bad, but can be either. Ladders can take one either up or down. Modern music is a mix of music that is uplifting and that which is degrading. Much of the martial music of totalitarian regimes and some of today's popular music bring out beastly tendencies. It is up to the individual to select music that uplifts and avoid whatever degrades. A further distinction was made by Shoghi Effendi in a letter written on his behalf:

> In the teachings there is nothing against dancing, but the friends should remember that the standard of Bahá'u'lláh is modesty and chastity. The atmosphere of modern dance halls, where so much smoking and drinking and promiscuity goes on, is very bad, but decent dances are not harmful in themselves. There is certainly no harm in classical dancing or learning dancing in school. There is also no harm in taking part in dramas. Likewise in cinema acting. The harmful thing, nowadays, is not the art itself but the unfortunate corruption which often surrounds these arts. As Bahá'ís we need avoid none of the arts, but acts and the atmosphere that sometimes go with these professions we should avoid.[10]

In another letter written on behalf of Shoghi Effendi there is a caution against applying rigid standards:

> Music, as one of the arts, is a natural cultural development, and the Guardian does not feel that there should be any cultivation of 'Bahá'í Music' any more than we are trying to develop a Bahá'í school of painting or writing. The believers are free to paint, write and compose as their talents guide them. If music is written, incorporating the sacred writings, the friends are free to make use of it, but it should never be considered a requirement at Bahá'í meetings to have such music. The further away the friends keep from any set forms, the better, for they must realize that the Cause is absolutely

universal, and what might seem a beautiful addition to their mode of celebrating a Feast, etc., would perhaps fall on the ears of people of another country as unpleasant sounds – and vice versa. As long as they have music for its own sake it is all right, but they should not consider it Bahá'í music.[11]

The most memorable and uplifting Feasts, Holy Days and other gatherings have been those in which the arts have been incorporated. One Feast stands out in my memory where a few soft musical chords were played after each reading during the devotional portion. It provided a meditative atmosphere to reflect on what was just read. Obviously, this would not suit everyone's taste. There are a variety of ways to create an appropriate atmosphere and it is important to do whatever contributes to that.

Bahá'u'lláh stated that there is a connection between this world and the next through the arts and sciences. Referring to souls that have gone on into the next world, He wrote:

> The light which these souls radiate is responsible for the progress of the world and the advancement of its peoples. They are like unto leaven which leaveneth the world of being, and constitute the animating force through which the arts and wonders of the world are made manifest.[12]

I'm sure I am not the only Bahá'í who, while trying to do something creative, has felt assistance beyond myself.

Finally, there is this statement of encouragement:

> Let the loved ones of God, whether young or old, whether male or female, each according to his capabilities, bestir themselves and spare no efforts to acquire the various current branches of knowledge, both spiritual and secular, and of the arts.[13]

Work

The beasts of the fields and even the tiny insects spend most of their time foraging for a living. It seems that toiling for survival has been an incessant demand of life on earth for all creatures. Bahá'u'lláh elevated work from the strictly material realm. First, He confirmed the need to work. Then, He made it sacred. In the *Kitáb-i-Aqdas*. He wrote:

> O people of Bahá! It is incumbent upon each one of you to engage in some occupation – such as a craft, a trade or the like. We have exalted your engagement in such work to the rank of worship of the one true God. Reflect, O people, on the grace and blessings of your Lord, and yield Him thanks at eventide and dawn. Waste not your hours in idleness and sloth, but occupy yourselves with what will profit you and others. Thus hath it been decreed in this Tablet from whose horizon hath shone the day-star of wisdom and utterance. The most despised of men in the sight of God are they who sit and beg. Hold ye fast unto the cord of means and place your trust in God, the Provider of all means.[14]

Not only did He condemn idleness, He forbids begging. This is different from revealed religions of the past in which mendicancy was an acceptable part of normal life.

How does this fit with 'Abdu'l-Bahá's legendary giving to the poor? In Akka, on Fridays he would go to the Mosque and give alms to the poor in the Islamic tradition. During His trip to America, His visit to the Bowery is often told. He got a large bag of coins and freely gave a coin or two to each man in the Bowery. Is this enabling and a form of encouragement that contradicts the condemnation of begging?

Two things stand out. In the first place, 'Abdu'l-Bahá generally did not give money to those who asked or begged for a handout. He selected those to whom He would give. Another key point: 'Abdu'l-Bahá, as Centre of the Covenant, was Himself an institution. His actions demonstrated the fact that institutions have a responsibility for the poor.

There is an obligation to give to the poor without encouraging begging. This can be done in several ways. Giving money to a bona fide charity is excellent. Some Bahá'ís will take a beggar asking for money into a store or restaurant to buy food, paying for something to eat without giving money directly – sometimes to the disappointment of the beggar, who may have had other plans for the money.

Helping someone with school expenses, or people facing emergencies, is appropriate. It is especially helpful to ask them not to pay back, but pay forward – that is, helping someone else as needed.

At this stage in the development of the Faith, the Bahá'í institutions have such meagre resources that giving all they have to charity would not make a dent in the problem of poverty. That does not mean poverty is something to ignore. One course of action is to direct those in need, or take them, to institutions (whether government, religious or secular), that are in a better position to address their material needs. Serious as the immediate problems may be, only the establishment of the teachings of Bahá'u'lláh will bring long-term solutions, and only Bahá'ís can bring that about.

According to the Writings, this is a responsibility that cannot be ignored. Once again, there is a direct blessing and protection from the Covenant. The Universal House of Justice sets the pace in two ways. Currently it has an International Fund, used at its discretion for specific situations. When the time is right, it will let believers know when and how to take a different course of action.

In the meantime it is better to help individuals find some means to earn a livelihood. Bahá'u'lláh wrote:

> that man should know his own self and recognize that which

leadeth unto loftiness or lowliness, glory or abasement, wealth or poverty. Having attained the stage of fulfilment and reached his maturity, man standeth in need of wealth, and such wealth as he acquireth through crafts or professions is commendable and praiseworthy in the estimation of men of wisdom, and especially in the eyes of servants who dedicate themselves to the education of the world and to the edification of its peoples.[15]

He also wrote, 'To engage in some profession is highly commendable, for when occupied with work one is less likely to dwell on the unpleasant aspects of life.'[16]

Leisure time

One of the characteristics of Western civilization is that many people have more discretionary time than ever before in history. The challenge of using it beneficially is greater than most people realize. Advertising today is full of lures for self-indulgence. Ads are couched in terms suggesting that if you go on this trip, or buy this or that, you will find the secret to happiness. The uncomfortable truth is that leisure time can become a waste-time that leads to dissatisfaction, a desire for more diversions and leisure time, and away from spiritual and humanitarian activities.

In His book *The Secret of Divine Civilization*, 'Abdu'l-Bahá highlighted the problem of non-productive time. While addressed to Persia, its truths are universal. He wrote:

> How long will your torpor and lethargy last? . . .How does it seem, when your neighbours are at work by day and night with their whole hearts, providing for their advancement, their honour and prosperity, that you, in your ignorant fanaticism, are busy only with your quarrels and antipathies, your indulgences and appetites and empty dreams?[17]

ARTS, SCIENCE, WORK AND LEISURE

In *The World Order of Bahá'u'lláh*, Shoghi Effendi lists 'the lapse into luxurious indulgence'[18] as one of the hallmarks of this age of social deterioration.

Bahá'ís who are walking in the light of the Covenant have found an endless number of ways to make creative and spiritual use of their time. So much so, that a common lament is that more time is not available for the Faith. More than one new Bahá'í has complained that before they embraced the Faith, they had more vacation time than they knew what to do with. Once they became Bahá'ís, they found there was not enough time to do all they wanted.

The Bahá'í Writings give some insights. Bahá'u'lláh spoke of the true meaning of 'Resurrection', and stepping into 'the realm of complete detachment'. This is not a matter of forsaking everything in pursuit of some spiritual ideal. Instead, it is related to action: 'One righteous work performed in this Day, equalleth all the virtuous acts which for myriads of centuries men have practised.' He went on to state that those who forsake all earthly pleasure, in the name of piety, miss the point. 'They deny themselves every moment of leisure, and utterly ignore Him, Who is the Essence of all learning, and the one Object of their quest!'[19]

Leisure time is not a bad thing. There is a saying from the days of bow and arrow hunting, 'Even the strongest bow needs to be unbent at times.' There is no better way to build relationships and trust with other people than by spending leisure time together. How many people have been led to Bahá'u'lláh by a fishing trip, working on a recreational project, or through a quilting or singing project?

Napoleon Bergamaschi was a pioneer to the Yup'ik Eskimo village of Savoonga on St Lawrence Island in the Bering Sea. I was there for the formation of its Spiritual Assembly, even though Napoleon had been killed in a car accident before then. His simple teaching materials were still visible: prayer books and pinochle decks – all well worn. He used the leisure card game of pinochle to lead those precious souls into the Faith.

The passing of the Greatest Holy Leaf, was a great sorrow for Shoghi Effendi. In her biography we find, 'The Guardian feels her loss tremendously because the greatest part of his leisure hours he used to spend in her company.'[20]

The standard is clear:

> In their homes, in their hours of relaxation and leisure, in the daily contact of business transactions, in the association of their children, whether in their study-classes, their playgrounds, and club-rooms, in short, under all possible circumstances, however insignificant they appear, the community of the followers of Bahá'u'lláh should satisfy themselves that in the eyes of the world at large and in the sight of their vigilant Master they are the living witnesses of those truths which He fondly cherished and tirelessly championed to the very end of His days.[21]

When asked if recreational games were bad, 'Abdu'l-Bahá replied, 'No, some games are innocent, and if pursued for pastime there is no harm. But there is danger that pastime may degenerate into waste of time. Waste of time is not acceptable in the Cause of God.'[22]

It is a question of balance. What could be better than using the arts, science, work and leisure time in pursuit of socio-economic development projects? The next chapter will explore this.

16

Socio-Economic Development: Bahá'í-inspired Projects

> *All social action seeks to apply the teachings and principles of the Faith to improve some aspect of the social or economic life of a population, however modestly. Such endeavours are distinguished, then, by their stated purpose to promote the material well-being of the population, in addition to its spiritual welfare. That the world civilization now on humanity's horizon must achieve a dynamic coherence between the material and spiritual requirements of life is central to the Bahá'í teachings. Clearly this ideal has profound implications for the nature of any social action pursued by Bahá'ís, whatever its scope and range of influence.*
> The Universal House of Justice[1]

Even before their respective ministries, the Twin Manifestations – the Báb and Bahá'u'lláh – exemplified the importance of both economic justice and social commitment. The Báb was born in Shiraz to a prominent family of merchants. When He was a teenager, He was put in charge of the family business in Bushihr where He was noted for His integrity, honesty and piety.

Years later, when first a prisoner in Máh-Kú, He was not allowed visitors. When restrictions were eased, some of His followers could visit Him and were eager to do anything to serve their Lord.

In this unusual circumstance He stated two fundamental economic principles:

One day the Báb asked that some honey be purchased for Him. The price at which it had been bought seemed to Him exorbitant. He refused it and said: 'Honey of a superior quality could no doubt have been purchased at a lower price. I who am your example have been a merchant by profession. It behoves you in all your transactions to follow in My way. You must neither defraud your neighbour nor allow him to defraud you. Such was the way of your Master.' The shrewdest and ablest of men were unable to deceive Him, nor did He on His part choose to act ungenerously towards the meanest and most helpless of creatures. He insisted that the attendant who had made that purchase should return and bring back to Him a honey superior in quality and cheaper in price.[2]

At the time of the Báb's Declaration, Bahá'u'lláh was living in Núr, not far from Tehran. One of the Báb's first actions was to have Mullá Ḥusayn deliver a Tablet to an unidentified person, someone of 'transcendent holiness'. Mullá Ḥusayn had only a description of His character, not a name. Yet, he found a man from Núr to whom he explained his mission. This man gave the following description of the One Whom the Báb intended, Mírzá Ḥusayn 'Alí Núrí, who later came to be known as Bahá'u'lláh. He was known for 'His virtuous life, His high attainments, His loving-kindness and liberality'. When asked about His occupation, the man said, 'He cheers the disconsolate and feeds the hungry.' When asked further about His rank and position, the reply was, 'He has none . . . apart from befriending the poor and the stranger.'[3]

The lives of the Báb and Bahá'u'lláh illustrate two responsibilities under the Covenant: economic responsibility and serving social needs. 'Abdu'l-Bahá stated it this way:

> The essence of the Bahá'í spirit is that, in order to establish a better social order and economic condition, there must be allegiance to the laws and principles of government.[4]

He also said,

> The fundamentals of the whole economic condition are divine in nature and are associated with the world of the heart and spirit. This is fully explained in the Baháʼí teaching, and without knowledge of its principles no improvement in the economic state can be realized.[5]

Baháʼís frequently talk about a 'spiritual solution to the economic problem' even though there is little in the Writings that specifically addresses that issue. What is known is that a major shift in thinking is needed. That change goes far beyond existing economic systems or models. The Writings focus on spiritual realities. As the Guardian explained:

> There are practically no technical teachings on economics in the Cause, such as banking, the price system, and others. The Cause is not an economic system, nor [can] its Founders be considered as having been technical economists. The contribution of the Faith to this subject is essentially indirect, as it consists of the application of spiritual principles to our present-day economic system. Baháʼu'lláh has given us a few basic principles which should guide future Baháʼí economists in establishing such institutions which will adjust the economic relationships of the world . . .
> Social inequality is the inevitable outcome of the natural inequality of man. Human beings are different in ability and should, therefore, be different in their social and economic standing. Extremes of wealth and poverty should, however, be abolished.[6]

There is an understandable desire on the part of many Baháʼís to establish social and economic justice RIGHT NOW! In response to a question on this point, the Guardian's secretary wrote on his behalf eight decades ago:

> Shoghi Effendi fully sympathizes with the desire of some of the members to . . . find ways and means to put into practice the economic teachings of the Cause, as explained in some of the recorded Writings and Sayings of Bahá'u'lláh and the Master. But he believes that the time is not yet ripe for such activities. First we have to study the economic teachings in the light of modern problems more thoroughly so that we may advocate what the Founders of the Faith say and not what we conjecture from Their Writings. There is great difference between sounding a great general principle and finding its application to actual prevailing conditions.
>
> Secondly, the Cause is not financially in a position to launch itself in such undertakings at present. Such plans need great financial backing to be worked out in a permanent form . . . For the present we have to consolidate our basic institutions and spread the teachings and spirit of the Faith among the public.[7]

Today, grassroots initiatives, with the encouragement of the Universal House of Justice, can and do make significant inroads on both economic and social matters. They are also early experiments and models for the future. While the Bahá'í institutions retain overall guidance and encourage socio-economic development, it is not appropriate for them to expend significant resources on these matters. Individual believers who see a need are the ones to conceive and execute solutions. The Writings give both inspiration and guidance, but the needs, identified by individuals, are addressed locally.

The scope of both the challenges and the needed changes can be seen in secular efforts to assist developing countries. For six decades the industrialized countries of the world have provided assistance to impoverished nations. Yet the gap between the have and have-not nations has increased. Why? Granted, there is corruption, inefficiency and incompetence, but that alone does not explain the growing gap.

If country A helps country B to increase its growth rate to 3 per cent, that is good. However, if, at the same time, country A's economy increases by 3½ per cent, it means that even though gains have been made by country B, the gap gets bigger.

The problem is not sinister; it is the simple fact that creativity, innovation and success beget more creativity, innovation and success. The most advanced country is bound to continue to grow more rapidly than the one lagging behind. Material catch-up does not seem possible.

Even if the rate of growth for country B is higher, the size of the economy of country A means that the gap will still widen. If A grows at a rate of 3 per cent and B grows at 4 per cent, the gap still increases. That is, 3 per cent of 1,000 is 30, while 4 per cent of 100 is only 4. So the largest economy grows more, even when the growth rate for the smaller one is higher. In order for country B to catch up with country A, it needs to exceed the growth rate of country A by a substantial amount over an extended period of time. That is yet to be seen and is highly unlikely.

The real problem is that this is *an attempt to solve spiritual problems with material solutions.* In our materialistic and economic intensive world there is an excessive focus on material gain rather than quality of life. Rephrased, this means that today even well-meaning people apply economic solutions to spiritual problems, instead of spiritual solutions to economic problems. It doesn't work.

The definition of success is part of the trouble. In the Western world, success, described as the 'bottom line', is in financial terms – meaning net profit. If the standard of the bottom line was seen in terms of service delivered, the results would be different.

Adherence to the Covenant provides the needed shift in thinking. This is demonstrated in Bahá'í-inspired socio-economic projects. These differ from most projects undertaken by governments or other social agencies, be they for-profit or not-for-profit, because in most Bahá'í-inspired projects spiritual principles are the highest priority. They are generally distinctive for the following reasons:

> They are based on the application of spiritual principles. Many projects by other organizations have political or economic concerns as well as humanitarian objectives.
> Rectitude of conduct marks all activities. Corruption has sabotaged far too many otherwise well-intended secular or governmental projects.
> Consultation is the primary decision-making tool. The key element is that once the decision is made, everyone supports it, regardless of previous views. There is a long list of projects carried out by public and private development agencies that have been abandoned or severely compromised because participants could not work together.

Profit is a tainted word in some people's minds, yet it is essential for survival. Even so-called 'not-for-profits' need to make a profit in order to provide services, let alone pay bills and grow. Bahá'í-inspired projects need resources. Enough money must be generated or the enterprise goes out of business, no matter how noble and worthy. There is usually a substantial drain of both energy and finances from those starting a project. Bahá'í funds are rarely available, nor should they be; there are already too many demands on them. Even with meagre resources, these Bahá'í-inspired underfunded, grass-roots projects are one means of making profits tools for service.

Sometimes, individuals with means see the value of a project and provide funds. Many schools around the world were started this way. In some cases grants are available from governments or other institutions. When profits are generated, they can contribute to the ongoing success. In the Netherlands, the Bahá'ís own a wonderful summer school facility. When Bahá'ís are not using it, it is rented out to other organizations. It is self-sustaining.

During the 19th century the standard for financial transactions was *caveat emptor* ('let the buyer beware'). During the 20th century most companies realized that in order to be profitable, they needed to deliver service. Service became a tool for profitability. Economic stability in the 21st century is dependent upon the next step of reversing priorities so that profit becomes a tool for service.

The importance of evaluating results cannot be overemphasized. Bahá'í-inspired initiatives providing services also need to be measured. It is foolish to assume that goals or objectives are being met; an impartial assessment is needed to determine if services should be sustained, modified or abandoned. Assessing effectiveness is part of a spiritual solution to an economic problem. Only then can difficult decisions be made for necessary improvements and adjustments. It is a mistake to assume that the project is serving its intended purpose without setting specific goals and measuring its progress. In the secular world, business leaders such as Bill Gates and a few others have made a major impact by making evaluation an important part of noble projects.

In its 2010 Riḍván Message, the Universal House of Justice pointed out several principles to keep in mind in relation to socio-economic enterprises that are Bahá'í-inspired:

- The fundamental need is to provide education.
- The primary concern should be capacity building. Social change is not a project that one group of people carries out for the benefit of another.
- Action must be in terms of human and other resources available within the respective area.
- Projects should begin on a modest scale and be allowed to grow as the capacity of the community develops.
- Effective social action serves to enrich participation in community discourses.

➢ The success of projects is not to be measured by the number of new believers. Enrolments are not the purpose. Sincerity in this respect is imperative.

In 2003 the Bahá'í International Community published a booklet called *For the Betterment of the World*. That brochure outlined a worldwide approach to social and economic development. Its opening paragraph states:

> The Bahá'í community's commitment to social and economic development is rooted in its sacred scriptures, which state that all human beings 'have been created to carry forward an ever-advancing civilization'. Bahá'u'lláh wrote, 'Be anxiously concerned with the needs of the age ye live in, and center your deliberations on its exigencies and requirements'. Fundamental to Bahá'í belief is the conviction that every person, every people, every nation has a part to play in building a peaceful and prosperous society . . .
>
> Bahá'í experience in the field of development stretches back to the beginnings of the Faith in Iran during the nineteenth century. In that country, the community of adherents were able, in just a few generations, to advance from a population consisting largely of illiterate villagers to one whose members were in the forefront of many areas of endeavor. By 1973, for example, Iranian Bahá'ís had achieved a 100 percent literacy rate among women followers under the age of 40, in contrast to a national literacy rate among women of less than 20 percent.[8]

The booklet further stresses the point that since proselytizing is prohibited, 'development projects are not conducted for the purpose of public relations or as a means of converting people'.[9]

In an email to me dated 19 March 2013, the Office of Social and Economic Development said,

SOCIO-ECONOMIC DEVELOPMENT: BAHÁ'Í-INSPIRED PROJECTS

> ... at present, the vast majority of Bahá'í social and economic development efforts are small-scale activities, generally of fixed duration, that are carried out at the grassroots by individuals or groups of believers who are striving to apply the Teachings to improve some aspect of the life of their communities. Over time, some of these grassroots initiatives may grow in size and complexity, as circumstances and resources allow, and begin to function as sustained social and economic development projects. In certain cases, a Bahá'í development organization may be established, which generally carries out several lines of action in a coherent fashion and influences a wider segment of the population. Our Office does not maintain a comprehensive list of Bahá'í development projects, of which there are several thousand around the world at any one time.

In its 2015 Riḍván Message, the Universal House of Justice announced a development that will better apply the teachings to social and economic issues. It announced a seven-member International Advisory Board to assist the Office of Social and Economic Development.

While many of the thousands of ongoing projects are of short duration, the Office stated there were approximately 400 sustained projects in various parts of the world. A few of these are sponsored by Bahá'í institutions, but the majority are initiatives that one or a few individuals conceived. Here are some of the kinds of projects that are under way.[10]

> ➤ **Literacy:** Throughout the world, groups and individuals have worked on projects to improve the literacy rate wherever they are. In Guyana the "On the Wings of Words" project has trained more than 3,000 volunteers who have reached more than 10,000 young people from villages. In St Lucia, there was pride in the eyes of a woman who had been illiterate. When a Bahá'í taught

her to read and she read a prayer at a Bahá'í Feast for the first time, her face glowed.
- **Schools:** In many parts of the world, public education is inadequate or non-existent. Bahá'ís working as individuals or in groups have started many schools, from elementary to university level. In one primary school launched in Africa, it was not possible to tell a child's age since birth records were non-existent. Young children have short arms compared to the size of their heads. To see if a child was old enough to start school, the child was to reach an arm over its head. If the fingers touched the top of the ear on the opposite side the head, the child was considered old enough for school.*
- **Moral education:** Morality is not restricted to any religion. Bahá'ís have had great success in teaching universal values and improving the quality of life wherever this is done. Education without a moral rudder is dangerous. Illiterate people do not design weapons of mass destruction or create elaborate Ponzi schemes. The Bahá'í Academy in Panchgani, India has been highly successful in designing and presenting workshops on 'Universal Human Values' to universities and colleges in the area. These, in turn, start study groups of students and faculty to conduct workshops developed by the academy.
- **Elimination of prejudice:** Bahá'ís frequently work in concert with other organizations to advance racial harmony. They often have leadership roles in various human rights observances, such as Martin Luther King Day in the United States. They are also at the forefront of special events for Race Unity Day.
- **Advancement of women:** Bahá'ís are prominent in both individual activities and working with established groups. Some Bahá'ís routinely seek to support

---

* It was a thrill for the author to see one of this school's first students cast a ballot at an election for the Universal House of Justice.

businesses and professions that are run by women, as a means of encouragement. Bahá'ís have been involved with micro-lending projects, providing small loans, generally to rural women, to help them with income-producing crafts and services. This has proved to be an important step away from poverty.

- ➢ **Environment:** This is another area in which Bahá'ís work with other individuals and existing organizations, as well as taking personal steps intended to reduce environmental degradation. Several Bahá'í families who own bed and breakfast facilities have extensive gardens. Their intent is to produce as much as possible for their guests while minimizing environmental impact. Many young Bahá'ís enroll in environmental studies in universities. It is not unusual to find a Bahá'í in a leadership position in environmental organizations.
- ➢ **Agriculture:** Bahá'ís have started public gardening projects throughout the world from Bucharest, Romania to the mountains in California. This is another area that attracts young Bahá'ís in academic choices.
- ➢ **Health:** A number of Bahá'í health workers volunteer their services with organizations involved with health in developing countries. "Health for Humanity" in the United States was started by two Bahá'í physicians in 1992. It partners with local institutions to help communities around the world build the capacity to meet their own health needs. Other health projects have been started by Bahá'í medical professionals. This includes a Bahá'í in Nasik, India who owns and operates a homeopathic college and hospital. His brother owns and operates a nearby school. Another Bahá'í, in Bangalore, owns a medical clinic. Both families are where they are because their forebears answered an appeal from the Guardian to pioneer to places where there were no Bahá'ís.

In addition to these sustained projects, there are a great number of stable and sustainable organizations created to promote Bahá'í principles. Most projects were launched through the personal initiative of individuals, rather than institutions, sometimes by a single person with an idea. At other times, a number of people combine resources, expertise, networking and other skills. Among the significant organizations are:

> ➢ **Nur University:** Opened in 1985 in Santa Cruz, Bolivia, it has become one of the country's most prominent universities, featuring a wide range of disciplines, including residential, semi-residential and distance learning programmes. It emphasizes service to the community. Among its offerings are participatory adult literacy, youth empowerment, and village health care.
> ➢ **Barli Development Institute for Rural Women:** In 1985 the National Spiritual Assembly of India founded the Barli Institute for vocational training. Barli is the name of the central pillar that supports tribal houses, and women are the central pillars of society. Based in Indore, India, it has trained over 6,700 young tribal women from more than 600 villages, providing skills for them to become agents of change for the advancement of women. Many of the arriving students are semiliterate; nearly all go home functionally literate. There is practical training and experience in: personality development; literacy; health and hygiene; vocational training; the environment; cooking with solar cookers; and strengthening family relationships. About 95 per cent of the students completing the course of studies use their new skills to generate income. About half of these set up small businesses. The others become employed, work for themselves or assist their families in business or farming.[11]
> ➢ **FUNDAEC:** In 1974 FUNDAEC was established in

Colombia. Among its purposes is enabling local communities to establish the institutions and structure to carry out local objectives. Alternative systems of production, viable systems of formal education and the strengthening of local economies have been started by FUNDAEC. The impact has been felt in many South American countries.

➢ **Tahirih Justice Center:** This center, headquartered in the United States, was established to assist women and girls facing dire and/or abusive situations. In 1997, about five years after the founder, as a law student, assisted a girl in need, the Center was formally organized and incorporated as a non-profit organization. Over the years, thousands of women from many countries and cultures who have faced serious abuse have received assistance. The Center networks with other organizations, mainly legal firms, willing to do pro-bono work for cases referred to them.

➢ **New Era Development Institute:** Located in central western India, NEDI was started in 1987. Its driving force has been the conviction that sustainable development is most likely to take place when individuals and communities are empowered to make informed decisions about their own lives. One- and two-year certificates are available for vocational or small business courses and teacher training. NEDI encourages both cultural identity and appreciation of unity in diversity. Local initiatives have been started for environmental protection, sanitation, health, child education and small-scale income generation. Students trained at NEDI are in high demand throughout India.

➢ **Badi Foundation:** Since 1990 the Badi Foundation has been networking with similar organizations throughout the world, but mainly in China. A major project has been the School of the Nations in Macau. A focus is to help people identify local needs. It offers training in social service projects.

> **William Mmutle Masetlha Foundation:** Operating since 1983 in Zambia, its focus involves vocational training in rural technology, farming, food production, arts and crafts, health and hygiene and other practical skills. From its beginning the Foundation has been committed to the equality of men and women. All its programmes retain that principle as an underlying objective. Its Primary Health Care Project has trained more than 150 community workers to promote preventive health measures in their own communities, increase the level of immunization coverage and diffuse general health information with an emphasis on HIV/AIDS and malaria prevention. It also has a one-year tutorial programme to reinforce language and scientific skills and knowledge in primary schools. The aim is to increase the capacity of rural youth in Zambia to pursue higher-level education.

> **Parent University:** Motivation for this enterprise started in 1998 when racial strife was tearing the school system apart in Savannah, Georgia, United States. In 2000 it was formally established as a non-profit organization with a four-fold objective to: maximize student learning; enable parents to teach one another; involve whole families in the learning process as a unit; and provide nurturing support and guidance so that families can realize their own success. Too often school officials and parents were wary of one another and each group viewed the other with suspicion. After just a few years of operation, it was reported: 'Schools were once enemy territory where they (parents) entered only when their kids were in trouble. Not any more. They're (the parents) committed to their children's education. One mother reported, "Being a single mom working, trying to provide for my daughter, it has been somewhat hard trying to make it.

You always feel that you are alone. Being a part of Parent University you feel that you are not alone.'"[12]

In the summer of 2015, Fortune magazine named Michael O'Neal, the Bahá'í who conceived and launched the Parent University Program, as one of 55 'Heroes' for this work. The selected 55 were chosen from among the 27 million employees of the Fortune 500 top companies.

These are just a few examples of what Bahá'ís are doing to provide spiritual solutions to economic and social problems.

In its 1985 document *The Promise of World Peace*, the Universal House of Justice wrote:

> The inordinate disparity between rich and poor, a source of acute suffering, keeps the world in a state of instability, virtually on the brink of war. Few societies have dealt effectively with this situation. The solution calls for the combined application of spiritual, moral and practical approaches.[13]

While that document was a plea to the world, it is individual Bahá'ís who are leading the way to its implementation. This calls to mind the following observation by 'Abdu'l-Bahá:

> In short, O ye believers of God! Exalt your effort and magnify your aims. His Holiness Christ says: 'Blessed are the poor, for theirs shall be the Kingdom of Heaven.'[14] In other words: Blessed are the nameless and traceless poor, for they are the leaders of mankind. Likewise it is said in the Qur'án: 'And We desire to show favor to those who were brought low in the land, and to make them spiritual leaders among men, and to make of them Our heirs.'[15] Or, we wish to grant a favor to the impotent souls and suffer them to become the inheritors of the Messengers and Prophets.[16]

This is another area in which change does not come from those in authority, or the existing power structure. This change takes place 'through the poor and lowly'.¹⁷ These 'poor and lowly' are a cross-section of mankind. They are the ones who build Baháʼí institutions. These 'impotent souls' are also at the forefront of applying spiritual principles to economic issues.

Ordinary folks, like you and me, are the ones to see a need and, inspired by the Writings, take practical steps toward solutions. Furthermore, this is done without the disputations, wrangling and partisan interests that often inhibit people and institutions of position and authority in the secular world.

This is an important part of how the New World Order will be built – not like manna coming down from heaven, but by the activities of ordinary people in local, simple settings, finding areas of need and proceeding in a meaningful and constructive way to find solutions.

This is a unique opportunity and bounty available to anyone who chooses to walk in the light of the Covenant and thereby become a stabilizing factor in a world in turmoil.

These and other efforts will continually be marked by both crises and victories, as we will explore in the next chapter.

17

Crisis and Victory

Shoghi Effendi perceived in the organic life of the Cause a dialectic of victory and crisis . . . Let every Bahá'í in the world be assured that whatever may befall this growing Faith of God is but incontrovertible evidence of the loving care with which the King of Glory and His martyred Herald, through the incomparable Centre of His Covenant and our beloved Guardian, are preparing His humble followers for ultimate and magnificent triumph.
The Universal House of Justice[1]

In sports, people talk about the 'thrill of victory and agony of defeat'. After defeat it can often be heard, 'Wait till next year'. Gains and losses are just a normal part of life.

There is one major difference in the unfolding of the Divine Plan. Even apparent reversals contain the seeds of further progress. People have a natural yearning for smooth, sustained and uninterrupted growth – but that is not the way it works.

Shoghi Effendi called the *Seven Valleys* Bahá'u'lláh's greatest mystical composition.[2] In the 'Valley of Knowledge' Bahá'u'lláh suggests that contrasts should be considered as part of the whole. The traveller will

> come out of doubt into certitude . . . in this station [the believer] is content with the decree of God, and seeth war as peace, and findeth in death the secrets of everlasting life . . . He beholdeth justice in injustice, and in justice, grace. In ignorance he findeth many a knowledge hidden, and in knowledge a myriad wisdoms manifest . . . if he meeteth with injustice he shall have patience, and if he cometh upon

wrath he shall manifest love.³

Specifically concerning this Revelation, Bahá'u'lláh wrote:

> No sooner had that Revelation been unveiled to men's eyes than the signs of universal discord appeared among the peoples of the world, and commotion seized the dwellers of earth and heaven, and the foundations of all things were shaken. The forces of dissension were released, the meaning of the Word was unfolded, and every several atom in all created things acquired its own distinct and separate character. Hell was made to blaze, and the delights of Paradise were uncovered to men's eyes. Blessed is the man that turneth towards Thee, and woe betide him who standeth aloof from Thee, who denieth Thee and repudiateth Thy signs in this Revelation wherein the faces of the exponents of denial have turned black and the faces of the exponents of truthfulness have turned white . . . ⁴

Life is a matter of challenge and response. No one can control all the challenges that will have to be faced. The best that can be done is to respond in the most appropriate manner given the circumstances. It is a matter of seeing order in chaos and chaos in order. Still, there is an enormous difference between external and internal problems.

External opposition

Referring directly to the ultimate victory of the Cause, Bahá'u'lláh wrote, 'Verily God rendereth His Cause victorious at one time through the aid of His enemies, and at another by virtue of the assistance of His chosen ones.'⁵

Bahá'ís today face a variety of conditions. In some parts of the world they are openly persecuted. In other places they are ignored or dismissed as naïve, if harmless and ideological eccentrics. There are also many places where the authorities have praised and honoured the Bahá'ís for the work they are doing. Whatever the circumstance: persecution, being ignored or honoured, the Faith is thriving.

Results often appear later. Recently a Muslim couple from Iran moved to the United States for their education. They contacted the Bahá'ís and asked to enrol in the community. They felt they could do so in America without endangering themselves or their families in Iran.

The Guardian explained a fundamental advantage that Bahá'ís have:

> I am however, assured and sustained by the conviction, never dimmed in my mind, that whatsoever comes to pass in the Cause of God, however disquieting in its immediate effects, is fraught with infinite Wisdom and tends ultimately to promote its interests in the world. Indeed, our experiences of the distant past, as well as of recent events, are too numerous and varied to permit of any misgiving or doubt as to the truth of this basic principle – a principle which throughout the vicissitudes of our sacred mission in this world we must never disregard or forget.[6]

Expanding further, he wrote:

> We have only to refer to the warnings uttered by 'Abdu'l-Bahá in order to realize the extent and character of the forces that are destined to contest with God's holy Faith. In the darkest moments of His life, under 'Abdu'l Hamíd's regime, when He stood ready to be deported to the most inhospitable regions of Northern Africa, and at a time when the auspicious light of the Bahá'í Revelation had only begun to break upon the West, He, in His parting message to the cousin of the Báb, uttered these prophetic and ominous words: 'How great, how very great is the Cause! How very fierce the onslaught of all the

peoples and kindreds of the earth. Ere long shall the clamour of the multitude throughout Africa, throughout America, the cry of the European and of the Turk, the groaning of India and China, be heard from far and near. One and all, they shall arise with all their power to resist His Cause. Then shall the knights of the Lord, assisted by His grace from on high, strengthened by faith, aided by the power of understanding, and reinforced by the legions of the Covenant, arise and make manifest the truth of the verse: "Behold the confusion that hath befallen the tribes of the defeated"'[7]

In a long letter to the Bahá'ís of East, the Guardian gave a literal explanation. Parts of the letter follow.

> He ['Abdu'l-Bahá] said, 'How very fierce the onslaught of all the peoples and kindreds of the earth.' There is no doubt whatsoever that resistance to the advancement of the Cause and attacks on all that it holds sacred will come from both the generality of people and rulers in the East, West, South and North; also, from church leaders in Europe and America, from Christian missionaries in Australia and Africa, and from chieftains and heads of ancient religions of India and China in southeast Asia and the Far East ... There is not and will never be any doubt that this resistance and onslaught will increase with the passage of time; this collision between the battalion of the abyss and the army of life will spread and intensify, its reverberations will be felt throughout the globe, its aftermath effects will cause the whole world to be stirred and shaken, will astound the human race and, in the most conspicuous way, will proclaim the Cause of God. The truth of the verses: "Behold the confusion that hath befallen the tribes of the defeated" and "And We desire to show favor to those who were brought low in the land, and to make them spiritual leaders among men, and to make of them Our heirs" will be made manifest.'[8]

An indirect level of opposition, 'to resist His Cause', can be thought of as resistance to the divine teachings for this age, such as the oneness of mankind, economic justice, the emancipation of women and so on. Throughout the world entrenched forces fight vigorously against those developments.

Resisting the spirit of the oneness of mankind, for example, is 'to resist His Cause'. As recently 'liberated' groups assert their own cultural identity in opposition to others, the 'cry' spoken of by 'Abdu'l-Bahá can be heard in the very places He mentioned. It is no wonder that so much 'confusion' results as tribal, ethnic, religious and national rivalries combat one another and the anguish lingers on. As this drama plays out, it can be seen as another turbulent stage mankind must pass through on its journey to accepting the oneness of mankind.

In 1985 the Universal House of Justice wrote the following to a National Spiritual Assembly:

> as the Faith becomes known, we can expect opposition and persecution. Nevertheless, in our presentations and relationships, we should always try to build bridges so that our beautiful Teachings can be understood and accepted, and the power which they have to establish unity amongst men will be exemplified.[9]

Where do attacks come from? How should they be met? What can be done to prepare for them? What should be done about the attacks themselves?

In many places it is the clergy who mount the greatest opposition even though, ironically, their primary responsibility is to prepare people for the new Messenger from God. In the words of 'Abdu'l-Bahá:

> This day, the powers of all the leaders of religion are directed towards the dispersion of the congregation of the All-Merciful, and the shattering of the Divine Edifice. The hosts

of the world, whether material, cultural or political are from every side launching their assault, for the Cause is great, very great. Its greatness is, in this day, clear and manifest to men's eyes.[10]

Bahá'u'lláh mentioned some of the motives of this vehement and direct opposition:

> Some for the lust of leadership, others through want of knowledge and understanding, have been the cause of the deprivation of the people . . . Content with a transitory dominion, they have deprived themselves of an everlasting sovereignty.[11]

Many clergymen are sincere in their efforts to protect their followers from what they perceive as the 'evils' being brought by the Bahá'ís. It just so happens that they are sincerely wrong![12]

An open attack by the clergy fulfils God's plan in several ways. A woman stopped by the home of a Bahá'í one day and said she had just come from church where the preacher was talking about the 'devil people' who were preaching in their midst. She said, 'I thought he must be talking about you so I came to find out what you have to say.' The result was that within a very short time, this lovely lady and her whole family embraced the Cause of Bahá'u'lláh.

Another result of attacks from the clergy is to demonstrate their own behaviour compared to the Bahá'ís. Frequently, the way Bahá'ís respond to attacks validates their claim in the eyes of onlookers. During a public meeting, a Bahá'í was being attacked by a 'born-again' Christian. The Bahá'í calmly responded to the onslaught. When it was over someone who was listening, but had said nothing, asked for an enrolment card.

One woman was reluctant to join the Faith because her priest had assured her she would go to Hell if she did. When asked to describe the priest, she described someone who was arrogant and condescending. When asked if she would rather be in heaven with him or in hell with her Baháʼí friends, she laughed and readily agreed that she did not want to be anywhere that the priest would be. It wasn't long before she became a strong Baháʼí.

In recent times, the governments that have acted in greatest opposition to the Faith have been those that tried to control the thoughts and consciousness of the people. Specifically this was true of the Soviet Union, starting in the 1920s, and Nazi Germany in the 1930s. From time to time – over more than a century and a half – the Government of Iran has been swayed by the fanatical clergy who unleashed their hatred of the Baháʼís. Most recently in 1955 and again since the Islamic Revolution in 1979, there have been ongoing and horrible persecutions stirred up by government leaders and the clergy. While this is the action of authority figures, there are many instances in which Muslims have quietly come to the aid of Baháʼís in local situations.

Dysfunctional governmental systems eventually encounter defeat, not by Baháʼís, but by the hand of destiny. The separation of church and state is a highly prized principle in parts of the Western world. This has served as a protection for Baháʼís. This time of relative calm will not last. In the future, when open opposition occurs, some weak Baháʼís will fall away and the strong will become even stronger. This has happened in the past and will likely be the case in the future. Those who withstand the coming ordeals will turn to each other for strength, reinforce the foundations of loyalty in their hearts, and build stronger communities through increased bonding. This show of strength will attract new seekers.

In one of His talks in the United States, ʻAbduʼl-Bahá gave a delightful illustration of what happens when there are attacks. He said of them, 'this is only as the harmless twittering of sparrows that will soon pass away'.[13] The Guardian wrote:

Viewed in the light of past experience, the inevitable result of such futile attempts, however persistent and malicious they may be, is to contribute to a wider and deeper recognition by believers and unbelievers alike of the distinguishing features of the Faith proclaimed by Bahá'u'lláh. These challenging criticisms, whether or not dictated by malice, cannot but serve to galvanize the souls of its ardent supporters, and to consolidate the ranks of its faithful promoters. They will purge the Faith from those pernicious elements whose continued association with the believers tends to discredit the fair name of the Cause, and to tarnish the purity of its spirit. We should welcome, therefore, not only the open attacks which its avowed enemies persistently launch against it, but should also view as a blessing in disguise every storm of mischief with which they who apostatize their faith or claim to be its faithful exponents assail it from time to time. Instead of undermining the Faith, such assaults, both from within and from without, reinforce its foundations, and excite the intensity of its flame. Designed to becloud its radiance, they proclaim to all the world the exalted character of its precepts, the completeness of its unity, the uniqueness of its position, and the pervasiveness of its influence.[14]

In some ways, indirect attacks from outside the Faith are more difficult to deal with than direct attacks because they are not as clearly seen as threats or are subtle or hard to prove. Both the malicious and the uninformed have accused Bahá'ís of everything from subversion to immorality to criminal connections. The best precaution, after living a true Bahá'í life, is for Bahá'ís to establish friendly relations with people in prominent positions. Often Bahá'ís have been protected because someone in authority knew something about the Faith from a personal relationship with a Bahá'í. On several occasions, detrimental material has come to the attention of people in positions of importance who happened to know some Bahá'ís and had some basic information about the Faith. They were able to dismiss the false charges easily rather than unwittingly accept the misinformation as true. Being known as responsible and optimistic people gives Bahá'ís protection that will become increasingly important, as more severe attacks are unleashed.

'Abdu'l-Bahá gave explicit advice for what to do in the face of onslaughts:

> In these days the Cause of God, the world over, is fast growing in power and, day by day, is spreading further and further to the utmost bounds of the earth. Its enemies, therefore, from all the kindreds and peoples of the world, are growing aggressive, malevolent, envious and bitterly hostile. It is incumbent upon the loved ones of God to exercise the greatest care and prudence in all things, whether great or small, to take counsel together and unitedly resist the onslaught of the stirrers up of strife and the movers of mischief.[15]

Finally, confidence and encouragement are found in these words of Bahá'u'lláh:

> Gird up the loins of your endeavour, O people of Bahá, that haply the tumult of religious dissension and strife that agitateth the peoples of the earth may be stilled, that every trace of it may be completely obliterated.[16]

While it is encouraging to know that external threats actually aid the Cause, it is important to be also mindful of internal problems.

Internal problems

Dangers can arise within the Bahá'í community that are at least as serious as external attacks. Bahá'u'lláh wrote:

Nothing whatever can, in this Day, inflict a greater harm upon this Cause than dissension and strife, contention, estrangement and apathy, among the loved ones of God. Flee them, through the power of God and His sovereign aid, and strive ye to knit together the hearts of men, in His Name, the Unifier, the All-Knowing, the All-Wise.[17]

Bahá'ís, in common with all other human beings, can become preoccupied with secondary interests or envious at the successes of others. The Guardian wrote: 'True, the Cause as every other movement has its own obstacles, complications, and unforeseen difficulties.'[18] Some of these may stem from the following human weaknesses.

Disobedience

One of the worst problems Bahá'ís can inflict on the Faith is outright disobedience to Bahá'u'lláh's teachings. 'Abdu'l-Bahá said:

> Those who speak falsehoods, who covet worldly things and seek to accumulate the riches of this earth are not of me. But when you find a person living up to the teachings of Bahá'u'lláh, following the precepts of the Hidden Words, know that he belongs to Bahá'u'lláh; and, verily, I proclaim that he is of me. If, on the other hand, you see anyone whose deeds and conduct are contrary to and not in conformity with the good pleasure of the Blessed Perfection and against the spirit of the Hidden Words, let that be your standard and criterion of judgment against him, for know that I am altogether severed from him no matter who he may be. This is the truth.[19]

However, it is not up to individuals to judge whether or not someone else is living up to being a Bahá'í. Everyone falls short. The differences are in the nature of the misdeed and a matter of degree.

There is no such thing as 'bending' the laws of Bahá'u'lláh. Breaking the divine law is breaking the divine law! The effect is just as sure as trying to defy the law of gravity. The British orientalist E.G. Browne was greatly attracted to the Bahá'ís and had a personal audience with Bahá'u'lláh. Disenchantment came through the activities of some few of the Bahá'ís whom he encountered. While most of the Bahá'ís he met were law-abiding and pleasing to be with, there were some unfortunate episodes with a few believers which may have played a significant role in preventing him from a whole-hearted embrace of the Cause.[20]

Even worse than disobedience to Bahá'u'lláh's teachings is criticism of the Bahá'í institutions. This is a virulent and destructive type of backbiting. Of this the Guardian's secretary wrote on his behalf: 'Vicious criticism is indeed a calamity. But its root is lack of faith in the system of Bahá'u'lláh, i.e. the administrative order – and lack of obedience to Him – for He has forbidden it.'[21] Mistakes can and will be made. There are proper ways to deal with these. Nowhere is criticism of the institutions listed among the acceptable methods.

When an individual brings a problem before a Spiritual Assembly, that person must be prepared to follow the advice given. It is easy to follow advice when you like what you hear. It can be a great test when you don't like the advice. To follow guidance when you like it, and reject it when you don't, is to trifle with a divine institution. Appeals can be made, but every effort must be made to be obedient.

The solution to disobedience is easy in theory, but hard in practice. It starts with a love for the Central Figures of the Faith and an intense desire to please them. With love for them, reliance on prayer, a yearning to do what is right and, when appropriate, assistance from others, the struggle can be won, one day and one event at a time. Put disappointment behind and move on to find new ways to serve Bahá'u'lláh.

Thirst for leadership

Leadership skills have great value when the talent is channelled in appropriate ways. The same skills can be disastrous when used for personal recognition. The Hands of the Cause were outstanding examples of individuals who had great leadership qualities, but no interest in acclaim for themselves. Because they were so firm in the Covenant, their conspicuous talent was an asset and not a liability.

Study circles and youth projects require someone to take the initiative to get them going. Teaching projects flounder when no one leads the way. Socio-economic activities and other innovative initiatives are the results of people using their leadership abilities appropriately in the path of service. Sometimes this is done in spite of criticism from other Bahá'ís.

Humility can be a two-edged sword. Obviously, no one should be boastful. On the other hand, it is a false humility to claim you cannot do something just because it seems difficult, or refuse to use your talents to serve the Faith because someone might object. In the *Hidden Words*, Bahá'u'lláh writes, 'Transgress not thy limits, nor claim that which beseemeth thee not.'[22] Not putting your best foot forward in the path of service – even when it seems beyond you – is transgressing your limits.

True humility is placing your best efforts and best talents in the service of promoting the Cause. When you do your best, not for acclaim or pride of accomplishment, but to serve Bahá'u'lláh, it is a form of true humility.

Some Bahá'ís have a desire to be elected to a Spiritual Assembly or appointed to one of a number of positions. Some people have entered the Faith looking for leadership opportunities. Finding no positions available to them, they leave the Faith. There have been Christian ministers who led their followers to an acceptance of Bahá'u'lláh. A few of them, accustomed to their previous role as leaders, became frustrated when there were no positions open to them. Some of them withdrew, but often their followers remained.

There is a delightful story of someone in a developing country who wrote to the National Spiritual Assembly about his enthusiasm in finding the Faith and eagerness to be active. He said, 'Let me know when there is a vacancy on the NSA.' Hopefully, he found more appropriate areas in which to invest his enthusiasm. If not, he was in for serious disappointment.

Some people, finding no avenue for their thirst for leadership, simply fade away and are rarely seen or heard from again. There are a few, thankfully very few, who eventually became Covenant-breakers because they did not receive the acclaim in the Faith that they wanted.

Poor judgement

There are many Bahá'ís who love Bahá'u'lláh, love the Faith, and would never deliberately or knowingly harm the Cause. Yet these same people, through some action or lack of wisdom, do things contrary to the best interests of the Faith they love.

Among the problems of poor judgement is taking action outside of the institutions or attempting to solve administrative problems by some other means or acting like Spiritual Assemblies in relation to each other. Trying to 'help' others by telling them what to do and that 'this is for your own good' is a common bad example of individuals acting like Spiritual Assemblies.

It is not unusual to see something in others that is troubling. The problem is what to do about it. In Western culture, gossiping or backbiting are normal. Since this activity is forbidden in the Bahá'í Faith, a dilemma is created. It is not always easy just to forget about it. As a member of a Spiritual Assembly, I once got a call from a woman who wanted to let the Assembly know something about someone. She concluded by saying, 'I'm so glad I'm a Bahá'í. Now you (the Assembly) can deal with it and I don't have to think about it anymore.' She did the right thing: taking her concern to the institution and leaving it alone.

Improper consultation is another aspect of poor judgement. Mistakes will be made while learning this art. However, good judgement involves constantly seeking to improve. Being content with a low level of consultation is poor judgement. This stems from many things: retaining old habits of discussion; lack of reliance on prayer; insufficient love and harmony; lack of unity of purpose; impact of strong personalities; dealing with each other on a power basis; failure to gain an understanding of the true nature of the problems discussed; inadequate understanding of the Writings in relationship to the problem concerned; assuming you know all you need to know about consultation; and so on. By constantly seeking to improve consulting skills, improvements will be made.

Judgement becomes most clouded when issues become emotional or when things are done impulsively. Reason is robbed of its power when issues become emotional. Acting out of feeling or impulse can add energy to anything, but is fraught with danger.

It is hard to spot poor judgement in yourself. At the same time, it is inappropriate to look for faults in others. Understanding and patience are needed. In the words written in behalf of the Guardian:

> So many misunderstandings arise from the passionate attachment of the friends to the Faith and also their immaturity. We must therefore be very patient and loving with each other and try to establish unity in the Bahá'í family. The differences . . . which you describe in your letter he feels are caused by the above and not by enmity to the Faith or insincerity.[23]

There is some protection from bad judgement. It starts with being in tune with the spirit of the Covenant. Patience and stepping back from a situation makes it possible to put things in a better perspective and restrain one from an unfortunate act. A loving and caring community is a protective network that keeps poor judgement in check. Reliance on consultation with trusted friends and the proper use of the institutions are enormously important bulwarks of stability that can lead to better judgement.

Apathy

If you love someone, you continually think about how special that person is. When your preoccupation stops, the special feeling starts to erode. Then, like any garden that goes untended, the garden of love is overcome with weeds. That which was once lovely and a source of delight turns ordinary, taken for granted, then becomes ignored and unattractive.

So too with the love of God, His Messengers, and the Faith They bring. That love must never be taken for granted. It must be nurtured, tended and fussed over. Neglected, it will slip into an untended corner of the heart. Even the garden of the love of God can fall prey to the weeds of neglect. This may be one of the reasons why daily reciting of the Words of Bahá'u'lláh, prayer and bringing oneself to account each day are commands.

Distractions

There are many worthwhile and valuable interests that consume vast amounts of time, money and energy. The struggle for survival in the modern world consumes an inordinate amount of time and vitality. A result of the decaying moral, social, political, economic and environmental conditions of the world places Bahá'ís and others in a frantic swirl of activities from which there is no easy escape. They sap the energy and desire needed to serve the Cause. The results lead to lethargy and/or a desire to be left alone to seek simpler pursuits or pleasure-producing diversions. That can be spiritually lethal.

Recreation, hobbies and pleasant pastimes have their place and value, as we have seen earlier in this book. The danger comes when a pastime becomes a waste of time. Even a person's job or profession can consume more time, emotional and physical energy than it ought to.

Danger lurks, even for activities that are humanitarian, spiritually fulfilling or personally gratifying. These activities can take on exaggerated importance that not only consume resources and vitality, but can ultimately lead some Bahá'ís away from the Faith and further from those very things that the individual was trying to achieve.

Concern with the crying needs of human suffering, peace movements, racial and gender inequities, poverty, environmental issues, substance abuse, injustices, etc., are all worthy causes. Many Bahá'ís participate effectively within other organizations that are working for these noble pursuits. It is a good thing to join forces with likeminded people on matters of mutual concern as long as there is no compromise of Bahá'í principles. The Guardian set an example by being one of the first 'Men of the Trees' in Israel in support of reforestation. In 1987 the Universal House of Justice joined the Network on Conservation and Religion, an alliance with the World Wide Fund for Nature.[24]

There are also movements that promise 'self-fulfilment', 'peace of mind', 'mindfulness' or 'spiritual well-being' through specialized meditation practices and introspection. These can lure otherwise faithful believers into preoccupation with their own spiritual welfare, which may lead to a blind alley of frustration and wasted effort, and delay the progress of the Cause.

None of the items mentioned above are bad or harmful in themselves. But, when pursued without incorporating the greater purpose of serving Bahá'u'lláh, they can cripple the spiritual life of both the individual and the community.

Bahá'ís are the ones given the task of building the Kingdom

of God on earth. Activities in peripheral areas should not be allowed to overshadow that longterm objective.

If the house you live in is falling apart, you can fix it or build another one. Today's secular institutions and cultural activities are like a house that is so badly in need of repair that it is falling apart. Thank God, there are legions of good-hearted people who are working hard to make the best of a bad situation.

At the same time, it is the Bahá'ís, and only the Bahá'ís, who are building the foundation for the new. Granted, the old is falling apart faster than the new is being built, and it is tempting to put a lot of effort into obvious and immediate needs. Bahá'ís should lend their efforts to these problems, but not at the expense of laying aside the greater work for mankind's future.

One value of bringing oneself to account each day[25] is an opportunity to reassess priorities on a regular basis.

Envy and jealousy

> O My servants, defile not your wings with the clay of waywardness and vain desires, and suffer them not to be stained with the dust of envy and hate, that ye may not be hindered from soaring in the heavens of My divine knowledge.[26]

People with innovative ideas, especially if they are also successful financially, are sometimes accused of being self-serving. Bahá'ís with wealth need to be especially strong to withstand both the jealousy and requests – sometimes demands – for their resources from other believers. One couple purchased a building for a Bahá'í Centre and the Spiritual Assembly decided that neither husband nor wife should serve on the facility committee. Fortunately, they were strong and deepened Bahá'ís and able to rise above the shortsighted decision without complaint or criticism. In the meantime, the community was deprived of the enthusiasm, creativity and leadership ability they could have provided.

'Abdu'l-Bahá cautioned, 'Envy closes the door of Bounty, and jealousy prevents one from ever attaining to the Kingdom of Abhá.'[27]

Every devoted Bahá'í finds himself at some time faced with a situation in which serving the Cause seems to bring more frustration than satisfaction; when other Bahá'ís do not act like Bahá'ís; or are not doing their share of the work; or there seem to be reversals in the evolving Bahá'í community. Other activities look more appealing.

Apathy or indifference develops slowly and subtly. While inactivity may reduce tensions for the moment, it produces a much larger problem for both the individual and for the Cause. It is like a soldier being absent without leave in the heat of battle. Difficulties from fellow believers can be endured when what is being done is for Bahá'u'lláh.

Bahá'ís of today are subject to all the problems afflicting the human race. They also happen to be the trustees of the solutions given to mankind to overcome its many problems. Immediate problems give experience for long-term solutions. As individuals and institutions confront and resolve these difficulties, enormous strides are made in the maturation of the Bahá'í communities. These are victories snatched from the jaws of crisis.

When reversals are encountered it is well to remember the example of the Guardian during the Ten Year Plan. One goal of the Plan was to build a Bahá'í temple in Baghdad. Even though the site had been purchased and building materials were available, persecution of the Bahá'ís in Iraq made the goal impossible within the time of the Plan. The Guardian's reaction was to replace the one impossible objective with two others: temples in Africa and Australia.

But crises such as these, severe though they may be, pale in comparison to Covenant-breaking, which will be discussed in the next chapter.

18

Covenant-breaking

> *Today no power can conserve the oneness of the Bahá'í world save the Covenant of God; otherwise differences like unto a most great tempest will encompass the Bahá'í world. It is evident that the axis of the oneness of the world of humanity is the power of the Covenant and nothing else. Had the Covenant not come to pass, had it not been revealed from the Supreme Pen and had not the Book of the Covenant, like unto the ray of the Sun of Reality, illuminated the world, the forces of the Cause of God would have been utterly scattered and certain souls who were the prisoners of their own passions and lusts would have taken into their hands an axe, cutting the root of this Blessed Tree. Every person would have pushed forward his own desire and every individual aired his own opinion!*
> 'Abdu'l-Bahá[1]

The virulent disease of Covenant-breaking has been with the people of God at least since the beginning of recorded history. Even the conflict between Cain and Abel involved the Covenant. Both were to make sacrifices to the Lord from their labours. Abel, the herdsman, sacrificed the best cuts of lamb. Cain, the farmer, offered the cull of his crops. Cain became jealous, because Abel's offerings were accepted by God and his were not. Therefore, he killed his brother.[2]

There is probably no more severe reaction to a violation of the Covenant than found during the exodus of the Hebrew people from Egypt. The second time Moses went into the mountains to talk with God, He was delayed in His return. His followers grew impatient and the rebellious among them encouraged them to return to idol worship. They made a golden calf. When Moses returned, He cried out in righteous anger, 'Who is on the Lord's side? Let them come unto Me.' All the sons of Levi gathered together with Him. Then Moses had them take up their swords and slay the Covenant-breakers, 'And the children of Levi did according to the Word of Moses, and there fell, of the people that day, about three thousand men.'[3]

Three thousand men! All killed in a single day because of Covenant-breaking. Once purified of this element, the followers of Moses went forward. Over the generations, and in spite of many subsequent tests and obstacles, a great civilization was built.

The onerous disease of Covenant-breaking continued. The betrayal of Christ by Judas was a clear case of violating the Covenant.

Muhammad knew scorn, ridicule and abuse from the moment that He proclaimed that He was the Prophet of God. However, the fiercest problems occurred after His death. Differences of opinion, including over the successorship, resulted in a vicious split among the followers that continues to this day. Each group claims the other violated the Covenant.*

Bahá'u'lláh's life was plagued by the actions of Covenant-breakers. According to 'Abdu'l-Bahá, Covenant-breakers markedly delayed the growth of the Faith. Shoghi Effendi had to expel members of his own family because of their activities.

Breaking the Covenant should not be confused with breaking a Bahá'í law. It is altogether different. It is not just a matter of degree. There is no comparison. Violating a law may be because of weakness, immaturity, ignorance, carelessness or some other human factors. Such indiscretions can be part of a growth process. Nor should Covenant-breaking be confused with external opposition.

The Universal House of Justice writes:

---

* The Sunnis accepted the Caliphate with Abu Bakr as the first Caliph. The Shi'ih follow the Imamate with 'Ali as the first Imam.

COVENANT-BREAKING

When a person declares his acceptance of Bahá'u'lláh as a Manifestation of God he becomes a party to the Covenant and accepts the totality of His Revelation. If he then turns round and attacks Bahá'u'lláh or the Central Institution of the Faith he violates the Covenant. If this happens every effort is made to help that person to see the illogicality and error of his actions, but if he persists he must, in accordance with instructions of Bahá'u'lláh Himself, be shunned as a Covenant breaker.[4]

When there is suspicion of Covenant-breaking, an investigation needs to be made. Generally, one or more Counsellors are given the assignment. After evidence is gathered, the House of Justice makes a final determination.

Covenant-breakers have often been well-known Bahá'ís who have given great service to the Cause before open defection. Why does a capable and strong Bahá'í become a Covenant-breaker?

Every human being has certain flaws in his character. The one thing Covenant-breakers have in common is that whatever prayer, fasting and service they may have practised was insufficient to overcome the growing character flaws. The fault often revolves around a boundless desire for leadership and the adulation of others, or some uncontrolled passion of hate, rancour, envy or egotism.

Mirzá Yaḥyá, Bahá'u'lláh's half-brother, was essentially raised by Bahá'u'lláh. The Báb conferred upon him the mantle of temporary leadership of the Bábís as a protection for Bahá'u'lláh. Despite all this, it was not enough for Mirzá Yaḥyá. He wanted adulation, so he claimed for himself the station that only Bahá'u'lláh could fulfil.

Muḥammad-'Alí, 'Abdu'l-Bahá's half-brother, had great capacity. Otherwise, Bahá'u'lláh would not have bestowed on him the potential of being second only to 'Abdu'l-Bahá. However, this was not good enough for Muḥammad-'Alí. His character flaws grew and as a result he forfeited his spiritual destiny.

During His lifetime, 'Abdu'l-Bahá did much to protect the believers from the poison of Covenant-breaking. With His passing, it became necessary for the believers to take a major leap toward a mature understanding of the problem. The stern language in His Will and Testament underscored the importance of this issue and the need for believers to take a strong stance of vigilance. In unambiguous language He described its pernicious nature.

Unfortunately, people so afflicted tend to be clever and knowledgeable about the Faith. For their own reasons, they rise up against it. With their twisted thinking they try to lure others to their support as they denounce the very basis of the divine institutions. There is nothing more dangerous to the Cause of God than this treacherous attack from those who were once believers. For this reason, unlike others with whom we might disagree, they should be avoided completely and their literature left untouched. They need to be put out of the Cause in the same way that cancerous tissue needs to be removed from an otherwise healthy body.

In the words of 'Abdu'l-Bahá in His Will and Testament: 'For so grievous is the conduct and behaviour of this false people that they are become even as an axe striking at the very root of the Blessed Tree,' and He warns: 'And now, one of the greatest and most fundamental principles of the Cause of God is to shun and avoid entirely the Covenant breakers, for they will utterly destroy the Cause of God, exterminate His Law and render of no account all efforts exerted in the past.'[5]

These people are spiritually sick, with a disease they have consciously harboured. Covenant-breaking can be compared to an apple gone bad. When one apple rots, the apples near it start to rot. The bad one never catches wholesomeness from the healthy ones. The only way to protect the apples that are not spoiled is to remove the ones that have rotted.

COVENANT-BREAKING

When someone is declared a Covenant-breaker, the believers in the part of the world affected are informed, and they are instructed to have no further dealings with the person identified. Those who have broken the Covenant know what must be done to set things right. Leave them alone. Good intentions do not persuade them, but they could infect others – no one is immune.

I've known Bahá'ís who have become physically nauseated from just holding Covenant-breaking literature, even before they knew what it was. While at Bahjí with Eugene King, who was blind and unusually sensitive, I had him stand safely by a tree while I took some pictures. When I came back and led him away from the tree, he asked where he had been, because he felt uncomfortable and slightly nauseated, but when he moved away from that spot, he felt all right. We asked our guide what had been there. He said Eugene was standing where a Covenant-breaker's house had been. The guide described how he had destroyed the house himself on the instructions of the Guardian. Then, we understood why Eugene had not felt well while standing on that spot where a Covenant-breaker had lived.

No one is immune to this detestable condition. As mentioned earlier, even one Hand of the Cause, Mason Remey, was so afflicted. He had served the Guardian in Haifa and had even been appointed as chairman of the International Bahá'í Council – forerunner to the Universal House of Justice.

After the passing of the Guardian, the Hands of the Cause, including Remey, affirmed that there was no second Guardian. However, Remey's personal ambition exceeded whatever love He had for the Faith. He announced to the other Hands that he should be the second Guardian. The stunned Hands had no choice but to put him out of the Cause.

It did not stop there. He sent a letter to believers all over the world announcing his claim as second Guardian. He had a few followers for a brief time, but he expelled most of them as people who broke his covenant. When he died in Italy a few years later, at the age of 100, he was alone, having lost or excommunicated all his followers. He had a civil rather than a religious burial. There wasn't even the customary funeral service.

After the problems associated with Mason Remey, I have heard Hands of the Cause ask believers to pray that they may be steadfast to the end. In a casual conversation with Hand of the Cause John Robarts, he mentioned how he envied those faithful Hands who had already passed on, because they were steadfast to the end.

While the numbers of Covenant-breakers are small, they do damage in several ways:

- ❖ They undermine the authority that is the only means of bringing divine order to this dysfunctional world and setting mankind on the pathway to its spiritual destiny.
- ❖ They build nothing. They have no grand teaching plans, no scheme for the redemption of humankind. Their only object is to undermine the legitimate aims of the Faith for their own nefarious purposes.
- ❖ They cause division and confusion among the friends, frustrating positive efforts and slowing down progress.
- ❖ They cause confusion among those who are not Bahá'ís. When non-believers hear the contentions of Covenant-breakers, they get a distorted view of the Faith that obscures the magnitude and grandeur of the divine teachings.
- ❖ They waste a lot of precious time and resources. That is, believers must spend time and energy to combat their unpredictable actions.

Occasionally a sincere seeker will become a Bahá'í after first hearing of Bahá'u'lláh through Covenant-breakers. Each case should be pursued with great care, and with guidance from an Auxiliary Board member or a Counsellor.

'Abdu'l-Bahá was explicit in describing the dynamics of this process:

> The tests of every dispensation are in direct proportion to the greatness of the Cause, and as heretofore such a manifest Covenant, written by the Supreme Pen, hath not been entered upon, the tests are proportionately more severe. These trials cause the feeble souls to waver while those who are firm are not affected. These agitations of the violators are no more than the foam of the ocean, which is one of its inseparable features; but the ocean of the Covenant shall surge and shall cast ashore the bodies of the dead, for it cannot retain them. Thus it is seen that the ocean of the Covenant hath surged and surged until it hath thrown out the dead bodies – souls that are deprived of the Spirit of God and are lost in passion and self and are seeking leadership. This foam of the ocean shall not endure and shall soon disperse and vanish, while the ocean of the Covenant shall eternally surge and roar . . .
>
> From the early days of creation down to the present time, throughout all the divine dispensations, such a firm and explicit Covenant hath not been entered upon. In view of this fact is it possible for this foam to remain on the surface of the ocean of the Covenant? No, by God! The violators are trampling upon their own dignity, are uprooting their own foundations and are proud at being upheld by flatterers who exert a great effort to shake the faith of feeble souls. But this action of theirs is of no consequence; it is a mirage and not water, foam and not the sea, mist and not a cloud, illusion and not reality. All this ye shall soon see.[6]

No one should either become complacent or get paranoid about the danger of becoming a Covenant-breaker. Here are some steps that should help anyone remain firm in the Covenant:

- ❖ Unfailingly use the obligatory prayers and read from the Writings.
- ❖ Follow the Baháʼí laws, both in spirit and letter, to the best of your ability.
- ❖ Deepen as much as possible to gain a better understanding and appreciation of the Faith.
- ❖ Invest energy in projects sponsored by the institutions.
- ❖ Use initiative and creativity to find ways to serve the Faith that get you excited.

In short, the greatest protection is to follow the example of ʻAbduʼl-Bahá. Obviously, no one can serve to His level, but everyone has the capacity to serve according to her or his own potential.

While it is dangerous to minimize the pernicious evil of Covenant-breaking, the most essential component for the protection and growth of the Cause is vigorous teaching, and we will focus on that in the next chapter.

19

Teaching

> *If it be Our pleasure We shall render the Cause victorious through the power of a single word from Our presence . . . However, since Our loving providence surpasseth all things, We have ordained that complete victory should be achieved through speech and utterance, that Our servants throughout the earth may thereby become the recipients of divine good. This is but a token of God's bounty vouchsafed unto them. Verily thy Lord is the All-Sufficing, the Most Exalted.*
> Bahá'u'lláh[1]

As this book draws to its conclusion, it is appropriate to stress the greatest gift and greatest mandate: teaching. 'Abdu'l-Bahá explained:

> . . . let the loved ones . . . say: 'Of all the gifts of God the greatest is the gift of Teaching. It draweth unto us the Grace of God and is our first obligation. Of such a gift how can we deprive ourselves? Nay, our lives, our goods, our comforts, our rest, we offer them all as a sacrifice for the Abhá Beauty and teach the Cause of God.' Caution and prudence, however, must be observed even as recorded in the Book. The veil must in no wise be suddenly rent asunder.[2]

In the Preface to this book, the Báb was quoted as promising that the Cause would be victorious. In His final address to the Letters of the Living He echoed that promise when He said, 'be assured of ultimate victory'.[3] The Báb's statements guaranteed victory. Then, Bahá'u'lláh said He wanted you and me to do it. This creates a dilemma:

- ➤ The Báb promised the victory of this Cause.
- ➤ Bahá'u'lláh said it could be done with a single word, but tells His followers to do it, as a benefit to them.
- ➤ 'Abdu'l-Bahá said this is not only a bounty and a mandate, but that 'the greatest is the gift of Teaching'.
- ➤ Then, He said it must be done with 'caution and prudence'.

We would not be asked to do anything that could not be accomplished. The Covenant is what makes it possible for ordinary believers to win 'ultimate victory'. It is like a do-it-yourself kit for building the New World Order, to be accomplished 'through speech and utterance'. Instructions come complete with a warning that it will not be easy and the results will not be seen right away. However, divine assistance is always available. Bahá'u'lláh told us how by simply saying, 'Seize the chance . . .'[4]

The universal responsibility for everyone to teach is so important that Bahá'u'lláh even included it as a mandate in his Tablet to Napoleon III. He not only made this a requirement – although Napoleon forfeited what could have been a high spiritual destiny – but He also emphasizes that a praiseworthy character must come first:

> God hath prescribed unto every one the duty of teaching His Cause. Whoever ariseth to discharge this duty, must needs, ere he proclaimeth His Message, adorn himself with the ornament of an upright and praiseworthy character, so that his words may attract the hearts of such as are receptive to his call. Without it, he can never hope to influence his hearers.[5]

Shoghi Effendi gave the magic formula for accomplishment:

> Not by the force of numbers, not by the mere exposition of

a set of new and noble principles, not by an organized campaign of teaching – no matter how worldwide and elaborate in its character – not even by the staunchness of our faith or the exaltation of our enthusiasm, can we ultimately hope to vindicate in the eyes of a critical and sceptical age the supreme claim of the Abhá Revelation. One thing and only one thing will unfailingly and alone secure the undoubted triumph of this sacred Cause, namely, the extent to which our own inner life and private character mirror forth in their manifold aspects the splendour of those eternal principles proclaimed by Bahá'u'lláh.[6]

He further related teaching to martyrdom when he wrote, 'To live to teach in the present day is like being martyred in those early days. It is the spirit that moves us that counts, not the act through which that spirit expresses itself; and that spirit is to serve the Cause of God with our heart and soul.'[7] To seek a martyr's death at this time is to have a passion for teaching.

The martyrs had no way of knowing the results of their acts of devotion and ultimate sacrifice. None of the Letters of the Living saw the 'ultimate victory' that the Báb promised. Today, the teacher is to teach, whether or not there are apparent results. In a letter to the Bahá'ís of the East, Shoghi Effendi

> attributed all the great victories of the Cause in the western world . . . to the mysterious forces released by the blood of countless martyrs in Persia. However, in this Dispensation Bahá'u'lláh has exhorted His followers not to seek martyrdom. He has instead decreed that the believers should live to teach the Faith, and has exalted the reward of teaching to that of martyrdom.[8]

It still happens that a teacher in one part of the world may not have obvious successes, but is responsible for victories elsewhere even when there is no physical connection.

There is a catch. 'Abdu'l-Bahá both warned and predicted persecutions when He said,

> Turn all your thoughts and devote all your powers to the Divine Covenant. Unless a servant in the Cause of God is subjected to all these persecutions he is not fitted to spread the Heavenly Message of Glad Tidings. Follow 'Abdu'l-Bahá! Let nothing hinder or defeat you. God is your helper and God is invincible.[9]

Again, the 'secret weapon' for teaching is 'the extent to which our own inner life and private character mirror forth in their manifold aspects the splendour of those eternal principles proclaimed by Bahá'u'lláh'.

It is clear that teaching is not just talking about the Faith. I have heard from several reputable sources a story of two Bahá'ís who walked from Persia to the Bahá'í World Centre in the days of 'Abdu'l-Bahá, teaching all the way. One was an eloquent and powerful speaker. The other rarely said anything, but would pray silently while the more polished one was teaching the Faith. As they approached 'Abdu'l-Bahá, He is said to have stretched out His arms and said, 'Here comes that marvellous teacher.' He walked past the eloquent speaker and embraced the silent pray-er. Teaching is not so much what we say, but what we have in our hearts and how we live our lives.

A guaranteed way to get fired up for teaching is to read and ponder the Fire Tablet which concludes: 'Should all the servants read and ponder this, there shall be kindled in their veins a fire that shall set aflame the worlds.'

There is probably no stronger set of practical teaching instructions than what is found in the Tablet of Aḥmad.[10] Aḥmad had walked more than 1,000 miles to be in the presence of Bahá'u'lláh. When he was a short distance away from his destination, he received this famous Tablet.

He described his reaction: 'I received the Tablet of "The

TEACHING

Nightingale of Paradise" and reading it again and again, I found out that my Beloved desired me to go and teach His Cause. Therefore I preferred obedience to visiting Him.'[11] He could have walked just a short distance further to be in His presence. Instead, Aḥmad turned the other way and walked nearly two thousand miles to teach the Faith among the Bábís in Persia, which he did with unparalleled vigour.

There are many valid ways of understanding this marvellous Tablet. One way is to study the entire Tablet with the view of how it relates to teaching. True, believers rely on it for many other purposes, and that is all right. But the instruction for teaching is paramount, and that is the way Aḥmad understood it. A few passages are considered below.

Bahá'u'lláh starts by speaking in the voice of 'the King' – that is the supreme authority of the universe. A loyal subject does whatever his King says without hesitation or question. That is the level of obedience that is expected of anyone who wishes to spread this Divine Message. The importance of what is to follow is emphasized when He said the message was being delivered with both complete knowledge and ultimate understanding – from 'the All-Knowing, the Wise'. This is not a casual or perfunctory opening.

He proceeds by saying that 'the Nightingale of Paradise singeth upon the twigs of the Tree of Eternity, with holy and sweet melodies'. How can that be? How can one nightingale be on more than one twig at a time?

First of all, the 'Tree of Eternity' implies a connection to all Revelations of the past as well as all mankind. When direct quotations from Bahá'u'lláh are used, it has the effect of being the voice of the Nightingale singing from whatever 'twig' – or place – those Sacred Words are uttered. When quoting Bahá'u'lláh, it is as if the 'Nightingale' is singing at that time and place. The manner of delivering His Words is crucial: 'with holy and sweet melodies.

One, but only one, way to consider those terms is as different approaches to different kinds of people. Four significant terms relating directly to delivering the Message follow: 'proclaiming', 'calling', 'informing' and 'guiding'. These can be associated with four different kinds of people: 'sincere ones', 'believers in the Divine Unity', 'severed ones', and 'lovers'. Four different aspects of the Revelation are mentioned: 'the glad tidings of the nearness of God', 'the court of the Presence of the Generous One', 'the Message Revealed by God', and 'the seat of sanctity'.

- A *proclamation* can be made to the 'sincere ones'. They need to be told 'the glad tidings of the nearness of God' because that is what they are sincerely searching for.
- A *call* should be made to people who are believers in the 'Divine Unity'. That is, people who are spiritually sensitive and attracted to spiritual, or metaphysical, matters. Let them know that they can enter 'the court of the Presence of the Generous One'.
- People can be 'severed' or detached either because they have freed themselves from material attachments or because they feel alienated or disenfranchised from the rest of humanity and are thirsting for comfort and security. Either way, they may be receptive to being *informed* of 'the Message revealed by God'.
- Those who are the 'lovers' of either spiritual realities or mankind, and are concerned about social justice, really have a yearning to be *guided* to the 'seat of sanctity' for all humanity.

These examples are reminders to be alert to the yearning of the people being taught. We all have favourite themes, and Anna's story in the Ruhi Book 6 is a good model. However, it is important to speak to the needs and interests of the listener, rather than talking about our own favourite themes. We should teach according to the needs of the listener, not what appeals to the speaker.

TEACHING

Everyone can find within the Baháʼí teachings something with special meaning for them. Those different dimensions show that this Tablet is addressed to everyone, regardless of the specific part of the Revelation that touches each one's heart. Everyone is summoned, each with her or his individual relationship to God.

Another way to view this is as a four-step process. There is the general statement of *proclaiming,* that is, letting people know that the Baháʼí Faith exists. When interest is shown, the next step is *calling* upon people to hear more. As interest increases, it is time to *inform* seekers of the verities of the Faith. Once there is a degree of recognition of Baháʼu'lláh, it is time for *guiding* the new soul into the ocean of God's word. The Ruhi system focuses on the last two steps.

This section of the Tablet concludes by giving the teacher added confidence, affirming that Baháʼu'lláh is the standard 'through Whom truth shall be distinguished from error and the wisdom of every command shall be tested'.

Aḥmad felt that the Tablet was telling him to return to Persia and teach among the Bábís. His instructions were to acknowledge the supremacy of the Báb and use their Holy Book, the *Bayán* – 'the Mother Book' – as a means of teaching according to what was dear to their hearts. Baháʼu'lláh used this same approach in the *Kitáb-i-Íqán*. Most of that Book was focused on explaining divine truth based on what the person who raised the questions already knew and believed. This suggests building bridges to where people are in their spiritual journey. Had Aḥmad been sent among the Christians, it is possible that he would have been told to validate Christ as the Son of God[12] and the Word made flesh,[13] and to teach the true meaning of the Gospel as explained in the Baháʼí Writings.

The Tablet goes on to say that the teacher is to teach without concern over how it is received: 'He hath but to deliver this clear message. Whosoever desireth, let him turn aside from this counsel.' This is a reminder that whether anyone accepts or rejects the Cause it is not the responsibility of the teacher – don't fret over it.

We are promised that there will be entry by troops and mass conversion to Bahá'u'lláh's Revelation. That time has not yet come in most parts of the world, which can be discouraging for people who love to teach and are energetically trying to spread the Faith with meagre results. A peanut farmer in the south of the United States said, 'Our job is to plant the peanuts. When the rain comes, the peanuts will grow.' At this stage, most Bahá'ís are still planters, not harvesters. Since I tend to be results-oriented, I need to remind myself of this often. Whether or not anyone embraces the Faith is not my concern. Delivering the Message is!

It is also important to remember '. . . and whosoever desireth let him choose the path to his Lord'. There are as many valid ways to reach God as there are people. This statement is a reminder to allow new believers the freedom to find their own ways. That does not mean to abandon them to their own devices, but with loving assistance help them deepen in the spirit of the Faith and let them apply their newly acquired love and knowledge as they see fit, not as you think they should.

We are told, through Aḥmad, not to be deterred even if 'all the heavens and the earth arise against thee', or if overtaken by 'afflictions'. Don't let other Bahá'ís, the institutions, material issues or personal problems get in your way – 'rely upon God, thy God and the Lord of thy fathers', nothing else. As the Guardian stated, 'Let him not wait for any directions, or expect any special encouragement, from the elected representatives of his community, nor be deterred by any obstacles which his relatives, or fellow-citizens may be inclined to place in his path, nor mind the censure of his critics or enemies.'[14]

After an allegorical reference to fire and a river,* there is a strong caution in the Tablet against discouragement, no matter

---

* It is useful to think of the physical characteristics of fire and water and apply them directly to various methods of delivering the Message.

what happens. The basic difficulty in recognizing the Faith is stated as people 'wandering in the paths of delusion' fuelled by 'superstitions' that 'become as veils'. Bahá'u'lláh explained the true nature of 'veils' elsewhere, when He wrote, 'It is the veil of idle imaginations which . . . hath intervened, and will continue to intervene, between [the Manifestations] and the rest of mankind.'[15] The crux of teaching is helping people remove or see through their own veils so that each soul can make its natural connection with its Lord.

Another key point is: 'Learn well this Tablet . . . Chant it during thy days.' This implies both internalizing its deeper meanings and putting forth a serious effort to live by the spirit it can generate.

As to the 'reward of a hundred martyrs', there are many ways to view this. Least likely is receiving a benefit someone else earned. One possible understanding is that since this prayer is a mandate to teach, and teaching has been equated to martyrdom, by chanting or reciting this prayer and teaching, the reward would be the same as that which a martyr would receive. A martyr yields life once. Teaching, with a martyr's level of devotion, can be done over and over – a hundred or more times – hence, multiple rewards.

Another possibility is that the reward for chanting this Tablet is that one hundred martyrs may be assigned to help you. 'Abdu'l-Bahá stated that 'The triumphant hosts of the Celestial Concourse,* arrayed and marshalled in the Realms above, stand ready and expectant to assist and assure victory to that valiant horseman who with confidence spurs on his charger into the arena of service.'[16]

Just think of that! If you have ever been asked a question about the Faith and words came out of your mouth that you didn't know you knew, the chances are that one of the 'hosts'– perhaps a martyr – is inspiring you.

Amatu'l-Bahá Rúḥíyyih Khánum took this literally. She

---

* Obviously, that includes martyrs.

often mentioned that she would cry out to specific individuals from the next world to assist her in time of need, often calling by name on her mother – whom Shoghi Effendi described as a martyr –, Martha Root and others. In many of her talks she spoke of a time in Africa when she was having car trouble on her monumental teaching trip. She said she cried out, 'There must be a mechanic among you somewhere. Now, push!' She explained that they did and, with help from on high, she got to where she could get her Land Rover fixed.[17] More than once I've been stuck on something I've been doing when there has been an unexpected inspiration. I prefer to think one of the 'hosts' was whispering in my ear and I was lucky enough to listen.

There are several ways to consider the following passage: 'Should one who is in affliction or grief read this Tablet with absolute sincerity, God will dispel his sadness, solve his difficulties and remove his afflictions.'

Many people have reported how their sadness had been dispelled, problems solved, and difficulties removed when they arose to teach. I can't say how often I have been stuck in my own perplexing concerns when an opportunity to talk about the Faith arose. All the concerns of the moment vanished, as by magic, just as promised in the Tablet. All that was important at that moment was the teaching opportunity.

Another consideration is that by concentrating with absolute sincerity, particularly in regard to teaching, a better perspective is gained on sadness, difficulties and afflictions and a power is generated within the person to deal with them. While sitting in a dentist's chair once, without the benefit of Novocain, I shielded myself from the pain of the approaching drill by deliberately thinking of the teaching effort. It worked. Not only was the dental work relatively painless, I had a great inspiration that led to great events at our pioneering post.*

---

* On the way to the dentist's office I stopped by Pete Simple's place. He had asked me to help him learn to read better. When I walked in he

TEACHING

Have you ever wondered whom to teach? After intense use of the Tablet of Aḥmad, many people have deployed some of their 100 martyrs to locate receptive souls and arrange for a meeting. That has a proven track record. Whenever the indomitable Martha Root would arrive in a new locale, she would recite the Tablet NINE times, before venturing out to teach the Cause.

How about those people who seem ready to become Bahá'ís but don't take that final step? By using the Tablet of Aḥmad some of the martyrs can be dispatched to give the reluctant ones a needed nudge. Often Bahá'ís have said something like, 'I didn't know what else to do, so I said the Tablet of Aḥmad and they enrolled!' After all, those martyrs already gave up their lives and are now eager to be of 'service in both worlds'. Put them to work. Frequent use of the Tablet of Aḥmad lets you make it possible for some martyrs to serve the Cause in both worlds. What a wonderful partnership! Use it! This is full employment at its best.

There is another aspect of prayer that is easily overlooked. A wonderful way to deploy those martyrs is by praying out loud when no one is around. This can be awkward and not easy for many Westerners. However, Bahá'u'lláh wrote,

> Intone, O My servant, the verses of God that have been received by thee, as intoned by them who have drawn nigh unto Him, that the sweetness of thy melody may kindle thine own soul, and attract the hearts of all men. Whoso reciteth, in the privacy of his chamber, the verses revealed by God, the scattering angels of the Almighty shall scatter

---

was speaking in the Athabascan Indian language to his cousin and he told me he was telling his cousin that he intended to learn all about the Bahá'í Faith and become the interpreter of it for his people. Seeing the dentist's drill approach made me search for something else to think about. That is when I decided Pete and I would start our reading lessons that afternoon, using the Writings of 'Abdu'l-Bahá. He became a strong, dedicated Bahá'í.

abroad the fragrance of the words uttered by his mouth, and shall cause the heart of every righteous man to throb. Though he may, at first, remain unaware of its effect, yet the virtue of the grace vouchsafed unto him must needs sooner or later exercise its influence upon his soul. Thus have the mysteries of the Revelation of God been decreed by virtue of the Will of Him Who is the Source of power and wisdom.[18]

Those martyrs become the 'scattering angels' whose job is it to 'scatter abroad the fragrance of the words uttered by his mouth, and shall cause the heart of every righteous man to throb'. When a Bahá'í prays out loud while alone it may be aiding the' heart' of someone she or he doesn't even know to 'throb', and thereby draw closer to an acceptance of Bahá'u'lláh. So, while intoning the verses of God in the privacy of his chamber, teaching is also taking place on a profound and mystical level.

Who should teach?

Who is qualified to teach? In one manner of thinking, no one is! That's tough. Qualified or not, you and I are the ones called upon to do it. The Universal House of Justice explains:

> Every individual believer – man, woman, youth and child – is summoned to this field of action; for it is on the initiative, the resolute will of the individual to teach and to serve, that the success of the entire community depends. Well-grounded in the mighty Covenant of Bahá'u'lláh, sustained by daily prayer and reading of the Holy Word, strengthened by a continual striving to obtain a deeper understanding of the divine Teachings, illumined by a constant endeavour to relate these Teachings to current issues, nourished by observance of the laws and principles of His wondrous World Order, every individual can attain increasing measures of success in teaching. In sum, the ultimate triumph of the

TEACHING

Cause is assured by that 'one thing and only one thing' so poignantly emphasized by Shoghi Effendi, namely, 'the extent to which our own inner life and private character mirror forth in their manifold aspects the splendour of those eternal principles proclaimed by Bahá'u'lláh'.[19]

How to teach?

While there is no one teaching method that fits all, there is a great deal of guidance. First and foremost are these instructions from Bahá'u'lláh:

> Consort with all men, O people of Bahá, in a spirit of friendliness and fellowship. If ye be aware of a certain truth, if ye possess a jewel, of which others are deprived, share it with them in a language of utmost kindliness and goodwill. If it be accepted, if it fulfil its purpose, your object is attained. If anyone should refuse it, leave him unto himself, and beseech God to guide him. Beware lest ye deal unkindly with him. A kindly tongue is the lodestone of the hearts of men. It is the bread of the spirit, it clotheth the words with meaning, it is the fountain of the light of wisdom and understanding.[20]

This solid relationship is the most effective preparation for teaching. The importance of being careful about your manner is pointed out in this statement from Bahá'u'lláh:

> O people of Baha! Ye are the dawning-places of the love of God and the daysprings of His loving-kindness. Defile not your tongues with the cursing and reviling of any soul, and guard your eyes against that which is not seemly. Set forth that which ye possess. If it be favourably received, your end is attained; if not, to protest is vain. Leave that soul to himself and turn unto the Lord, the Protector, the Self-Subsisting. Be not the cause of grief, much less of discord and strife. The

hope is cherished that ye may obtain true education in the shelter of the tree of His tender mercies and act in accordance with that which God desireth. Ye are all the leaves of one tree and the drops of one ocean.[21]

In a prayer for teaching, Bahá'u'lláh has us make this request:

> Do Thou destine for me, O my God, what becometh the greatness of Thy majesty, and assist me, by Thy strengthening grace, so to teach Thy Cause that the dead may speed out of their sepulchers, and rush forth towards Thee, trusting wholly in Thee, and fixing their gaze upon the orient of Thy Cause, and the dawning-place of Thy Revelation.[22]

What if people won't listen?

Just because no one is paying attention is no reason to stop teaching. It is, however, a good time reassess what you are doing.

The fact that people ignore the divine call comes as no surprise to Bahá'u'lláh. In one of the prayers for the Fast He wrote:

> Thou seest me among Thy creatures who have rebelled and transgressed against Thee. Every time I invite them unto the ocean of Thy knowledge, their repudiation of Thy Cause increaseth and their rejection of the Dawning-Place of Thy Will waxeth greater.[23]

When people are persistent in their 'repudiation . . . and their rejection of the Dawning-Place of Thy Will', it creates a dilemma. Of course, Bahá'ís teach with the hope of leading people to Bahá'u'lláh. What greater thrill is there than to witness a dear one's moment of acceptance? Many Bahá'ís feel a sense of failure when those they are trying to teach do not enrol in the Faith, especially when they have been enduring

TEACHING

long years at a pioneering post with no tangible results. But there is more to it than that.

When enrolments are meagre, it does not necessarily mean that teaching is not effective. When proceeding with the proper motivation, there is still profound progress. Far-sighted people throughout the world have accepted many of Bahá'u'lláh's teachings without recognizing Him. It may take a long time – even generations – for connections to be made. But connections will be made. If we cannot lead people to Bahá'u'lláh, we can promote the reality of His Revelation. That, too, is an essential step.

In all the reports of 'Abdu'l-Bahá's teaching ventures, where did He insist that someone must accept Bahá'u'lláh? His approach was broader. Indeed, how many times have people signed an enrolment card claiming acceptance of Bahá'u'lláh, when they really missed the essence of His Faith and drifted away?

Part of the problem is confusion over what teaching really is. It is more than telling people that the Lord of the Age has come. Deepening, of course, is vital. There is also another dimension. For instance, in the Arabic *Hidden Words* it says: 'O Son of Man! Bestow My wealth upon My poor . . .'[24]

Bahá'ís are the wealthiest people on earth. They have the rich blessings of Bahá'u'lláh. They are commanded to share this wealth with those who are deprived. Even if it seems useless to speak directly of the station and majesty of Bahá'u'lláh, teaching includes sharing insights on what He brought to mankind. Proclaiming these gems of wisdom both enhances individual lives and builds blocks of the New World Order.

While it is best to mention the Author, delivering the Message has two other profound impacts that silently appear when people promote and demonstrate the oneness of mankind and religion; gender equality; harmony of science and religion; the idea of one world; the necessity of trustworthiness, courtesy and honesty in all doings; service to fellow human beings; and other divine truths.

First of all, these vital understandings lay the foundation

for that day when people are ready to accept Bahá'u'lláh. They will have been exposed to some of what He has brought to the world, making it easier for them to enter the continuous learning curve of a Bahá'í way of life.

At the same time, as these teachings are spread, humanity is inching forward toward the Most Great Peace. Our ultimate job is to move the entire population to an acceptance of this new Revelation. It is an uneven process that happens both directly and indirectly.

Bahá'u'lláh offered the most immediate and direct approach in His proclamation to the kings and rulers. That did not produce immediate results that were tangible. Rather than giving up, He offered a second option when He wrote to them, 'Now that ye have refused the Most Great Peace, hold ye fast unto this, the Lesser Peace.'[25] It is not clear how that will develop. No matter how it comes about, Bahá'ís have a vital role in bringing His teachings into more general awareness. In addition to spreading His teachings, the value of prayer cannot be overemphasized, whether focused or general. There are legions of stories of how prayer alone has opened doors that had seemed permanently locked. Hand of the Cause John Robarts loved to tell stories of how use of the Long Obligatory Prayer changed stagnant communities into ones of robust growth.

Bertha Dobbins and Katherine Harcus walked 14 kilometres to Alberta Park, outside Adelaide in South Australia, to spread the Message. There were no immediate results. Exhausted, on the way home they rested at a railway and road intersection. During their rest they repeated the Greatest Name, specifically asking that one of the homes nearby be opened to the Faith. They did not know that H. Collis and Madge Featherstone lived in the nearest house. A short time later, Madge was invited to and attended a Bahá'í meeting. She brought home some literature for Collis, and it wasn't long before they embraced the Faith. In 1957, the Guardian named Collis Featherstone a Hand of the Cause.[26]

TEACHING

In the Tablets of the Divine Plan 'Abdu'l-Bahá said that 'heavenly armies' would be raised up: 'By heavenly armies those souls are intended who are entirely freed from the human world, transformed into celestial spirits and have become divine angels . . .'[27]

The irony is that a person may or may not know the result of efforts as they are made. The beauty is that each of us is invited to be part of the 'heavenly armies', whether or not we see a desired outcome. The title is earned by the extent the individual arises to serve and directly or indirectly spreads the wealth of Bahá'u'lláh's Revelation.

A Bahá'í pioneer once met a new Bahá'í who had been living in the same village as the pioneer just a few years ealier. The new believer told the pioneer that his mother's dying words had been, 'look for the people of BE-HA'. When he was living in the village where the pioneers were and he first saw them, he felt they must have been the ones his mother was talking about. He watched them for three years, but was too timid to approach them. They did not meet at that time. However, he was convinced that his deeply sensitive and spiritual mother was talking about the Message they had. A few years later, in another village, he got to know a different Bahá'í and embraced the Cause. Only later did he meet the pioneer who had been his silent teacher.

No one can fully know how, when or whom she or he is teaching. With purity of motive, how one lives answers this prayer of 'Abdu'l-Bahá:

> O my God! O my God! O God! Thou seest me in my lowliness and weakness, occupied with the greatest undertaking, determined to raise Thy word among the masses and to spread Thy teachings among Thy peoples.[28]

The work is vital, whether or not anyone is listening. Which leads to the pathway being followed by all mankind.

20

The Pathway

The purpose underlying their revelation hath been to educate all men, that they may, at the hour of death, ascend, in the utmost purity and sanctity and with absolute detachment, to the throne of the Most High.
Bahá'u'lláh[1]

The Revelation of Bahá'u'lláh is for both this world and the next. In regard to this world He wrote:

> God's purpose in sending His Prophets unto men is twofold. The first is to liberate the children of men from the darkness of ignorance, and guide them to the light of true understanding. The second is to ensure the peace and tranquillity of mankind, and provide all the means by which they can be established.[2]

A letter from the Guardian to a National Spiritual Assembly contains an interesting warning and a prediction:

> The tests and trials which it [the NSA] must, sooner or later, experience in the course of its unfoldment and consolidation will severely challenge its spirit and resources. The path which it must tread ere the full evidence of its latent capacities are manifested will be long, tortuous and stony.[3]

The 'long, tortuous and stony' journey is true for both the Bahá'í community and individual believers. Both face a series of challenges calling for appropriate responses. Following are thoughts about both journeys, starting with the individual.

The individual pathway

The individual's spiritual journey begins in the mother's womb, courses through the challenges of life on earth, and continues on to the next world. Our time on planet Earth might be compared to the second part of a three-stage rocket to outer space. The first stage is that in the womb. Then, there is this life as the second stage. Finally, there is the third stage, life after death. The time in the womb can be compared to the preparations for the rocket's lift-off. The earthly lifespan is like the booster stage, guiding and propelling the rocket through atmospheric resistance and challenges to its destiny. The rocket finally reaches its orbit – its final stage and ultimate home.

In this, the second stage, the soul courses through earthly life. There are three major barriers in this journey:

- ➢ attachment to this world;
- ➢ attachment to the next world; and
- ➢ attachment to the 'Kingdom of names'.[4]

The dangers, hence the barriers, are not in the nature of these items. They lie in attachment to them, that is craving and loving their benefits and blessings too much.

The preceding chapters have had an underlying theme of reducing attachment to this world. Before discussing attachment to the next world, a few comments about attachment to names are in order. Here is what Bahá'u'lláh has to say about attachment to names:

> People for the most part delight in superstitions. They regard a single drop of the sea of delusion as preferable to an ocean of certitude. By holding fast unto names they deprive themselves of the inner reality and by clinging to vain imaginings they are kept back from the Dayspring of heavenly signs.[5]

A little later in the same Tablet, He gave an example of pious words uttered by a highly regarded person. The person's actions were contrary to what he said and demonstrated the point Bahá'u'lláh made.

It can be inferred that attachment to names includes placing undue importance on the symbols of excellence, such as titles, positions, labels, trophies, plaques, pomp, pageantry, ceremonies, awards, honour badges, accolades, degrees, certificates, achievements, and other signs and symbols. In describing this subtle phenomenon, Bahá'u'lláh quotes a verse from the poet Rumi, 'Love is a veil betwixt the lover and the loved one.'[6]

Most of the above names and processes were designed to enhance the value or prestige of something by making a clear distinction. The danger lies in emotional connections to the names or symbols – overshadowing, distracting from or even eclipsing that which they were intended to represent or support.

There are so many examples of attachment to names in the material world, such as seeking autographs from celebrities. In the art world, an original Rembrandt is worth millions while a copy is only worth a fraction of that even though the naked eye can't see the difference and it is just as aesthetically pleasing. The difference in price is a material measure of the attraction to names.

Even though the Bahá'í Writings are filled with exhortations to strive for excellence, there is a hidden danger. Excessive pride in achieving excellence in one's profession, avocation or anything else can take on such a high priority and consume so much thought and energy that it can become a formidable barrier to the divine. This attachment is the cause of a great deal of cheating to get credit that is not deserved.

High on the list of barriers in this category are strongly held ideologies, be they religious or sectarian. In addition to being an obstacle to God, Bahá'u'lláh said of strongly held religious ideology, 'Religious fanaticism and hatred are a world-devouring fire, whose violence none can quench.'[7]

Even when supposedly for religious purposes, excesses can take on a life of their own and become a subtle but powerful barrier. For some people, being known as a Jew, Christian, Muslim, Bahá'í or something else can become more important than living up to the teachings of the Faith. When that happens, the label – or the name – becomes a powerful barrier between the individual and his Lord.

Many people wear a Christian cross, a Star of David, a piece of clothing – such as a habit, head scarf or priestly vestments or collar, a Bahá'í symbol or some other religious adornment. That is all right. Danger comes when the symbol is cherished or even overshadows the desire to live a religious life.

The term 'patter' illustrates this. It means idle chatter or mumbling and is derived from the Latin *Pater Noster* or the Lord's Prayer. The term comes from the fact that some people repeat the Lord's Prayer mechanically, instead of thinking of its profound connection with the Divine. It is said without thinking seriously about its meaning, let alone the degree of commitment implicit in the words. Hence the 'name' of the Lord's Prayer becomes 'patter', meaning nonsense, and is a barrier to its essence.

The purpose of a degree or certificate is to indicate certain skills, knowledge or level of competence. While they often do that, they can become more essential than what they are intended to represent. Many people have valid certificates, but are incompetent. Degrees or certificates can become like badges of honour to be collected, and take on more significance than what they represent. The Universal House of Justice cautioned against certificates for completion of Bahá'í courses when it said: 'We are happy to note plans for the Institute, but we feel that it would not be appropriate to issue a certificate for those who have completed the course.'[8]

Bahá'ís are not immune to the seduction of names or titles. One person who was an energetic travel teacher mentioned that after she was appointed to the Auxiliary Board she was asked to stay in homes she had never been invited to before. A former member of the Universal House of Justice was warned that he would be asked extensively to speak at schools and conferences. Many summer school and conference committees look for 'names' as headliners. Content, or the quality of presentation, are secondary.

In contrast to the pageantry and ceremony that have become part of many religious practices, the Bahá'í Writings suggest the essence of simplicity for Feasts, Holy Days, weddings and funerals. This protects against excessive attachment to the name, form or trappings of the event.

The Guardian repeatedly admonished Bahá'ís to simplify their lives. He spoke of 'Setting aside all the shibboleths of present-day living, leaving behind the false standards of those endeavouring to solve the world's problems by weak platitudes, and demonstrating the new Bahá'í way of dynamic spiritual living . . . This will produce the results which the cries of humanity today require.'[9] Numerous pilgrims reported that he said Western Bahá'ís should reduce their standard of living.

Amatu'l-Bahá Rúhíyyih Khánum frequently lamented that Bahá'ís too often have weddings that reflect the flamboyance and romanticism of their culture instead of the simplicity suggested in the Writings. She spoke of her own marriage to Shoghi Effendi. They repeated the vows in the room of the Greatest Holy Leaf. Then, the two of them went to the Shrine of Bahá'u'lláh at Bahjí for prayers.[10]

One couple requested a meeting with the local Spiritual Assembly after a Feast without stating why. At the meeting they presented the necessary consent from living parents together with the marriage licence form required by the government, and asked to be married, which they were – all within 15 minutes. Their concern was the spiritual nature of the marriage, not the pageantry of the wedding. It is hard to get much simpler.

A prominent Bahá'í had praise heaped on her for a wonderful

presentation she gave at a conference. She put her hand to her face, palm out, and said, 'Please, not too much. I don't want to enjoy anything in this world so much that it could detract from what I need in the next world.'

There is nothing wrong with enjoying the benefits of this world, or striving to do our best at whatever we undertake. After Florence Mayberry had given a wonderful talk people rushed forward to heap praise on her. She was asked how she could keep her composure following such praise. She answered, 'Everyone likes to hear nice things about what they have done, but I think of the Tablet of Visitation by 'Abdu'l-Bahá, *Make me as dust in the pathway of Thy loved ones.*'

The foregoing are just a few examples indicating that attachment to names not only plays down the importance of what they are supposed to represent, but can be formidable barriers to God. Attachment to accomplishment, not the fact of what has been done, is the barrier.

What about attachment to the next world?

There are two prongs. One has to do with its very existence and nature. The other is an inordinate desire for its perceived benefits.

Belief in some form of life after death is ancient. Most descriptions of the next life are extensions of understandings and capacities of life on earth. Many items – tools, weapons, ornaments, even bodies of former servants – have been found in burial places in all parts of the world. This suggests both a universal belief in an afterlife, and that it is an extension of life on earth, often a glorification of some aspect of this life.

Notations of a future life appeared in the Jewish Scriptures (Old Testament) after their conquest by the Babylonians. The elements described are similar to beliefs held by the Babylonians. Many details that are part of Christian belief and tradition are not from the Bible, but can be traced to John Bunyan's *The Pilgrim's Progress from this world to that which is to come*, published in 1678.

In the Muslim view of Paradise, especially meritorious believers will have the company of 70 virgins. This is an emblem of purity – they would be called angels in Christian terminology. Despite that, many non-Muslims snicker and give it a sexual connotation.

Near-death experiences, even when real, have severe limitations. Frequently, there are reports of a bright light; feelings of rapture, peace and tranquillity; and reunions with loved ones. Whether or not these glimpses of the next world are valid, they tend to be understood in the context of the individual's own belief system. In other words, people who claim to glimpse the next world interpret what they experience according to what they have been taught to expect. At best, such flashes can be no more than a brief, incomplete taste. In would be similar to the knowledge a world traveller might have of a country by spending a few hours in its major airport.

Attachment to the next world is the danger of desiring, seeking and becoming overly attracted to its perceived blessings. As the Báb pointed out in a prayer,

> . . . shouldst Thou ordain evil for a servant by reason of that which his hands have unjustly wrought before Thy face, Thou wouldst test him with the benefits of this world and of the next that he might become preoccupied therewith and forget Thy remembrance.[11]

Little is really known about that world. How is possible to plan for a trip when no one knows what it will be like? All the Divine Messengers teach us how to live in this world. At the same time, that prepares us for the next without being attached to either. Universal spiritual principles such as the Golden Rule have been taught by all the Divine Educators. They are both prescriptions for the best way to live in this world, and literally the means of salvation for the next stage on the spiritual pathway.

THE PATHWAY

A child told to pack socks for a trip may or may not realize they will be needed later. That does not matter. The socks are to be packed. Following divine guidance is the right thing to do for effective living in this world and has even greater implications for the next stage. Just as the eyes of the foetus in the womb world are for greater future use, so too, obedience to the Divine Educators is the best preparation for that part of the spiritual pathway still hidden from view – like the child packing the socks whether or not he understands why.

Each transition is an experience of both death and birth. When born into this world, the individual dies to the world of the womb. Death to this world is a birth to the next. Bahá'u'lláh gave the most insightful analogy when He wrote, 'The world beyond is as different from this world as this world is different from that of the child while still in the womb of its mother.'[12]

That statement is a powerful window to understanding the relationship among the three worlds. The womb defines the limits of the world for the developing child. There is no way to describe the wonders of physical life beyond that existence – such as the beauty of a sunset. It is inconceivable that a child in the womb could know that the purpose of life in that world is to prepare for a life in a world it cannot imagine.

By the same token, earthlings have no way to understand what is beyond. Unlike the child in the womb, many people are conscious that something greater exists. However, every human idea of the next world is just an extension of experience in this life. Time and space in this world are like the confines of the womb – they limit conscious experience. In the same way, living in a world limited by time and space leaves little but wild speculation as to what might be beyond those limits.

The child in the womb does respond to soothing music and positive emotions. And in this second stage of life people can and do, generally unwittingly, respond to intercession from the Concourse on High.

How can the foetus be aware of either the purpose or

importance of its arms, legs and eyes? Any injury or deficiencies in those features have enormous impact on its life once it is born. By the same token, it is not possible to do much more than speculate on the importance in the next world of incomplete or improper development in this world. Caterpillars have been given non-fatal knife wounds. When the butterflies emerge from their cocoons, signs of knife wounds can be found. What we do, or do not do, in this world has much greater effect on the next life than is generally realized.

The umbilical cord in the womb is the child's most significant material possession. It is the source of life and development for the foetus, feeding it as it grows and preparing it for life in this world. The Covenant is a spiritual umbilical cord, providing guidance for both this life and preparation for the next. But there is a major difference. The integrity of the umbilical cord in the womb is protected by the laws of nature and is beyond the control of the child. In this world, the ability of the Covenant to provide needed spiritual nutrients is the result of human volition. People can spurn, ignore or be oblivious of their spiritual connection. In contrast, by following the teachings of the Divine Revelators, they can keep the connection vibrant and healthy.

As for the material elements of this world, from necessities to luxuries they have no more use in the next world than the umbilical cord has in this one. Attachment to them produces problems that linger beyond death. This relationship was stated by Bahá'u'lláh:

> Say: If ye be seekers after this life and the vanities thereof, ye should have sought them while ye were still enclosed in your mothers' wombs, for at that time ye were continually approaching them, could ye but perceive it. Ye have, on the other hand, ever since ye were born and attained maturity, been all the while receding from the world and drawing closer to dust. Why, then, exhibit such greed in amassing

the treasures of the earth, when your days are numbered and your chance is well-nigh lost? Will ye not, then, O heedless ones, shake off your slumber?'[13]

Just as we are born into this world with certain talents and capacities, entrance into the next world has the added ingredient of the spiritual development acquired in this life. Tests and difficulties, challenge and response are not just universal parts of life, they are needed exercises in preparation for the next. Those experiences shape the nature of what each one takes to the third and final stage, even though appreciation of their ultimate value is limited.

When born into this world each one has many gifts – organs, arms, legs, senses, intellect, genes and DNA. These are the tools to work with while facing the changes, chances and challenges of life on earth. How those tools are used in confronting life's issues is what influences spiritual development and may be specific preparation for whatever role is expected in the next world.

Bahá'u'lláh defines the purpose of this life in the short Obligatory Prayer: 'Thou hast created me to know Thee and to worship Thee.'[14] That should be the objective, not getting a softer berth in the next world. In the Tablet of Aḥmad the goal is expressed of being of service in both worlds.

This life can be thought of as a spiritual boot-camp, or training exercise: a preparation for the life to come. It is a time of challenges that are essential for gaining experience in the practical application of learning to know and worship God in everyday life with all its trials and tribulations. Without knowing a great deal about the next life, the way each person responds to the challenges of this life is part of the training needed for whatever may be expected of that soul in the next world.

It can also be thought of as a proving ground where souls are given certain tests and challenges to determine if they are suited for certain functions in the next world. 'Abdu'l-Bahá explained,

> The spirits of heavenly souls will find eternal life, that is, they will attain the highest and most great stations of perfection; but the spirits of the heedless souls, although they are eternal, yet they are in a world of imperfection, concealment and ignorance. This is a concise answer. Contemplate and meditate upon it, in order that thou mayest comprehend the reality of the mysteries in detail.[15]

What little can be gleaned about the next world indicates that gender, race, class, ethnic and physical distinctions are no longer relevant. Positive emotions such as joy, love and compassion, as well as continuing relationships, are retained. Negative emotions such as hate, jealousy, anger and rancour are no more. Sensual delights cease. Apparently those are necessary ingredients while navigating through the jungle of planet Earth, but are not needed for the next world. This is similar to the child leaving the womb. The most essential material feature, the umbilical cord, is left behind; even though life and development were impossible without it, it has no further use.

'Abdu'l-Bahá gave an explanation of the relationship between innate capacity and opportunities for betterment, saying:

> It is evident that although education improves the morals of mankind, confers the advantages of civilization and elevates man from lowest degrees to the station of sublimity, there is nevertheless a difference in the intrinsic or natal capacity of individuals.[16]

He also said:

> In the Bahá'í Cause arts, sciences and all crafts are . . . worship. The man who makes a piece of notepaper to the best

THE PATHWAY

of his ability, conscientiously, concentrating all his forces on perfecting it, is giving praise to God. Briefly, all effort and exertion put forth by man from the fullness of his heart is worship, if it is prompted by the highest motives and the will to do service to humanity. This is worship: to serve mankind and to minister to the needs of the people. Service is prayer.[17]

Some people have special physical, intellectual and moral equipment, based on their innate capacity and education. They do great things; other people, who have less, cannot achieve as much. At least a part of spiritual development is dependent upon how those gifts are used, given the circumstances. Having great capacity and using it for self-serving purposes is like having a ten-ton truck used only for going on picnics. Bahá'u'lláh wrote:

> The whole duty of man in this Day is to attain that share of the flood of grace which God poureth forth for him. Let none, therefore, consider the largeness or smallness of the receptacle. The portion of some might lie in the palm of a man's hand, the portion of others might fill a cup, and of others even a gallon-measure.[18]

Spiritual development is based on how these tools and capacities are used in service, not their unused potential. The Bible quotes Christ as saying, 'For unto whomsoever much is given, of him shall be much required . . .'[19]

If Melinda has a gallon measure of capacity and is primarily concerned with her own comfort, well-being and other self-serving purposes, it's her choice. If she uses two cups of her capacity in service to others, she has helped other people to that extent. Jeremy's capacity may be one cup and he may use all he has in service to others. On one level, Melinda is doing twice as much for the benefit of others as Jeremy since she is giving two cups compared to Jeremy's one. However, Jeremy is giving 100 per cent while Melinda is only using 12.5 per cent of her capacity. It is possible that in the next world they will be judged, not by how much they did, but what each did considering their tools or capacity and the challenges each faced.

No one can say he is ahead or behind anyone else spiritually. Not only is that inappropriate, there are no valid ways to compare either their circumstances or available talents and capacity. The fact that differences exist among us is clear from the following by Bahá'u'lláh:

> From the exalted source, and out of the essence of His favour and bounty He hath entrusted every created thing with a sign of His knowledge, so that none of His creatures may be deprived of its share in expressing, each according to its capacity and rank, this knowledge.[20]

There is an interesting question of where the next world is located. Images of up or down, celestial or underground are based on analogous statements that are descriptive, not literal.

The child in the womb is part of this world, but cannot know it. The thin membrane of the mother's abdomen both protects the child during that phase of development and keeps it ignorant of this life. In the same way, we may all be in the next world, but not know it. People other than the mother are aware of the child as it develops. Those who have already passed on are likewise aware of folks still on earth as they develop and do things that are both good and not so good. Bahá'u'lláh tells us, 'Ye are better known to the inmates of the Kingdom on high than ye are known to your own selves.'[21]

This raises the question of psychic phenomena. They are really features needed for the next world. A letter written on behalf of the Guardian explains:

> Briefly, there is no question that visions occasionally do come to individuals, which are true and have significance. On the

other hand, this comes to an individual through the grace of God, and not through the exercise of any of the human faculties. It is not a thing which a person should try to develop. When a person endeavours to develop faculties so that they might enjoy visions, dreams etc., actually what they are doing is weakening certain of their spiritual capacities . . . [22]

Extra-sensory perceptions are like the arms and legs for the next world. Other than natural, random movements, if someone tries to exercise a child's legs while the child is still in the mother's womb, it may do harm. The same principle applies to extra-sensory perceptions. Leave them alone. Let them develop on their own.

Marcus Bach, a professor of religion from the University of Iowa, was not a Bahá'í, but he had a rare interview with Shoghi Effendi. He asked the Guardian why the Faith was growing more slowly in the United States than other religious communities that started about the same time. The Guardian gave this surprising answer.

'Our influence cannot be counted in numbers,' he declared. 'But the Bahá'í world population is very large and very strong.'

Dr Bach persisted. He mentioned Christian Science, the Adventists, the Mormons, the Jehovah's Witnesses and others that started about the same time and were growing much faster in America. He wrote that Shoghi Effendi answered, 'The trouble with these new religions . . . is that they are always offering the people something. People too often join a new religion, or even an old one, because they expect to get something out of it. Bahá'ís believe they have something to give.'

Dr Bach further said of the Guardian, 'He contended that the westernization of the Christian faith tended to make it opportunistic. "The western concept is, 'What can I get out of religion? What is in it for me?' The Baha'i religion asks, 'What am I willing to give?' What did the first followers of Jesus expect to get out of the Christian faith? A cross."'[23]

Echoing the Guardian's words to Dr Bach, I have sometimes told people that if they expect the Faith to solve their problems, make life easier for them or guarantee a safe birth in the next world, they will be disappointed. Indeed, they may encounter problems never even dreamed of before. There are plenty of religions promising a better life here or in the next world, if that is what they are after. However, if they desire to answer the call of God for this age, to serve the Lord under conditions ranging from miserable to fantastic, to help build the foundation for the Christ-promised Kingdom of God on earth even though they will never bask in its benefits, they will gain unimaginable spiritual insights, often because of enduring enormous difficulties: this is the place.

Instead of offering an easier life, what other modern religion refers to God, at the end of the Long Healing Prayer, as: 'O Thou Who slayest the Lovers, O God of Grace to the wicked?'[24] In another prayer, followers are told,

> But for the tribulations which are sustained in Thy path, how could Thy true lovers be recognized; and were it not for the trials which are borne for love of Thee, how could the station of such as yearn for Thee be revealed? Thy might beareth Me witness! The companions of all who adore Thee are the tears they shed, and the comforters of such as seek Thee are the groans they utter, and the food of them who haste to meet Thee is the fragments of their broken hearts . . . By Thy glory! I wish only what Thou wishest, and cherish what Thou cherishest.[25]

In no less than the *Hidden Words* believers are advised,

> O Son of Being! Seek a martyr's death in My path, content with My pleasure and thankful for that which I ordain, that thou mayest repose with Me beneath the canopy of majesty behind the tabernacle of glory.[26]

Instead of an easy life, tests, difficulties and hardships often come with being a Bahá'í. This has two important features. One is the spiritual development of the individual, acquiring what is needed for the final stage of existence, not comfort in this fleeting one. The other is the necessary process of building the Kingdom of God on earth on a sound, not superficial foundation.

The collective pathway

When I first accepted Bahá'u'lláh, I wondered how long it would be before the whole world would recognize this obvious truth. My calculation was it would take two years and I wondered what would happen to all the church buildings.

Years later it was a thrill to see that Bahá'u'lláh had made the same calculation. However, He added a note of reality. He wrote,

> . . . whenever there was any slight evidence of progress and advancement, those concealed behind the veils would sally forth and utter calumnies more wounding than the sword. They cling unto misleading and reprehensible words and suffer themselves to be deprived of the ocean of verses revealed by God.
>
> If these obstructing veils had not intervened Persia would, in some two years, have been subdued through the power of utterance.[27]

Two years! Think of that. That's how long it would take if it weren't for those 'concealed behind the veils'. But the veils are many. They range from open opposition to indifference; from clinging to traditions to 'pursuit of that which is vain and trivial',[28] from habits to whatever is popular; from seeking personal, material advantage to finding inner enlightenment. Those veils are hard to penetrate, like trying to find your way through an extraordinarily dense fog.

It would seem that once the veils are penetrated, the Faith would be so self-evident that no one could hold back. Since God can put every situation to advantage, there may be something else going on.

True, we are growing more slowly than some of us would like! 'Abdu'l-Bahá said, 'all the forces of the universe, in the last analysis serve the Covenant.'[29] And Bahá'u'lláh quotes the poet Sadi to the effect that despite what happens, 'Even or odd, thou shalt win the wager.'[30] Perhaps even slow growth, given the 'intervening veils', serves a purpose.

During my first pilgrimage I had the privilege of a private lunch with Amatu'l-Bahá Rúḥíyyih Khánum. As an eager Bahá'í in my 20s, I expressed concern over slow growth. She wisely gave perspective by casually responding, 'Well, five hundred years really isn't very long in the history of man.' We are not building just for tomorrow or the day after tomorrow, but for at least 1,000 years for this phase. Ultimately, we are building the foundation for the next 500,000 years. It has to be done right and at the proper pace to endure the test of time. That is a deliberate, and not a speedy, process.

Dr Bach's interview with Shoghi Effendi was mentioned earlier. That was the Guardian's response to a serious religious scholar who was not a Bahá'í. When Mihdi Samandarí was on pilgrimage,* the Guardian gave a different answer to a similar question about the slow growth of the Faith. Mihdi told me that the Guardian said that slow growth was a protection for the Faith. If the Faith grew too rapidly, corruption could seep in, even to the Universal House of Justice. This comment, while only a second-hand pilgrim note, astounded me. But, the more I thought about it, the more it rang true.

'Abdu'l-Bahá contemplated forming the Universal House of Justice as early as 1906, but He realized that some strong, self-seeking Bahá'ís might well be elected. The Bahá'í community was not sufficiently developed to prevent corruption from

---

* Mihdi Samandari was later appointed a Counsellor for Africa.

infecting even that august body.

During a time of intense and energetic teaching in Alaska, a chant heard at a National Convention was that by next year, all of Alaska would have accepted the Bahá'í Faith. What terrified me was that it might happen. What would be the results? Were mass enrolment to happen that suddenly, the delegates to the next National Convention would most likely be well-known and prominent people with activist and political backgrounds and personal agendas. The National Spiritual Assembly would probably be comprised of people who had been prominent political figures and would bring with them many of their old habits and methods.

I once served on a Spiritual Assembly with a devoted Bahá'í who had been part of the inner circle of a national political party in a small country. He had put about 90 per cent of his old ways behind him, but try as he might, the old habits would occasionally creep into deliberations. With one out of nine going through that transition, it was possible to keep the general flow on a Bahá'í level. But what would happen if all nine were going through that learning process at the same time?

When someone accepts Bahá'u'lláh, no matter how sincere and earnest he or she may be, it is unlikely that all the baggage of bad habits and old ways of thinking are immediately and completely left behind. How often has a devoted believer reverted to some inappropriate behaviour patterns from the past, during times of stress?

Enrolling as a Bahá'í starts a process. It is not a switch that changes someone into a spiritual being. The life-long challenge of becoming a Bahá'í is filled with advances and reversals, trials and tribulations. Gradually new insights and perspectives are gained, even though some of those insights might be forgotten from time to time.

One Bahá'í scientist offers the following analogy from nature:

The longleaf pine is a tall majestic pine found in the [North] American southeast. It is the longest lived of the southern pines. It is found on sandy soils where fire is frequent due to drought conditions . . . Instead of getting taller each year as most trees do, the seedling gets thicker around each year but stays right at ground level, producing a thicker and thicker cluster of needles . . . During this stage it grows a deep taproot down to a level where it finds permanent water, often more than 15 feet deep. While in the grass stage, it is quite resistant to fire. The growing tip of the tree is close to the ground where temperatures are lowest during a fire and it is further protected by the thick cluster of green needles. When the seedling is sufficiently robust and has deep enough roots, it suddenly shoots up at the rate of three to six feet in height per year. In just a few years it is tall enough and has thick enough bark to survive most brush fires.[31]

The institutions of the Faith facilitate the process of driving the roots of certitude deep into the hearts of its adherents. At the same time, the relative obscurity of the Faith shields it to some extent from the destructive social storms that are currently wreaking havoc throughout the world. Entry by troops is inevitable. WHEN the time is right, the Faith will burst into visibility. That will be a dramatic sight to behold. Increasingly people will seek its shade and shelter.

During the Ten Year Plan, which the Guardian described as a 'spiritual Crusade', he referred to the great outflow of pioneers and travel teachers. He wrote:

> This flow, moreover, will presage and hasten the advent of the day which, as prophesied by 'Abdu'l-Bahá, will witness the entry by troops of peoples of divers nations and races into the Bahá'í world – a day which, viewed in its proper perspective, will be the prelude to that long-awaited hour when a mass conversion on the part of these same nations

and races, and as a direct result of a chain of events, momentous and possibly catastrophic in nature, and which cannot as yet be even dimly visualized, will suddenly revolutionize the fortunes of the Faith, derange the equilibrium of the world, and reinforce a thousandfold the numerical strength as well as the material power and the spiritual authority of the Faith of Bahá'u'lláh.[32]

Nowhere did he say that those intrepid pioneers would witness the triumphant results. When the time is ripe, like the longleaf pine, there will be an unprecedented burst of growth, first entry by troops, then mass conversion. It is unlikely that any of the pioneers who took part in the Ten Year Crusade will live to witness it.

During the mass teaching days of the 1960s and 70s I realized that the world was ready for Bahá'u'lláh, but the Bahá'ís were not ready to welcome and absorb the world. A major feature of the current Institute process is building the capacity to accommodate the masses when accelerated growth happens. The flow of pioneers was an early and essential step. Bahá'u'lláh predicted:

> When the victory arriveth, every man shall profess himself as believer and shall hasten to the shelter of God's Faith. Happy are they who in the days of world-encompassing trials have stood fast in the Cause and refused to swerve from its truth.[33]

Those who suddenly claim to be believers will have to be integrated into the Bahá'í community. It is no wonder the House of Justice, through the Institute process, is preparing today's believers to deal with that challenge.

Still, from one perspective, the Faith is growing rapidly. In 1988 the Encyclopedia Britannica called it the fastest growing religion in the world. Even more impressive, it reported that the Faith is found in more places of the world than any religion except Christianity.³⁴ Only a hopeless cynic would deny that progress has been made. Only an advanced Pollyanna would think the process is complete.

One of the beauties of this work in progress is that if a person pauses for a moment, looks both back and ahead, it is possible to see that while the journey has been tortuous, stony, and filled with pain and difficulties, there have been dramatic changes characterized by bursts forward followed by periods of little or no obvious change. During the 2001 Bahá'í Conference in Milwaukee, Wisconsin, I was struck by the fact that more Bahá'ís were attending that one conference than there were enrolled in the entire United States when I embraced the Faith nearly a half-century earlier.

Every human's physical life is characterized by growth cycles. The most dramatic change after birth is during adolescence about a decade and a half after birth. The Guardian eloquently drew attention to the process when he wrote:

> Humanity is now experiencing the commotions invariably associated with the most turbulent stage of its evolution, the stage of adolescence, when the impetuosity of youth and its vehemence reach their climax, and must gradually be superseded by the calmness, the wisdom, and the maturity that characterize the stage of manhood. Then will the human race reach that stature of ripeness which will enable it to acquire all the powers and capacities upon which its ultimate development must depend.³⁵

Adolescents frequently swing between being responsible adults to demanding children. Where is he to be found who is at his best at all times? Who is there who is never saddled by fits of depression? Who is there who doesn't love to be with people at one moment and wants to be left alone at another? It is no wonder that the Guardian also referred to this time in history as a 'turbulent age'[36] and the 'age of frustration'.[37]

The only thing certain about this age of uncertainty, turbulence and frustration, is that it will end. Timing and the exact role Bahá'ís will play as the drama unfolds are far from certain. The Guardian indicated one outcome that is both reassuring and frightening. He wrote to the American Bahá'í community:

> In a world writhing with pain and declining into chaos this community – the vanguard of the liberating forces of Bahá'u'lláh – succeeded in the years following 'Abdu'l-Bahá's passing in raising high above the institutions established by its sister communities in East and West what may well constitute the chief pillar of that future House – a House* which posterity will regard as the last refuge of a tottering civilization.[38]

It is impossible to conceive of the Universal House of Justice being 'the last refuge of a tottering civilization' without recognizing enormous destabilizing conditions in every locality of the world. The Covenant has provided three survival tools to sustain Bahá'ís in tumultuous times. One is applying the divine guidance that comes from the Writings. The second is following the infallible directions given by the Universal House of Justice. The third will become increasingly important in local responses to the challenges from the 'tottering civilization' that will affect every community. That is skill in using the divine law of consultation. Those three tools will not only be the means of coping with the unpredictable fallout of the 'tottering civilization', but are the best survival tools for any unpredictable disaster.

Calamities have been predicted in the Bahá'í Writings. Their exact times and natures have not. How can anyone prepare for an emergency that is unknown? Many people think guns,

---

* The Universal House of Justice had not yet been formed when this was written.

bunkers, food storage or other devices will be useful. They may or may not be of value. That which will be most useful is the ability to consult. Those who have learned how to consult will be the ones who will survive and can make the best out of unknown future dire situations.

Consulting well is of enormous importance in the 'majestic process' that the Guardian outlined in his second letter to the Jubilee launching the Ten Year Crusade. He looked forward to the establishment of the Universal House of Justice and said it would signalize the major and most significant consummation of spiritual events:

> Then, and only then, will the vast, the majestic process, set in motion at the dawn of the Adamic cycle, attain its consummation – a process which commenced six thousand years ago, with the planting, in the soil of the divine will, of the tree of divine revelation, and which has already passed through certain stages and must needs pass through still others ere it attains its final consummation. The first part of this process was the slow and steady growth of this tree of divine revelation, successively putting forth its branches, shoots and offshoots, and revealing its leaves, buds and blossoms, as a direct consequence of the light and warmth imparted to it by a series of progressive dispensations associated with Moses, Zoroaster, Buddha, Jesus, Muḥammad and other Prophets, and of the vernal showers of blood shed by countless martyrs in their path. The second part of this process was the fruition of this tree, 'that belongeth neither to the East nor to the West', when the Báb appeared as the perfect fruit and declared His mission in the Year Sixty in the city of Shíráz. The third part was the grinding of this sacred seed, of infinite preciousness and potency, in the mill of adversity, causing it to yield its oil, six years later, in the city of Tabríz. The fourth part was the ignition of this oil by the hand of Providence in the depths and amidst the

darkness of the Síyáh-Chál of Ṭihrán a hundred years ago. The fifth, was the clothing of that flickering light, which had scarcely penetrated the adjoining territory of 'Iráq, in the lamp of revelation, after an eclipse lasting no less than ten years, in the city of Baghdád. The sixth, was the spread of the radiance of that light, shining with added brilliancy in its crystal globe in Adrianople, and later on in the fortress town of 'Akká, to thirteen countries in the Asiatic and African continents. The seventh was its projection, from the Most Great Prison, in the course of the ministry of the Center of the Covenant, across the seas and the shedding of its illumination upon twenty sovereign states and dependencies in the American, the European, and Australian continents. The eighth part of that process was the diffusion of that same light in the course of the first, and the opening years of the second, epoch of the Formative Age of the Faith, over ninety-four sovereign states, dependencies and islands of the planet, as a result of the prosecution of a series of national plans, initiated by eleven national spiritual assemblies throughout the Bahá'í world, utilizing the agencies of a newly emerged, divinely appointed Administrative Order, and which has now [1953] culminated in the one hundredth anniversary of the birth of Bahá'u'lláh's Mission. The ninth part of this process – the stage we are now entering – is the further diffusion of that same light over one hundred and thirty-one additional territories and islands in both the Eastern and Western Hemispheres, through the operation of a decade-long world spiritual crusade whose termination will, God willing, coincide with the Most Great Jubilee commemorating the centenary of the declaration of Bahá'u'lláh in Baghdád.* And finally the tenth part of this mighty process must be the penetration of that light, in the

---

* Political conditions made that impossible. Instead, the First Bahá'í World Congress, celebrating the successful conclusion of the Ten Year Crusade, was held in London.

course of numerous crusades and of successive epochs of both the Formative and Golden Ages of the Faith, into all the remaining territories of the globe through the erection of the entire machinery of Bahá'u'lláh's Administrative Order in all territories, both East and West, the stage at which the light of God's triumphant Faith shining in all its power and glory will have suffused and enveloped the entire planet.

This present Crusade, on the threshold of which we now stand, will, moreover, by virtue of the dynamic forces it will release and its wide repercussions over the entire surface of the globe, contribute effectually to the acceleration of yet another process of tremendous significance which will carry the steadily evolving Faith of Bahá'u'lláh through its present stages of obscurity, of repression, of emancipation and of recognition – stages one or another of which Bahá'í national communities in various parts of the world now find themselves in – to the stage of establishment, the stage at which the Faith of Bahá'u'lláh will be recognized by the civil authorities as the state religion, similar to that which Christianity entered in the years following the death of the Emperor Constantine, a stage which must later be followed by the emergence of the Bahá'í state itself, functioning, in all religious and civil matters, in strict accordance with the laws and ordinances of the Kitáb-i-Aqdas, the Most Holy, the Mother-Book of the Bahá'í Revelation, a stage which, in the fullness of time, will culminate in the establishment of the World Bahá'í Commonwealth, functioning in the plenitude of its powers, and which will signalize the long-awaited advent of the Christ-promised Kingdom of God on earth – the Kingdom of Bahá'u'lláh – mirroring however faintly upon this humble handful of dust the glories of the Abhá Kingdom.

This final and crowning stage in the evolution of the plan wrought by God Himself for humanity will, in turn, prove to be the signal for the birth of a world civilization, incomparable in its range, its character and potency, in the history of mankind – a civilization which posterity will, with one voice, acclaim as the fairest fruit of the Golden Age of the Dispensation of Bahá'u'lláh, and whose rich harvest will be garnered during future dispensations destined to succeed one another in the course of the five thousand century Bahá'í Cycle.[39]

It is awesome to contemplate that sublime scheme in which ordinary Bahá'ís, like you and me, are privileged to take part. While we are still few in numbers and the problems of a dysfunctional world perplex and frustrate the most able and conscientious world statesmen, we can take heart in these words of the Master, 'Abdu'l-Bahá:

> O ye believers of God! Be not concerned with the smallness of your numbers, neither be oppressed by the multitude of an unbelieving world . . . One pearl is better than a thousand wildernesses of sand, especially this pearl of great price, which is endowed with divine blessing. Erelong thousands of other pearls will be born from it. When that pearl associates and becomes the intimate of the pebbles, they also all change into pearls.[40]

And this prayer of 'Abdu'l-Bahá:

> O Lord! O Lord! Protect them in every test, make every foot firm in the pathway of Thy love, and help them to be as mighty mountains in Thy Cause so that their faith shall not be wavering, their sight shall not be dimmed nor hindered from witnessing the lights emanating from Thy supreme Kingdom. Verily, Thou art the Generous. Thou art the Almighty. Verily, Thou art the Clement, the Merciful.[41]

There is a formula for protecting 'them in every test' in order to 'make every foot firm in the pathway of Thy love'. That formula includes daily prayer; fasting; taking account of our actions each day; teaching; and deepening in knowledge and understanding of the Faith and its capacity to transform mankind.

These tools do two special things: First and foremost, they bring the Báb's promise to fruition. While doing that, they enable you and me to walk more easily in the light of the Covenant, thereby fulfilling our individual spiritual destinies.

Hand of the Cause Horace Holley was asked how to attain wisdom. His answer was to read from the *Hidden Words* every day. Adib Taherzadeh claimed that the *Hidden Words* contained the germ or the seed of all the future teachings of Bahá'u'lláh, and Shoghi Effendi referred to them as 'that marvellous collection of gem-like utterances'.[42]

Therefore, it is fitting to end this reflection on walking in the light of the Covenant with both the prologue and epilogue of that most precious book.

> *This is that which hath descended from the realm of glory, uttered by the tongue of power and might, and revealed unto the Prophets of old. We have taken the inner essence thereof and clothed it in the garment of brevity, as a token of grace unto the righteous, that they may stand faithful unto the Covenant of God, may fulfil in their lives His trust, and in the realm of spirit obtain the gem of Divine virtue.*

* * * * *

> *. . . I bear witness, O friends! that the favour is complete, the argument fulfilled, the proof manifest and the evidence established. Let it now be seen what your endeavours in the path of detachment will reveal.*

Bibliography

'Abdu'l-Bahá. *'Abdu'l-Bahá in London* (1912, 1921). London: Bahá'í Publishing Trust, 1982.
— *Abdul Baha on Divine Philosophy.* Comp. I. F. Chamberlain. Boston: The Tudor Press, 1918.
— *Memorials of the Faithful.* Trans. M. Gail. Wilmette, IL: Bahá'í Publishing Trust, 1971.
— *Paris Talks: Addresses given by 'Abdu'l-Bahá in 1911* (1912). London: Bahá'í Publishing Trust, 12th ed. 1995.
— *The Promulgation of Universal Peace: Talks Delivered by 'Abdu'l-Baha During His Visit to the United States and Canada in 1912* (1922, 1925). Comp. H. MacNutt. Wilmette, IL: Bahá'í Publishing Trust, 2nd ed. 1982.
— *The Secret of Divine Civilization.* Trans. M. Gail. Wilmette, IL: Bahá'í Publishing Trust, 1957.
— *Selections from the Writings of 'Abdu'l-Bahá.* Comp. Research Department of the Universal House of Justice. Haifa: Bahá'í World Centre, 1978.
— *Some Answered Questions* (1908). Comp. L. Clifford Barney. Rev ed. Haifa: Bahá'í World Centre, 2015.
— *Tablets of Abdul-Baha Abbas.* 3 vols. Chicago: Bahá'í Publishing Society, 1909–1916.
— *Tablets of the Divine Plan.* Wilmette, IL: Bahá'í Publishing Trust, rev. ed 1977.
— *A Traveler's Narrative Written to Illustrate the Episode of the Báb* (1891). Trans. E. G. Browne. Wilmette, IL: Bahá'í Publishing Trust, rev. ed. 1980.
— *Will and Testament of 'Abdu'l-Bahá.* Wilmette, IL: Bahá'í Publishing Trust, RP 1990.

Able, John. *Apocalypse Secrets: Bahá'í Interpretation of the Book of Revelation.* CreateSpace Independent Publishing Platform, 2013.

The Báb. *Selections from the Writings of the Báb.* Comp. Research Department of the Universal House of Justice. Haifa: Bahá'í World Centre, 1976.

Bach, Marcus. *Circle of Faith*. New York: Hawthorne Books, 1957.

Bahá'í International Community. *For the Betterment of the World*, 2003. Available at: www.bic.org.

Relationship Between Disarmament and Development, 24 August 1987. Available at: https://www.bic.org/social-and-sustainable-development/statement-archive.

Bahá'í News. Periodical. National Spiritual Assembly of the United States, December 1924.

Bahá'í Prayers: A Selection of Prayers Revealed by Bahá'u'lláh, The Báb, and 'Abdu'l-Bahá. Wilmette, IL: Bahá'í Publishing Trust, rev. ed. 2002.

Bahá'í Studies Notebook. Vol. 2, nos. 1 & 2. Ottawa: Association for Bahá'í Studies, 1983.

Bahá'í World Faith: Selected Writings of Bahá'u'lláh and 'Abdu'l-Bahá. Wilmette, IL: Bahá'í Publishing Trust, rev. ed. 1956.

Bahá'u'lláh. *Epistle to the Son of the Wolf*. Trans. Shoghi Effendi. Wilmette, IL: Bahá'í Publishing Trust, rev. ed. 1976.

— *Gems of Divine Mysteries: Javáhiru'l-Asrár*. Haifa: Bahá'í World Centre, 2002.

— *Gleanings from the Writings of Bahá'u'lláh*. Trans. Shoghi Effendi. Wilmette, IL: Bahá'í Publishing Trust, 2nd ed. 1976.

— *The Hidden Words of Bahá'u'lláh*. Trans. Shoghi Effendi. Wilmette, IL: Bahá'í Publishing Trust, 1970; New Delhi: Bahá'í Publishing Trust, 1987.

— *The Kitáb-i-Aqdas: The Most Holy Book*. Haifa: Bahá'í World Centre, 1992.

— *Kitáb-i-Íqán: The Book of Certitude*. Trans. Shoghi Effendi. Wilmette, IL: Bahá'í Publishing Trust, 2nd ed. 1950, 1981.

— *Prayers and Meditations by Bahá'u'lláh*. Trans. Shoghi Effendi. Wilmette, IL: Bahá'í Publishing Trust, 1938, 1987.

— *The Seven Valleys and the Four Valleys*. Trans. M. Gail with A-K. Khan. Wilmette, IL: Bahá'í Publishing Trust, rev. ed. 1975.

— *The Summons of the Lord of Hosts: Tablets of Bahá'u'lláh*. Haifa: Bahá'í World Centre, 2002.

— *Tablets of Bahá'u'lláh Revealed after the Kitáb-i-Aqdas*. Comp. Research Department of the Universal House of Justice. Haifa: Bahá'í World Centre, 1978.

BIBLIOGRAPHY

Bahíyyih Khánum: The Greatest Holy Leaf. Haifa: Bahá'í World Centre, 1982.

Balyuzi, H. M. *'Abdu'l-Bahá: The Centre of the Covenant of Bahá'u'lláh.* Oxford: George Ronald, 1971.

Barthel, Trip. *Dynamic Consultation: 9 Keys to Synergy.* 9 Facets Publishing, 2013.

Cobb, Stanwood. *Character: A Sequence in Spiritual Psychology.* Washington DC: Avalon Press, 1938.

The Compilation of Compilations. Prepared by the Universal House of Justice 1963–1990. 2 vols. Sydney: Bahá'í Publications Australia, 1991.

Crisis and Victory. Comp. Research Department of the Universal House of Justice. London: Bahá'í Publishing Trust, 1988.

Cooper, Robert. 'The new product process: A decision guide for management', in *Journal of Marketing Management*, vol. 3, no. 3 (1988), pp. 238–55.

Davis, Stephen T. *Encountering Evil: Live Options in Theodicy.* Louisville: Westminster John Knox Press, 2001.

The Dawn-Breakers: Nabíl's Narrative of the Early Days of the Bahá'í Revelation. Trans. Shoghi Effendi. Wilmette, IL: Bahá'í Publishing Trust, 1932.

Developing Distinctive Bahá'í Communities. Evanston, IL: National Spiritual Assembly of the Bahá'ís of the United States, 1998.

Esslemont, J. E. *Bahá'u'lláh and the New Era.* Wilmette IL: Bahá'í Publishing Trust, 1980.

Frankl, Victor. *Man's Search for Meaning* (1946). Boston: Beacon Press, 2006.

Ford, Mary Hanford. *The Oriental Rose.* New York: Broadway Publishing Company, 1910.

Furútan, A.-A. *Stories of Bahá'u'lláh.* Oxford: George Ronald, 1986.

Gail, Marzieh. *Arches of the Years.* Oxford: George Ronald, 1991.

Gurinsky, H. Richard. *Learn Well This Tablet: A Commentary on the Tablet of Aḥmad.* Oxford: George Ronald, 2000.

Harper, Barron. *Lights of Fortitude: Glimpses into the Lives of the Hands of the Cause of God.* Oxford: George Ronald, rev. ed. 2007.

Hick, John. *Evil and the God of Love.* New York: Palgrave Macmillan, RP 2010.

Japan Will Turn Ablaze!: Tablets of 'Abdu'l-Bahá, Letters of Shoghi Effendi and Historical Notes About Japan. Tokyo: Bahá'í Publishing Trust, 1974.

Kolstoe, John. *Compassionate Woman: The Life and Legacy of Patricia Locke.* Wilmette, IL: Bahá'í Publishing Trust, 2011.

— *Consultation.* Oxford: George Ronald, 1985.

— *Developing Genius.* Oxford: George Ronald, 1995.

— *Pondering the Fire Tablet: Reflections on Bahá'u'lláh's 'Fire Tablet'.* 2015.

Kurzius, Brian. *Fire and Gold: Benefiting from Life's Tests.* Oxford: George Ronald, 1995.

Lights of Guidance: A Bahá'í Reference File. Comp. H. Hornby. New Delhi: Bahá'í Publishing Trust, 5th ed. 1997.

Living the Life. Wilmette, IL: Bahá'í Publishing Trust, 1981.

Loehle, Craig. *On the Shoulders of Giants.* Oxford: George Ronald, 1994.

Maxwell, May. *An Early Pilgrimage* (1917). Oxford: George Ronald, rev. ed. 1969.

Matthews, Gary. *The Metropolis of Satan.* Knoxville: Stonehaven Press, 1998.

Miller-Munro, Layli. 'Knowledge into action: The Bahá'í imperative to serve humanity', in *Journal of Bahá'í Studies*, vol. 14, no. 1 /2 (March–June).

Momen, Moojan (ed). *The Bábí and Bahá'í Religions, 1844–1944: Some Contemporary Western Accounts.* Oxford: George Ronald, 1981.

Nakhjavani, Violette. *The Great African Safari: The Travels of Amatu'l-Bahá Rúḥíyyih Khánum in Africa, 1969–73.* Oxford: George Ronald, 2002.

National Spiritual Assembly of the Bahá'ís of the United States. *In Service to the Common Good,* December 2004.

Ocean Research Library. Available at: http://www.bahai-education.org/ocean/.

Parsons, Agnes. Unpublished diary, in United States National Bahá'í Archive.

The Power of the Covenant. 3 parts. National Spiritual Assembly of the Bahá'ís of Canada. Thornhill, ON: *Bahá'í Canada Publications, 1976–7.*

BIBLIOGRAPHY

Qur'án. *The Koran.* Trans. J. M. Rodwell. New York: Dutton, 1971.

Rabbani, Rúḥíyyih. *The Priceless Pearl.* London: Bahá'í Publishing Trust, 1969.

Redman, Earl. *'Abdu'l-Bahá in Their Midst.* Oxford: George Ronald, 2011.

Ruiz, Don Miguel. *The Four Agreements: A Practical Guide to Personal Freedom.* Amber-Allen Publishing, 1997.

Sears, William. *Thief in the Night: The Case of the Missing Millennium* (1961). Oxford: George Ronald, RP 2002.

Shoghi Effendi. *The Advent of Divine Justice* (1939). Wilmette, IL: Bahá'í Publishing Trust, 1984.

— *Arohanui: Letters from Shoghi Effendi to New Zealand.* Suva, Fiji: Bahá'í Publishing Trust, 1982.

— *Bahá'í Administration: Selected Messages 1922-1932.* Wilmette, IL: Bahá'í Publishing Trust, 1980.

— *Citadel of Faith: Messages to America, 1947–1957.* Wilmette, IL: Bahá'í Publishing Trust, 1965.

— *Dawn of a New Day: Messages to India 1923-1957.* New Delhi: Bahá'í Publishing Trust, n.d.

— *Directives from the Guardian.* New Delhi: Bahá'í Publishing Trust, 1973.

— *God Passes By* (1944). Wilmette, IL: Bahá'í Publishing Trust, rev. ed. 1974.

— *High Endeavours.* Anchorage: National Spiritual Assembly of the Bahá'ís of Alaska, 1976.

— *Letters from the Guardian to Australia and New Zealand, 1923-1957.* Sydney: Australian Bahá'í Publishing, 1971.

— *The Light of Divine Guidance: The Messages from the Guardian of the Bahá'í Faith to the Bahá'ís of Germany and Austria.* 2 vols. Hofheim-Langenhain: Bahá'í-Verlag, 1982, 1985.

— *Messages to the Bahá'í World 1950–1957.* Wilmette, IL: Bahá'í Publishing Trust, 2nd ed. 1971.

— *Messages of Shoghi Effendi to the Indian Subcontinent 1923-1957.* Comp. Iran Furútan Muhajír. New Delhi: Bahá'í Publishing Trust, rev. ed. 1995.

— *The Promised Day Is Come* (1941). Wilmette, IL: Bahá'í Publishing Trust, rev. ed. 1980.

— *The World Order of Bahá'u'lláh: Selected Letters by Shoghi Effendi* (1938). Wilmette, IL: Bahá'í Publishing Trust, 2nd rev. ed. 1974.

Siegel, B. S. *Love, Medicine and Miracles*. New York: Harper and Row, 1988.

Sparey Fox, Carolyn. *The Half of It Was Never Told*. Oxford: George Ronald, 2015.

Speer, Albert. *Inside the Third Reich*. New York: Simon and Schuster, 1970.

Star of the West: The Bahai Magazine. Periodical, 25 vols. 1910–1935. Vols. 1–14 RP Oxford: George Ronald, 1978. Complete CD-ROM version: Talisman Educational Software/Special Ideas, 2001.

Taherzadeh, Adib. *The Revelation of Bahá'u'lláh*. 4 vols. Oxford: George Ronald, 1974–1987.

The Universal House of Justice. *A Wider Horizon: Selected Messages of the Universal House of Justice 1983–1992*. Comp. Paul Lample. Riviera Beach, FL: Palabra Publications, 1992.

— Letter to the Bahá'ís of Iran, 2 March 2013. Available at: http://www.bahaiebooks.org/letter-to-the-baha%E2%80%99is-of-iran-2-march-2013.

— *The Ministry of the Custodians 1957–1963*. Haifa: Bahá'í World Centre, 1992.

— *The Promise of World Peace*. Haifa: Bahá'í World Centre, 1985.

— Riḍván Messages, available on *Ocean*.

— *Wellspring of Guidance: Messages from the Universal House of Justice 1963–1968*. Wilmette, IL: Bahá'í Publishing Trust, 1976.

Waters, Frank. *The Book of the Hopi*. Penguin, 1977.

Webster's New World Dictionary. New York and Cleveland: The World Publishing Company, 1972.

Woolson, Gayle. *Divine Symphony*. New Delhi: Bahá'í Publishing Trust, 1988.

Yapp, M. E. *The Making of the Modern Near East 1792–1923*. London: Pearson Educational, 1987.

References

Foreword
1. 'Abdu'l-Bahá, on arriving in America, 11 April 1912, in *Star of the West*, vol. III, no. 3 (28 April 1912), p. 3; also in Esslemont, *Bahá'u'lláh and the New Era*, p. 71.
2. 'Abdu'l-Bahá, quoted by Shoghi Effendi, *God Passes By*, p. 238.
3. Reported words of 'Abdu'l-Bahá, 1900, in *Star of the West*, vol. VIII, no. 16 (31 Dec. 1917), p. 215.
4. 'Abdu'l-Bahá, *The Promulgation of Universal Peace*, p. 183.

Preface
1. Shoghi Effendi, in *Living the Life*, p. 11; also in *The Compilation of Compilations*, vol. II, no. 1274.

Introduction
1. Bahá'u'lláh, *Hidden Words*, Arabic no. 3.
2. Letter on behalf of Shoghi Effendi to an individual, 21 October 1921, in *Lights of Guidance*, p. 181, no. 593.
3. Letter from the Universal House of Justice to an individual, 23 March 1975, printed on the cover page of the compilation on the Covenant. Reprinted in *The Compilation of Compilations*, vol. I, p. 110.

1. The Eternal Covenant
1. Bahá'u'lláh, *Hidden Words*, Arabic no. 4.
2. A letter from the Research Department of the Universal House of Justice to the author, 20 May 1995, provided this information and listed *Biharu'l-Anvar*, vol. 11, p. 32 as the reference.
3. 'Abdu'l-Bahá, *Some Answered Questions*, no. 43, p. 164.
4. The copious writings of Joseph Campbell as well as other anthropologists provide a rich treasure trove of information about myths and their relevance.
5. 'Abdu'l-Bahá, *Selections from the Writing of 'Abdu'l-Bahá*, no. 192, p. 228.

2. The Greater Covenant

1. The Báb, Persian Bayán VI:16, in *Selections from the Writings of the Báb*, p. 87.
2. 'Abdu'l-Bahá, *Bahá'í World Faith*, p. 358.
3. Srimad Bhagavatam, vol. II, p. 654, translated by N. Raghunathan, quoted by Woolson, *Divine Symphony*, p. 12.
4. Shoghi Effendi, *God Passes By*, p. 95.
5. Vedas, ch. 1, p. 46. Quoted by Gayle Woolson in *Divine Symphony*, p. 39.
6. Shoghi Effendi, *God Passes By*, p. 95.
7. Isa. 2:4.
8. Matt. 10:34.
9. Isa. 9:6, 7.
10. John 16:12-13.
11. Luke 20:25.
12. A number of Bahá'ís have written detailed accounts about the fulfilment of Christian prophecies. Probably the most widely read is *Thief in the Night* by William Sears.
13. John 14:28.
14. Acts 7:55.
15. Qur'án 3:7 (Rodwell translation).
16. Qur'án 14:48 (Rodwell translation).
17. Bahá'u'lláh, *Gleanings from the Writings of Bahá'u'lláh*, LXXVI, p. 145.
18. A letter to the author from the Research Department of the Universal House of Justice, 20 May 1995, provided the information and listed *Biharu'l-Anvar*, vol. 11, p. 32 as the reference.
19. Kolstoe, *Compassionate Woman*, pp. 27-8.
20. 'Abdu'l-Bahá, *Selections from the Writings of 'Abdu'l-Bahá*, no. 40, p. 82.
21. See Mark, ch. 8, or Matt. ch.16.
22. See Sears, *Thief in the Night*, p. 5; Sparey Fox, *The Half of It Was Never Told*.
23. Bahá'u'lláh, *Kitáb-i-Íqán*, para. 88, p. 80.
24. While the Gospels contained many allusions to this, Matt. ch. 13 has the most complete coverage.
25. Bahá'u'lláh, *Kitáb-i-Aqdas*, para. 81, p. 49.
26. Dan. 12: 8-9.
27. See for example Bahá'u'lláh, *Tablets of Bahá'u'lláh Revealed after the Kitáb-i-Aqdas*, pp. 240-41.
28. Waters, *The Book of the Hopi*.
29. Bahá'u'lláh, *Kitáb-i-Íqán*, para. 86, p. 79.
30. See Friedrich Wilhelm Bessel in any standard encyclopedia.

REFERENCES

31 See Alvan Graham Clark in any standard encyclopedia.
32 Bahá'u'lláh, *Kitáb-i-Aqdas*, para. 37, p. 32.

3. The Lesser Covenant

1 Shoghi Effendi, *The World Order of Bahá'u'lláh*, p.145.
2 Matt. 20:16.
3 The institution of 'Hands of the Cause' was created by Bahá'u'lláh and specifically mentioned in the *Kitáb-i-Aqdas*. Both 'Abdu'l-Bahá, as Centre of the Covenant, and Shoghi Effendi, as Guardian, were able to appoint Hands. Appointments are no longer possible under the terms of the Covenant.
4 Shoghi Effendi, *Messages to the Bahá'í World, 1950-1957*, p. 127.
5 The Guardianship is the other institution of the Administrative Order; see Shoghi Effendi, *The World Order of Bahá'u'lláh*, p. 18.
6 Shoghi Effendi formed the International Bahá'í Council and appointed its first members; see Shoghi Effendi, *Citadel of Faith*, p. 90.
7 See *The Kitáb-i-Aqdas*, paras. 42, 121 and 174; and Notes 66, 67, 145, 183 and 184. A prayer for the Hands of the Cause (in *Lights of Guidance,* no. 1080), has the phrase: 'they who . . . spoke not save after Thy leave . . .' This is similar wording to that in Note no. 67 and reflects the description in Note no. 183.
8 For a full discussion of this relationship, see the letter from Shoghi Effendi of 8 February 1934 titled 'The Dispensation of Bahá'u'lláh'. It is the sixth letter found in *The World Order of Bahá'u'lláh*.
9 See Rabbani, *The Priceless Pearl*, pp. 213-18.
10 Shoghi Effendi, *God Passes By*, pp. 237-8.
11 ibid. p. 59.
12 Bahá'u'lláh, *Tablets of Bahá'u'lláh*, p. 108.
13 Letter from the Universal House of Justice to an individual, 22 August 1977, in *Lights of Guidance*, no. 1050, p. 311.
14 'Abdu'l-Bahá, *Will and Testament*, para. 25, p. 14.
15 ibid. para. 37, p. 20.
16 Letter from the Universal House of Justice to an individual, 22 August 1977, op. cit., no. 1051.
17 Shoghi Effendi, *God Passes By*, p. 325.
18 'Abdu'l-Bahá and a few other trusted believers made handwritten copies of Tablets revealed by Bahá'u'lláh and sent them to other believers according to Bahá'u'lláh's instructions.
19 Shoghi Effendi, *The World Order of Bahá'u'lláh*, p. 5.
20 Shoghi Effendi, *Bahá'í Administration*, pp. 17-25.
21 Bahá'u'lláh, quoted in Shoghi Effendi, *The Promised Day is Come*, p. 20.

22 Bahá'u'lláh, *Gleanings from the Writings of Bahá'u'lláh*, LIV, p. 108.
23 Bahá'u'lláh, Kitáb-i-'Ahd, in *Tablets of Bahá'u'lláh*, p. 221.
24 Note no. 183 in Bahá'u'lláh, *The Kitáb-i-Aqdas*, p. 245.
25 Bahá'u'lláh, *Gleanings from the Writings of Bahá'u'lláh*, CX, p. 216.
26 Quoted in US *Bahá'í News*, no. 429, p. 2, in *Lights of Guidance*, no. 1080.
27 Bahá'u'lláh, Kitáb-i-'Ahd, in *Tablets of Bahá'u'lláh*, p. 221.
28 Shoghi Effendi, *The World Order of Bahá'u'lláh*, pp. 156-7.

4. Behaviours

1 Bahá'u'lláh, *Hidden Words*, Persian no. 5.
2 'Abdu'l-Bahá, *The Promulgation of Universal Peace*, p. 177.
3 ibid. p. 41.
4 Bahá'u'lláh, *Gleanings from the Writings of Bahá'u'lláh*, LXXVI, p. 144-5.
5 'Abdu'l-Bahá, *Paris Talks*, no. 18, pp. 55-6.
6 Shoghi Effendi, *God Passes By*, p. 223.
7 Bahá'u'lláh, *The Kitáb-i-Aqdas*, para. 1, p. 19.
8 Bahá'u'lláh, *Gleanings from the Writings of Bahá'u'lláh*, LXXXVIII, p. 175.
9 'Abdu'l-Bahá, *The Promulgation of Universal Peace*, p. 204.
10 Bahá'u'lláh, *The Kitáb-i-Aqdas*, para. 66, p. 42.
11 Bahá'u'lláh, *Tablets of Bahá'u'lláh*, p. 27. Positive and negative reinforcement is at the basis of most schools of thought of behavioural psychology.
12 'Abdu'l-Bahá, *Selections from the Writings of 'Abdu'l-Bahá*, no. 227, pp. 302-3.
13 Stanwood Cobb, *Character: A Sequence in Spiritual Psychology*, p. 53.
14 The Báb, *Selections from the Writings of the Báb*, p. 192.
15 'Abdu'l-Bahá, words recorded in *Star of the West*, vol. 6, no. 6 (24 June 1915), p. 43.
16 Bahá'u'lláh, *Hidden Words*, Arabic no. 38.
17 Bahá'u'lláh, *Prayers and Meditations*, CLXI, p. 254.
18 Adib Taherzadeh, *The Revelation of Bahá'u'lláh*, vol. 4, p. 253.
19 'Abdu'l-Bahá, *Selections from the Writings of 'Abdu'l-Bahá*, no. 35, p. 71.
20 Bahá'u'lláh, *Gleanings from the Writings of Bahá'u'lláh*, XXXVIII, pp. 87-8.
21 'Abdu'l-Bahá, *Tablets of 'Abdu'l-Bahá*, vol. 1, p. 166.

II Reflections on Walking in the Light of the Covenant

1 Bahá'u'lláh, *Gleanings from the Writings of Bahá'u'lláh*, XXVII, p. 65.

REFERENCES

2 Bahá'u'lláh, *The Kitáb-i-Aqdas*, para. 1, p. 19.
3 Bahá'u'lláh, *Gleanings from the Writings of Bahá'u'lláh*, CXXVII, p. 272.
4 John 14:6.
5 Taherzadeh, *The Revelation of Bahá'u'lláh*, vol. 2, p. 113.
6 Bahá'u'lláh, Súriy-i-Haykal, para. 136, in *The Summons of the Lord of Hosts*, p. 70; also in *Epistle to the Son of the Wolf*, p. 49.
7 Bahá'u'lláh, *Gleanings from the Writings of Bahá'u'lláh*, CLIII, pp. 328–9..
8 Letter from the Universal House of Justice, 23 March 1975, printed on the cover page of the compilation on the Covenant. Reprinted in *The Compilation of Compilations*, vol. I, p. 110.
9 'Abdu'l-Bahá, quoted in Esslemont, *Bahá'u'lláh and the New Era*, p. 103.
10 Letter on behalf of the Guardian, 12 March 1949, in US *Bahá'í News*, No. 251 (Jan. 1952), p. 2; also in *Lights of Guidance*, no. 239, p. 68.
11 Bahá'u'lláh, *Gleanings from the Writings of Bahá'u'lláh*, CIX, p. 215.
12 'Abdu'l-Bahá, *The Promulgation of Universal Peace*, p. 157.
13 *Ministry of the Custodians*, pp. 104, 106.
14 Bahá'u'lláh, *Prayers and Meditations*, XXXI, p. 35.

5. Firmness in the Covenant

1 'Abdu'l-Bahá, *The Promulgation of Universal Peace*, p. 381.
2 Bahá'u'lláh, *The Kitáb-i-Aqdas*, para. 120, p. 62.
3 'Abdu'l-Bahá, *Tablets of the Divine Plan*, pp. 49–50.
4 'Abdu'l-Bahá, *The Promulgation of Universal Peace*, p. 191.
5 'Abdu'l-Bahá, *Selections from the Writings of 'Abdu'l-Bahá*, no. 10, pp. 26–7.
6 ibid. no. 96, p. 126.
7 Bahá'u'lláh, *Epistle to the Son of the Wolf*, p. 93; also in *Gleanings from the Writings of Bahá'u'lláh*, CXXX, p. 285.
8 Bahá'u'lláh, *Tablets of Bahá'u'lláh*, p. 175.
9 Bahá'u'lláh, *Hidden Words*, Persian no. 81.
10 Bahá'u'lláh, *Hidden Words*, Arabic no. 38.
11 Bahá'u'lláh, *The Seven Valleys*, p. 33.

6. Oneness of Mankind

1 'Abdu'l-Bahá, quoted by Shoghi Effendi, *The Promised Day Is Come*, p. 119.
2 Shoghi Effendi, *The World Order of Baha'u'llah*, pp. 42–3.
3 'Abdu'l-Bahá, *The Promulgation of Universal Peace*, pp. 190–91.
4 Letter from Shoghi Effendi to the National Spiritual Assembly of

India and Burma, 9 January 1934, in *Messages to the Indian Subcontinent*, p. 108; also in *The Compilation of Compilations*, vol. II, no. 1441.
5 Shoghi Effendi, *Bahá'í Administration*, p. 20.
6 Bahá'u'lláh, *Gleanings from the Writings of Bahá'u'lláh*, LXXXVII, p. 173.
7 ibid. XCII, p. 183.
8 'Abdu'l-Bahá, quoted by Shoghi Effendi, *God Passes By*, p. 238.
9 'Abdu'l-Bahá, *Selections from the Writings of 'Abdu'l-Bahá*, no. 65, p. 101.
10 Shoghi Effendi, *The Advent of Divine Justice*, pp. 29–30.
11 Shoghi Effendi, *The World Order of Bahá'u'lláh*, p. 47.

7. World Peace

1 Bahá'u'lláh, quote in Esslemont, *Bahá'u'lláh and the New Era*, pp. 39–40; also in *The Compilation of Compilations* vol. II, no. 1578.
2 The Universal House of Justice, *The Promise of World Peace*, section III.
3 'Abdu'l-Bahá, *Selections from the Writings of 'Abdu'l-Bahá*, no. 10, p. 26.
4 Bahá'u'lláh, *Gleanings from the Writings of Bahá'u'lláh*, CXVII, pp. 249–50.
5 The Universal House of Justice, *The Promise of World Peace*, para. 1.
6 'Abdu'l-Bahá, *The Promulgation of Universal Peace*, pp. 123–4.
7 'Abdu'l-Bahá, *Paris Talks*, no. 6, p. 19.
8 'Abdu'l-Bahá, *The Promulgation of Universal Peace*, pp. 11–12.
9 'Abdu'l-Bahá, *Tablets of the Divine Plan*, p. 33.
10 *The Dawn-Breakers*, p. 213.
11 Matt. 5:15.

8. Liberty, Submission and Guidance

1 Bahá'u'lláh, *The Kitáb-i-Aqdas*, para. 123, p. 63.
2 ibid. para. 122.
3 ibid. para. 123.
4 ibid. para. 124.
5 ibid. para. 125, pp. 63–4.
6 'Abdu'l-Bahá, *The Promulgation of Universal Peace*, p. 184.
7 Bahá'u'lláh, *Gleanings from the Writings of Bahá'u'lláh*, LXXXI, pp. 156–7.
8 For more information on the subject, see the compilation titled *Consultation* published by the Universal House of Justice in 1978. The entire compilation is included in *The Compilation of Compilations*, vol. I. See also my own books *Consultation* and *Developing Genius*, published by George Ronald in 1985 and 1995 respectively.
9 Bahá'u'lláh, *The Compilation of Compilations*, vol. I, p. 97.

REFERENCES

10 Bahá'u'lláh, 'Questions and Answers', no. 99, in *The Kitáb-i-Aqdas*, p. 136.
11 Bahá'u'lláh, *Gleanings from the Writings of Bahá'u'lláh*, CLXIII, pp. 342–3.
12 Bahá'u'lláh, *Prayers and Meditations*, CLXIII, p. 257.
13 Bahá'u'lláh, *The Kitáb-i-Aqdas*, para. 120, p. 62.
14 Bahá'u'lláh, *Epistle to the Son of the Wolf*, pp. 136–7.
15 Bahá'u'lláh, *Tablets of Bahá'u'lláh*, pp. 181–2.
16 Bahá'u'lláh, *Gleanings from the Writings of Bahá'u'lláh*, CXIV, p. 236.
17 Bahá'u'lláh, *Epistle to the Son of the Wolf*, p. 135.
18 Bahá'u'lláh, *Tablets of Bahá'u'lláh*, p. 38.
19 Bahá'u'lláh, *Epistle to the Son of the Wolf*, p. 11.
20 Bahá'u'lláh, *Tablets of Bahá'u'lláh*, p. 88.
21 Bahá'u'lláh, *Gleanings from the Writings of Baha'u'llah*, CLXIII, p. 342.

9. Two Processes

1 Bahá'u'lláh, *Gleanings from the Writings of Bahá'u'lláh*, IV, p. 7.
2 Shoghi Effendi, *The World Order of Bahá'u'lláh*, p. 134.
3 Bahá'u'lláh, *Gleanings from the Writings of Bahá'u'lláh*, XXXIV, pp. 79–80.
4 Bahá'u'lláh, *The Kitáb-i-Aqdas*, para. 181, p. 85.
5 Matt. 6:10.
6 Shoghi Effendi, *The Promised Day is Come*, p. 117.
7 Shoghi Effendi, *Citadel of Faith*, pp. 31–2.
8 Bahá'u'lláh, quoted by Shoghi Effendi, *God Passes By*, p. 194.
9 Shoghi Effendi, *Messages to the Bahá'í World, 1950–1957*, p. 102.
10 Shoghi Effendi, *The World Order of Bahá'u'lláh*, pp. 187–8.
11 ibid. p. 204.
12 Bahá'í International Community, *The Relationship Between Disarmament and Development*.
13 Letter from the Universal House of Justice to the Bahá'ís of Iran, 2 March 2013.
14 Bahá'u'lláh, Tablet of Ishráqát, quoted in *The Kitáb-i-Aqdas*, p. 91; for the whole Tablet see *Tablets of Bahá'u'lláh*, pp. 99–134.
15 Shoghi Effendi, *Citadel of Faith*, p. 39.
16 Shoghi Effendi, *God Passes By*, p. xvii.
17 John Able, *Apocalypse Secrets: Bahá'í Interpretation of the Book of Revelation*, p. 13.
18 Letter from the Universal House of Justice to the Bahá'ís of the world, Riḍván 163, 2006.
19 Bahá'u'lláh, *Gleanings from the Writings of Bahá'u'lláh*, XCVI, p. 196.
20 Shoghi Effendi, *The World Order of Bahá'u'lláh*, p. 169.

10. Three Protagonists

1. Message from the Universal House of Justice to the Bahá'ís of the world, Riḍván 152, 2013, p. 2.
2. Letter from the Universal House of Justice to the Conference of the Continental Counsellors, 153, 1995.
3. *The Dawn-Breakers*, pp. 92–4.
4. Letter on behalf of Shoghi Effendi to an individual, 6 July 1942, in *Lights of Guidance*, no. 250, p. 71.
5. Rabbani, *The Priceless Pearl*, p. 74.
6. The Fire Tablet is included in many Bahá'í prayer books. See also Kolstoe, *Pondering the Fire Tablet*.
7. Shoghi Effendi, *Directives from the Guardian*, no. 27, p. 9.
8. Shoghi Effendi, *Citadel of Faith*, pp. 148–9.
9. Bahá'u'lláh, *Gleanings from the Writings of Bahá'u'lláh*, CXXXII, p. 288.
10. Letter on behalf of Shoghi Effendi to an individual, 4 May 1942, in the compilation *The Power of Divine Assistance*; also in *The Compilation of Compilations*, vol. II, no. 1711.
11. 'Abdu'l-Bahá, *Selections from the Writings of 'Abdu'l-Bahá*, no. 208, p. 264; quoted by Shoghi Effendi in *Bahá'í Administration*, pp. 42–3.
12. Shoghi Effendi, *God Passes By*, p. 386.
13. Shoghi Effendi, *Bahá'í Administration*, pp. 63–4.
14. Bahá'u'lláh, Kitáb-i-'Ahd, in *Tablets of Bahá'u'lláh*, p. 222.
15. Letter on behalf of Shoghi Effendi to an individual, 6 July 1942, in *Lights of Guidance*, no. 250, p. 71.
16. Shoghi, Effendi, *Bahá'í Administration*, p. 64.
17. Letter on behalf of Shoghi Effendi to the National Spiritual Assembly of the United States and Canada, 30 August 1930, in the compilation *Local Spiritual Assemblies*; also in *The Compilation of Compilations*, vol. II, no. 1389.
18. Bahá'u'lláh, *Gleanings from the Writings of Bahá'u'lláh*, V, p. 9.

11. Living the Life

1. 'Abdu'l-Bahá, on arriving in America, 11 April 1912, in *Star of the West*, vol. 3, no. 3 (28 April 1912), p. 3; also in Esslemont, *Bahá'u'lláh and the New Era*, p. 71.
2. Bahá'u'lláh, *Gleanings from the Writings of Baha'u'llah*, XCVI, p. 196.
3. 'Abdu'l-Bahá, quoted by Mrs Florian (Grace) Krug, in *Star of the West*, vol. 13, p. 9.
4. Esslemont, *Bahá'u'lláh and the New Era*, p. 71.
5. Letter written on behalf of Shoghi Effendi to the National Spiritual Assembly of Central and East Africa, 8 August 1957, in *Lights of*

REFERENCES

   Guidance, no. 236, p. 67.
6 Letter written on behalf of Shoghi Effendi to an individual, 17 February 1938, in *Lights of Guidance*, no. 237, p. 68.
7 Bahá'u'lláh, *Gleanings from the Writings of Bahá'u'lláh*, XLIII, p. 97.
8 Gen.1:26.
9 'Abdu'l-Bahá, *Divine Philosophy*, pp. 83-4.
10 'Abdu'l-Bahá, quoted in Maxwell, *An Early Pilgrimage*, p. 42.
11 Shoghi Effendi, *God Passes By*, p. 193.
12 Bahá'u'lláh, *Hidden Words*, Persian no. 80.
13 Bahá'u'lláh, *Gleanings from the Writings of Bahá'u'lláh*, CXXXVI, p. 295.
14 Shoghi Effendi, *Directives from the Guardian*, no. 160, p. 60; also in many Bahá'í prayer books.
15 Bahá'u'lláh, in *Bahá'í Prayers*, p. 69.
16 Bahá'u'lláh, *Prayers and Meditations*, CLXXVIII, p. 299.
17 Bahá'u'lláh, *Gleanings from the Writings of Bahá'u'lláh*, CXXXVIII, p. 301.
18 ibid. p. 300.
19 'Abdu'l-Bahá, *Tablets of Abdul-Baha Abbas*, vol. 1, p. 207..
20 Taherzadeh, 'Growing in the Bahá'í Faith', recorded talk in Anchorage, Alaska.
21 Bahá'u'lláh, *Prayers and Meditations*, LXX, pp. 116-17.
22 Letter from Shoghi Effendi to an individual, in *The Compilation of Compilations*, vol. II, no. 1762..
23 'Abdu'l-Bahá, *The Promulgation of Universal Peace*, p. 246.
24 Bahá'u'lláh, *Prayers and Meditations*, CLII, p. 244.
25 Bahá'u'lláh, *Tablets of Bahá'u'lláh*, p. 173.
26 Note 29 in Bahá'u'lláh, *The Kitáb-i-Aqdas*, p. 178.
27 'Abdu'l-Bahá, *Selections from the Writings of 'Abdu'l-Bahá*, no. 102, p. 129; also in *The Compilation of Compilations*, vol. I, no. 23.
28 Bahá'u'lláh, *The Kitáb-i-Aqdas*, para. 37, p. 40.
29 'Abdu'l-Bahá, *Selections from the Writings of 'Abdu'l-Bahá*, no. 51, p. 91.
30 'Abdu'l-Bahá, in *Star of the West*, vol. IV, no. 7 (13 July 1913), p. 120; also in *The Compilation of Compilations*, vol. I, no. 933.
31 ibid.
32 ibid.
33 Bahá'u'lláh, *Gleanings from the Writings of Bahá'u'lláh*, LXXXVIII, p. 175.
34 Shoghi Effendi, *The Advent of Divine Justice*, p. 19.
35 ibid. p. 25.
36 *Webster's New World Dictionary*, p. 241.

37 Shoghi Effendi, *The Advent of Divine Justice*, p. 25.
38 Letter written on behalf of Shoghi Effendi to an individual, 28 September 1941, included in *A Chaste and Holy Life*, in *The Compilation of Compilations*, vol. I, no. 147.
39 Letter written on behalf of Shoghi Effendi to an individual, 13 December 1940, ibid. vol. I, no. 146.
40 Letter from the Universal House of Justice, 23 April 2013, forwarded to the author from the Bahá'í World Centre.
41 Bahá'u'lláh, *Kitáb-i-Íqán*, para. 92, p. 85.
42 Bahá'u'lláh, *The Kitáb-i-Aqdas*, para. 49, p. 37; see also Question no. 23, p. 114.
43 Letter written on behalf of Shoghi Effendi to an individual, 30 September 1949, included in *A Chaste and Holy Life*, in *The Compilation of Compilations*, vol. I, no. 149, and vol. II, no. 1323.
44 Letter from the Universal House of Justice, 27 October 2010, forwarded to the author from the Bahá'í World Centre.
45 Bahá'u'lláh, *Tablets of Bahá'u'lláh*, p. 138.
46 Available in *The Compilation of Compilations*, vol. I.
47 'Abdu'l-Bahá, *Selections from the Writings of 'Abdu'l-Bahá*, no. 84, p. 117.
48 Bahá'u'lláh, in *Bahá'í Prayers*, p. 103.
49 Letter written on behalf of Shoghi Effendi to an individual, 8 May 1939, included in *Marriage and Family Life*, in *The Compilation of Compilations* , vol. II, no. 2317.
50 'Abdu'l-Bahá, *Selections from the Writings of 'Abdu'l-Bahá*, no. 86, p. 118.
51 Letter written on behalf of Shoghi Effendi to an individual, 14 May 1929, included in *Family Life*, in *The Compilation of Compilations* , vol. I, no. 865.
52 Letter from the Universal House of Justice, 1 August 1978, included in *Women*, in *The Compilation of Compilations*, vol. II, no. 2160.
53 Khalil A. Khavari, 'Marriage and the Nuclear Family: A Bahá'í Persepctive', in *Bahá'í Studies Notebook,* vol. II, nos. 1 & 2 (March 1983), pp. 78–9.
54 Letter from the Universal House of Justice to the National Spiritual Assembly of the Bahá'ís of New Zealand, 28 December 1980, included in *Family Life*, in *The Compilation of Compilations*, vol. I, no. 916.
55 'Abdu'l-Bahá, from a Tablet translated from the Persian, included in *Marriage and Family Life*, in *The Compilation of Compilations*, vol. II, no. 1306.

12. Tests, Difficulties and a Radiant Life

1. Bahá'u'lláh, *Gleanings from the Writings of Bahá'u'lláh*, LXVI, p. 129.
2. 'Abdu'l-Bahá, *Paris Talks*, no. 31, p. 98.
3. 'Abdu'l-Bahá, in *Star of the West*, vol. VIII, no. 18 (7 February 1918), p. 235.
4. Bahá'u'lláh, *Tablets of Bahá'u'lláh* p. 164.
5. 'Abdu'l-Bahá, *Paris Talks*, no. 36, p. 114.
6. The Báb, *Selections from the Writings of the Báb*, p. 215.
7. 'Abdu'l-Bahá, *Paris Talks*, no. 14, pp. 42–3.
8. Bahá'u'lláh. *Gleanings from the Writings of Bahá'u'lláh*, XLV, p. 99.
9. Bahá'u'lláh. ibid. CXXXVI, p. 296.
10. This passage is consistent with the idea that the Manifestations are agents of change. The following passage from the long obligatory prayer suggests that the inert letters B and E become the action verb 'to be' when combined through the appearance of the Divine Messenger: 'He Who hath been manifested is the Hidden Mystery, the Treasured Symbol, through Whom the letters B and E (Be) have been joined and knit together.'
11. For a more comprehensive treatment of the subject, see the compilation from Bahá'í Writings collected by Brian Kurzius: *Fire and Gold: Benefiting from Life's Tests*.
12. Bahá'u'lláh, *Gleanings from the Writings of Bahá'u'lláh*, LIX, p. 117.
13. Agnes Parsons, unpublished diary, entry dated Sat. July 26.
14. Cooper, 'The new product process: A decision guide for management', pp. 238–55.
15. 'Abdu'l-Bahá, *The Promulgation of Universal Peace*, p. 310.
16. 'Abdu'l-Bahá, *Selections from the Writings of 'Abdu'l-Bahá*, no. 152, p. 179.
17. 'Abdu'l-Bahá, *Tablets of the Divine Plan*, p. 55.
18. Yapp, *The Making of the Modern Near East 1792–1923*, p. 290.
19. The Báb, *Selections from the Writings of the Báb*, p. 215.
20. Bahá'u'lláh, *Prayers and Meditations*, XX, p. 23.
21. Bahá'u'lláh, *Gleanings from the Writings of Bahá'u'lláh*, CLI, p. 320.
22. Bahá'u'lláh, *The Seven Valleys*, p. 15.
23. 'Abdu'l-Bahá, *Selections from the Writings of 'Abdu'l-Bahá*, no. 1, pp. 1–2.
24. Story told by 'Abdu'l-Bahá to Charles Tinsley, who had broken his leg, in *Star of the West*, vol. IV, no. 12 (16 October 1913), p. 205; also in *Lights of Guidance*, no. 2040, p. 601.
25. Bahá'u'lláh, *Gleanings from the Writings of Bahá'u'lláh*, V, pp. 8–9.
26. 'Abdu'l-Bahá, *The Promulgation of Universal Peace*, p. 453.
27. Ford, *The Oriental Rose*, p. 6.

THE COVENANT AND YOU

28 'Abdu'l-Bahá, in *Star of the West*, Vol. VI, no. 6 (24 June 1915), p. 44.
29 'Abdu'l-Bahá, ibid. vol. IV, no. 5 (5 June 1913), p. 89.
30 Bahá'u'lláh, quoted by Shoghi Effendi in *God Passes By*, p. 190.
31 Balyuzi, *'Abdu'l-Bahá: The Centre of the Covenant*, p. 31.
32 'Abdu'l-Bahá, *'Abdu'l-Bahá in London*, p. 120.
33 'Abdu'l-Bahá, *Tablets of Abdul-Baha*, vol. 1, p. 83.
34 'Abdu'l-Bahá, *Selections from the Writings of 'Abdu'l-Bahá*, no. 150, p. 177.
35 Bahá'u'lláh, *Gleanings from the Writings of Bahá'u'lláh*, CXLVI, p. 314.
36 'Abdu'l-Bahá, *Some Answered Questions*, no. 77, p. 309.
37 Siegel, *Love, Medicine and Miracles*, p. 195.
38 Matt. 6:12.
39 Letter on behalf of Shoghi Effendi to an individual, 18 December 1945, in *The Compilation of Compilations*, vol. II, no. 1308.
40 Letter on behalf of Shoghi Effendi, 22 July 1947, in *Letters from the Guardian to Australia and New Zealand*, p. 69.
41 'Abdu'l-Bahá, *Tablets of Abdul-Baha*, vol. III, p. 641.
42 Bahá'u'lláh, *The Kitáb-i-Aqdas*, para. 125, p. 64.
43 Furútan, *Stories of Bahá'u'lláh*, no. 60, p. 51.
44 Redman, *'Abdu'l-Bahá in Their Midst*, pp. 78–9, from Gail, *Arches of the Years*, pp. 106–7, and Balyuzi, *'Abdu'l-Bahá*, p. 452.
45 'Abdu'l-Bahá, *Some Answered Questions*, no. 35, p. 155.
46 Bahá'u'lláh. *Hidden Words*, Arabic no. 36.
47 'Abdu'l-Bahá, *The Promulgation of Universal Peace*, pp. 188–9.
48 Bahá'u'lláh, *The Compilation of Compilations*, vol. I, no. 1020; also in Esslemont, *Bahá'u'lláh and the New Era*, p. 108.
49 Bahá'u'lláh, *Prayers and Meditations*, XXXVIII, p. 54.

13. Words and Deeds

1 Bahá'u'lláh, *Tablets of Bahá'u'lláh*, p. 156.
2 Bahá'u'lláh, *The Kitáb-i-Aqdas*, para. 70, pp. 44–5.
3 Bahá'u'lláh, *Gleanings from the Writings of Bahá'u'lláh*, CXXXIX, p. 305.
4 Bahá'u'lláh, *The Summons of the Lord of Hosts*, p. 77.
5 See Ruiz, *The Four Agreements: A Practical Guide to Personal Freedom*.
6 See Barthel, *Dynamic Consultation: 9 Keys to Synergy*.
7 Bahá'u'lláh, *Gleanings from the Writings of Bahá'u'lláh*, CXVII, p.250.
8 'Abdu'l-Bahá, *Paris Talks*, no. 42, p. 142.
9 ibid. no. 58, pp. 193–4.
10 ibid. no. 45, p. 153.
11 ibid. no. 1, p. 2.
12 ibid. no. 9, p. 26.

REFERENCES

13　ibid. no. 58, pp. 193–5.
14　'Abdu'l-Bahá, in *Star of the West*, vol. VI, no. 6 (24 June 1915), p. 44.

14. Culture of Learning

1　Shoghi Effendi, *The World Order of Bahá'u'lláh*, p. 100.
2　Bahá'u'lláh, *Gleanings from the Writings of Bahá'u'lláh*, CLVI, p. 333.
3　Bahá'u'lláh, *Kitáb-i-Íqán*, para. 267, p. 238.
4　Letter from the Universal House of Justice, 31 January 1995. Available at: covenantstudy.org.
5　The Universal House of Justice, Riḍván Message, 1967, in *Wellspring of Guidance*, p. 114.
6　ibid. pp. 114–15.
7　Letter from the Universal House of Justice, 17 January 2003: 'Progress of Five Year Plan – Learning in Action,' p. 1. Available on *Ocean*.
8　Baha'u'llah, *Epistle to the Son of the Wolf*, pp. 10–11.
9　Bahá'u'lláh, *The Kitáb-i-Aqdas*, para. 126, p. 64.
10　ibid. para. 102, p. 57.
11　'Abdu'l-Bahá, in *The Compilation of Compilations*, vol. I, no. 627.
12　Furútan, *Stories of Bahá'u'lláh*, no. 60, p. 51.
13　'Abdu'l-Bahá, *The Promulgation of Universal Peace*, pp. 69–70.
14　ibid. p. 49.
15　ibid. pp. 226–7.
16　'Abdu'l-Bahá, quoted by Shoghi Effendi, *Japan Will Turn Ablaze*, p. 26.
17　'Abdu'l-Bahá, *Some Answered Questions*, pp. 34–5.
18　Dictionary app for Windows.
19　'Abdu'l-Bahá, *Some Answered Questions*, p. 43.
20　ibid. p. 44.
21　John 2:3–9.
22　Luke 5:37.
23　Matt. 14: 16–20; Mark 6:37–42; Luke 9:13–17; John 6:6–13.
24　Bahá'u'lláh, *Hidden Words*, Arabic no. 2.

15. Arts, Science, Work and Leisure

1　Bahá'u'lláh, *Tablets of Bahá'u'lláh*, p. 26.
2　'Abdu'l-Bahá, *The Promulgation of Universal Peace*, p. 316.
3　ibid. pp. 417–18.
4　Bahá'u'lláh, *The Kitáb-i-Aqdas*, para. 77, p. 48, and note 110, pp. 214–15.
5　'Abdu'l-Bahá, *The Promulgation of Universal Peace*, p. 92.
6　Bahá'u'lláh, *Tablets of Bahá'u'lláh*, pp. 168–9.
7　'Abdu'l-Bahá, *The Promulgation of Universal Peace*, p. 283.

THE COVENANT AND YOU

8 'Abdu'l-Bahá, *Selections from the Writings of 'Abdu'l-Bahá*, no. 74, p. 112.
9 Bahá'u'lláh, *The Kitáb-i-Aqdas*, para. 51, p. 38.
10 Letter written on behalf of Shoghi Effendi to the National Spiritual Assembly of India, Pakistan and Burma, 30 June 1952, in *The Compilation of Compilations*, vol. I, no. 132.
11 Letter written on behalf of Shoghi Effendi to the National Spiritual Assembly of the United States and Canada, 20 July 1946, in *The Compilation of Compilations*, vol, II, no. 1429.
12 Bahá'u'lláh, *Gleanings from the Writings of Bahá'u'lláh*, LXXXI, p. 157.
13 'Abdu'l-Bahá, in *The Compilation of Compilations*, vol. I, no. 578.
14 Bahá'u'lláh, *The Kitáb-i-Aqdas*, para. 33, p. 30.
15 Bahá'u'lláh. *Tablets of Bahá'u'lláh*, p. 35.
16 ibid. p. 175.
17 'Abdu'l-Bahá, *The Secret of Divine Civilization*, pp. 91–2.
18 Shoghi Effendi, *The World Order of Bahá'u'lláh*, p. 187.
19 Bahá'u'lláh, *Kitáb-i-Íqán*, para. 153, pp. 144–5.
20 *Bahíyyih Khánum*, no. 20, p. 86.
21 Shoghi Effendi, *Bahá'í Administration*, p. 130.
22 'Abdu'l-Bahá, quoted in Esslemont, *Bahá'u'lláh and the New Era*, p. 103.

16. Socio-Economic Development: Bahá'í-inspired Projects

1 Message from the Universal House of Justice, Riḍván 2010.
2 *The Dawn-Breakers*, p. 303.
3 ibid. pp. 104–6.
4 'Abdu'l-Bahá, *The Promulgation of Universal Peace*, p. 238.
5 ibid.
6 Letter on behalf of Shoghi Effendi to an individual, 26 December 1935, in *Directives from the Guardian*, no. 55; also partially in *Lights of Guidance*, no. 1868.
7 Letter on behalf of Shoghi Effendi to an individual, 11 January 1933, in *Directives from the Guardian*, no. 56.
8 Office of Social and Economic Development, Bahá'í International Community, *For the Betterment of the World*, pp. 2–3.
9 ibid. p. 6.
10 For an excellent description of the rationale and development of a Bahá'í-inspired project, See Layli Miller-Munro's article 'Knowledge Into Action: the Bahá'í Imperative to Serve Humanity', in *Journal of Bahá'í Studies*, vol. 14, no. 1 /2. This article is based on her presentation of the 31st Hasan M.Balyuzi Memorial Lecture at the 2013 Association of Bahá'í Studies (North America) Annual Conference.

REFERENCES

11 See Janak Palta McGilligan, *Barli Development Institute for Rural Women: An Alternative Model of Women's Empowerment in India* (Oxford, George Ronald, 2012).
12 National Spiritual Assembly of the Bahá'ís of the United States, *In Service to the Common Good*, p. 29.
13 The Universal House of Justice, *The Promise of World Peace*, section 2.
14 Matt. 5:3.
15 Qur'án 28:5.
16 'Abdu'l-Bahá, *Tablets of the Divine Plan*, pp. 33-4.
17 *The Dawn-Breakers*, p. 213.

17. Crisis and Victory

1 Letter from the Universal House of Justice to the Bahá'ís of the World, 2 January 1986, in *A Wider Horizon*, p. 41.
2 Shoghi Effendi, *God Passes By*, p. 140.
3 Bahá'u'lláh, *The Seven Valleys*, pp. 11-13.
4 Bahá'u'lláh, *Prayers and Meditations*, no. CLXXVIII, p. 296.
5 Bahá'u'lláh, in *Crisis and Victory*, no. 46; also in *The Compilation of Compilations*, vol. I, no. 303.
6 Shoghi Effendi, *Bahá'í Administration*, p. 27.
7 Shoghi Effendi, *The World Order of Bahá'u'lláh*, p. 17.
8 Shoghi Effendi, excerpt from a letter written to the Bahá'ís of Persia, provisional translation supplied to the author by courtesy of Adib Taherzadeh
9 Letter from the Universal House of Justice to the National Spiritual Assembly of the Bahá'ís of Tuvalu, 18 December 1985, in *Crisis and Victory*, no. 101; also in *The Compilation of Compilations*, vol. I, no. 358.
10 Shoghi Effendi, *The Advent of Divine Justice*, p. 5.
11 Bahá'u'lláh, *Kitáb-i-Íqán*, para. 15, p. 15.
12 The third of the three booklets published by the Canadian National Spiritual Assembly on the Power of the Covenant contains an illuminating exposition of why and how many clergymen attack the Faith; see *The Power of the Covenant*, part 3, pp. 24-51.
13 'Abdu'l-Bahá, *The Promulgation of Universal Peace*, p. 428.
14 Shoghi Effendi, *The World Order of Bahá'u'lláh*, p. 15.
15 'Abdu'l-Bahá, *Selections from the Writings of 'Abdu'l-Bahá*, no. 194, p. 233.
16 Bahá'u'lláh, *Epistle to the Son of the Wolf*, pp. 13-14.
17 Bahá'u'lláh, *Gleanings from the Writings of Bahá'u'lláh*, V, p. 9.
18 Shoghi Effendi, *Bahá'í Administration*, p. 28.
19 'Abdu'l-Bahá, *The Promulgation of Universal Peace*, p. 457.

THE COVENANT AND YOU

20 Momen, *The Bábí and Bahá'í Religions*, p. 35.
21 Letter written on behalf of Shoghi Effendi, in *Bahá'í News*, no. 233, July 1955, p. 2.
22 Bahá'u'lláh, *Hidden Words*, Arabic no. 24.
23 Letter written on behalf of Shoghi Effendi to an individual, 17 October 1944, in *The Compilation of Compilations*, vol II, no. 1301.
24 Special Report from the Bahá'í International Community Office of Public Information, 3 November 1987.
25 Bahá'u'lláh, *Hidden Words*, Arabic no. 31.
26 Bahá'u'lláh, *Gleanings from the Writings of Bahá'u'lláh*, CLIII, p. 327.
27 'Abdu'l-Bahá, in *Star of the West*, vol. VI, no. 6 (24 June 1915), p. 44.

18. Covenant-breaking

1 'Abdu'l-Bahá, *Tablets of the Divine Plan*, p. 49.
2 Gen. 4:2–8.
3 Exod. 32: 26, 28.
4 Letter from the Universal House of Justice to an individual, 23 March 1975, in *Developing Distinctive Bahá'í Communities*.
5 'Abdu'l-Bahá, *Will and Testament*, paras. 51, 38..
6 'Abdu'l-Bahá, *Selections from the Writings of 'Abdu'l-Bahá*, no. 185, pp. 210–11.

19. Teaching

1 Bahá'u'lláh, *Tablets of Bahá'u'lláh*, pp. 197-8.
2 'Abdu'l-Bahá, *Will and Testament*, para. 53.
3 *The Dawn-Breakers*, p. 94.
4 Bahá'u'lláh, *Gleanings from the Writings of Bahá'u'lláh*, CI, p. 206.
5 ibid. CLVIII, p. 334.
6 Shoghi Effendi, *Bahá'í Administration*, p. 66.
7 Letter from Shoghi Effendi to an individual, 3 August 1932, in *Bahá'í News*, no. 68, p.3; also in *The Compilation of Compilations*, vol. II, no. 1276.
8 Letter from Shoghi Effendi to the believers in the East, Riḍván 89 (1933), paraphrased by Taherzadeh, *The Revelation of Bahá'u'lláh*, vol. 3, p. 212.
9 'Abdu'l-Bahá, quoted in *Star of the West*, vol. IV, no. 5 (5 June 1913), p. 89.
10 The Tablet of Aḥmad can be found in most Bahá'í prayer books. For more information see Gurinsky, *Learn Well This Tablet*; Hatcher, *The Ocean of His Words*, Chapter 6; and Taherzadeh, *The Revelation of Bahá'u'lláh*, vol. 2, Chapter 5.There was a wonderful pamphlet, now long out of print, by Hand of the Cause A.-Q. Faizi, and his article in

REFERENCES

the US *Baháʼí News*, no. 443, April 1967, giving detailed information about the Tablet and its effect on Aḥmad.
11 Faizi, in *Baháʼí News*, no. 443, April 1967, p. 2.
12 John 5:20.
13 John 1:14.
14 Shoghi Effendi, *The Advent of Divine Justice*, p. 42.
15 Baháʼuʼlláh, *Gleanings from the Writings of Baháʼuʼlláh*, XXXV, p. 82.
16 ʻAbduʼl-Bahá, *Selections from the Writings of ʻAbduʼl-Bahá*, no. 208, p. 264.
17 I heard Rúḥíyyih Khánum tell this story on several occasions. This, and other instances of her calling on the Concourse on High, can be found in Nakhjavani, *The Great African Safari*.
18 Baháʼuʼlláh, *Gleanings from the Writings of Baháʼuʼlláh*, CXXXVI, p. 295.
19 Message from the Universal House of Justice, Riḍván 1998; also in *Promoting Entry by Troops*, p. 14.
20 Baháʼuʼlláh, *Epistle to the Son of the Wolf*, p. 15.
21 Baháʼuʼlláh, *Tablets of Baháʼuʼlláh*, p. 27.
22 Baháʼuʼlláh, *Prayers and Meditations*, XL, p. 56.
23 Baháʼuʼlláh, in *The Importance of Obligatory Prayer and Fasting*, no. IV.
24 Baháʼuʼlláh, *Hidden Words*, Arabic no. 57.
25 Baháʼuʼlláh, *Gleanings from the Writings of Baháʼuʼlláh*, CXIX, p. 254.
26 See Harper, *Lights of Fortitude*, pp. 387–99.
27 ʻAbduʼl-Bahá, *Tablets of the Divine Plan*, p. 47.
28 ibid. p. 68.

20. The Pathway

1 Baháʼuʼlláh, *Gleanings from the Writings of Baháʼuʼlláh*, LXXXI, p. 157.
2 ibid. XXXIV, pp. 79–80.
3 Shoghi Effendi, *High Endeavours: Messages to Alaska*, p. 37.
4 See Taherzadeh, *The Revelation of Baháʼuʼlláh*, vol. 2, p. 36.
5 Baháʼuʼlláh, *Tablets of Baháʼuʼlláh*, p. 58.
6 Baháʼuʼlláh, *The Seven Valleys*, p. 16.
7 Baháʼuʼlláh, *Gleanings from the Writings of Baháʼuʼlláh*, CXXXII, p. 288.
8 Letter from the Universal House of Justice to the National Spiritual Assembly of the Baháʼís of the Indian Ocean, 14 July 1965, in *The Compilation of Compilations*, vol. I, no. 112.
9 Letter written on behalf of Shoghi Effendi to the National Spiritual Assembly of the Baháʼís of the United States, 14 April 1954, in *The Compilation of Compilations*, vol. II, no. 1985.
10 Rabbani, *The Priceless Pearl*, p. 146.

THE COVENANT AND YOU

11 The Báb, in *Bahá'í Prayers*, p. 150.
12 Bahá'u'lláh, *Gleanings from the Writings of Bahá'u'lláh*, LXXXI, p. 157.
13 ibid. LXVI, p. 127.
14 Bahá'u'lláh, *Prayers and Meditations*, CLXXXI, p. 314.
15 'Abdu'l-Bahá, *Tablets of Abdul-Baha*, vol. 3, p. 550.
16 'Abdu'l-Bahá, *The Promulgation of Universal Peace*, p. 85.
17 'Abdu'l-Bahá, *Paris Talks*, no. 55, p. 189.
18 Bahá'u'lláh, *Gleanings from the Writings of Bahá'u'lláh*, V, p. 8.
19 Luke 12:48.
20 Bahá'u'lláh, *Gleanings from the Writings of Bahá'u'lláh*, CXXIV, p. 262.
21 ibid. CXLVII, p. 317.
22 Letter on behalf of Shoghi Effendi to an individual, 6 May 1952, in *Lights of Guidance*, no. 1745.
23 Bach, *Circle of Faith*, p. 76. In this book, Dr Bach reports on his 40,000 mile journey to interview what he thought were the outstanding spiritual leaders of the time. In addition to Shoghi Effendi, he interviewed Therese Neumann, Helen Keller, Pope Pius XII and Albert Schweitzer.
24 This prayer is found in most Bahá'í prayer books.
25 Bahá'u'lláh, *Epistle to the Son of the Wolf*, p. 95.
26 Bahá'u'lláh, *Hidden Words,* Arabic no. 45.
27 Bahá'u'lláh, *Tablets of Bahá'u'lláh*, p. 73.
28 Bahá'u'lláh, *Gleanings from the Writings of Bahá'u'lláh*, XCVI, p. 196.
29 'Abdu'l-Bahá, *Selections from the Writings of 'Abdu'l-Bahá*, no. 192, p. 228.
30 Bahá'u'lláh, in *The Compilation of Compilations*, vol. I, no. 304.
31 Loehle, *On the Shoulders of Giants*, pp. 131–2.
32 Shoghi Effendi, *Citadel of Faith*, p. 117.
33 Bahá'u'lláh, *Gleanings from the Writings of Bahá'u'lláh*, CL, p. 319.
34 *1988 Britannica Book of the Year*, p. 303.
35 Shoghi Effendi, *The World Order of Bahá'u'lláh*, p. 202.
36 Shoghi Effendi, *Bahá'í Administration*, p. 80.
37 Shoghi Effendi, *The World Order of Bahá'u'lláh*, p. 171.
38 ibid. p. 89.
39 Letter from Shoghi Effendi, 4 May 1953, in *Messages to the Bahá'í World 1950–1957*, pp. 153–6.
40 'Abdu'l-Bahá, *Tablets of the Divine Plan*, pp. 86–7.
41 'Abdu'l-Bahá, *The Promulgation of Universal Peace*, p. 442.
42 Shoghi Effendi, *God Passes By*, p. 140.

www.ingramcontent.com/pod-product-compliance
Lightning Source LLC
Chambersburg PA
CBHW070933230426
43666CB00011B/2424